The Structure of Light

The Structure of Light
Richard Kelly and the Illumination of Modern Architecture

Edited by Dietrich Neumann
Foreword by Robert A. M. Stern

With contributions by D. Michelle Addington, Sandy Isenstadt, Phyllis Lambert, Margaret Maile Petty, Dietrich Neumann, and Matthew Tanteri

Yale University Press, New Haven and London
in association with the Yale School of Architecture

yalebooks.com

Designed by Jena Sher

Set in type by Amy Storm
Printed in China by Regent Publishing Services Limited

Library of Congress Cataloging-in-Publication Data
The structure of light : Richard Kelly and the illumination of modern architecture / edited by Dietrich Neumann ; foreword by Robert A. M. Stern ; with contributions by D. Michelle Addington ... [et al.].
p. cm.
Includes bibliographical references and index.
ISBN 978-0-300-16370-4 (alk. paper)
1.Kelly, Richard, 1910–1977—Criticism and interpretation. 2.Light in architecture. 3.Lighting, Architectural and decorative. 4.Architecture, Modern—20th century. I.Kelly, Richard, 1910–1977. II.Neumann, Dietrich. III.Addington, D. Michelle. IV.Title: Richard Kelly and the illumination of modern architecture.
NA2794.S77 2010
729'.28092—dc22 2010026290

A catalog record for this book is available from the British Library.

This paper meets the requirements of ANSI/NISO Z39.48-1992 (Permanence of Paper).

10 9 8 7 6 5 4 3 2 1

Frontispiece: Portrait of Richard Kelly, ca. 1950
p. 106: Kimbell Art Museum, interior view with reflector installation; photograph, Roberto Schezen © Esto

Contents

Foreword

Robert A. M. Stern

To play with light is to play with magic.

Richard Kelly, "Lighting as an Integral Part of Architecture," *College Art Journal* 12 (Autumn 1952): 24–30

Light is critical to our perception of architecture. Yet its consideration remains peripheral to professional discourse and its role "invisible" to the general public. This holds true for both the effects of natural daylighting and that of artificial nighttime illumination.

Richard Kelly was a theorist of lighting and an immensely gifted lighting designer, creating images of such iconic power that they have become central to our understanding of modern architecture. His belief in the emotional power of light was given forceful expression in the lantern-like emanations of Philip Johnson's Glass House, the moody glow of Eero Saarinen's Dulles Airport seen at night, Mies van der Rohe's Seagram Building by day or night, the light-flooded galleries and interior courts of Louis I. Kahn's Center for British Art at Yale, and the reflections on the cycloidal arches of Kahn's Kimbell Art Museum in Fort Worth, among the many key monuments of twentieth-century architecture that benefited from his work.

When the Great Depression forced Kelly to drop his undergraduate studies in English, theater, and architecture at Columbia in 1931, he found work as a lighting designer in New York City. In 1942, seeking a deeper understanding of a discipline with strong roots in the theater but only in its infancy with respect to architecture, Kelly decided to complete his architectural education, enrolling at Yale under its wartime "accelerated program," and graduating with a bachelor's degree in October 1944. Yale's architecture program was then part of the School of Fine Arts, which was also home to programs in art and, most significantly for Kelly, theater. Indeed, as Dietrich Neumann suggests in his essay, Yale's theater program, with its close ties to the Architecture Department, may have been the reason Kelly chose to study in New Haven. Military service took Stanley McCandless, Yale's widely respected professor of lighting in the theater program, away from the university during Kelly's time, but Donald Oenslager, the set designer known for his imaginative stage lighting, and George C. Izenour were teaching. Kelly's interest in theater lighting is confirmed by his decision to undertake as his bachelor's thesis, supervised by William Wilson Wurster, the San Francisco Bay–area modernist, the design of a television studio, then the most technologically experimental form of theatrical stagecraft.

In the 1940s, the reputation of Yale's architecture program was deemed conservative by many, certainly as compared with Harvard's, where Walter Gropius was chairman of the Architecture Department and Marcel Breuer the leading studio teacher. Nonetheless, in addition to Wurster, Kelly was able to study with the planner Maurice Rotival, the Chicago-based modernist Richard Bennett, and Oscar Nitzchke, a brilliant German-born, Swiss-raised architect who, after an apprenticeship with Le Corbusier in Paris, had emigrated to New York where he was chief designer working under Wallace Harrison in the office of Harrison and Abramovitz. Kelly's interests were closely aligned with Nitzchke's, who, while still in Paris, had designed the Maison de la Publicité, a widely admired visionary project exploring electric illumination in the service of mass communication by means of a facade consisting of nothing but luminous advertising and a back projection screen for newsreels.

Five years after his graduation, Kelly once again became a part of the Yale milieu, closely collaborating with Louis I. Kahn on the design of the Art Gallery and Design Center, where his innovations included use of lighting tracks and the development of two sophisticated fixtures, the "Elipsol" and the "Parlite," designed and manufactured to his specifications by Edison Price, with whom he would productively collaborate over many years. In the 1950s and early 1960s, Kelly was also a frequent participant in Yale's architecture program, where he was welcomed into the studio, encouraging students to regard lighting design as part of the creative process and not just a technical subject to be mastered in a classroom. As a consequence, the role of both day and night lighting has become embedded as a constituent part of Yale's studio culture ever since, carried on at first by Professor King-lui Wu, whom Kelly overlapped with at Yale's architecture school for two terms in 1942, and since the 1990s by M. J. Long, who with faculty colleagues like Alexander Purves and I had the good fortune to study with Kelly in the 1960s and to experience and enjoy an evening of food and conversation in his New York apartment, culminating in the "play of brilliants" that Purves so beautifully describes in the letter quoted in the beginning of Dietrich Neumann's essay.

As if to counteract the fact that the material he worked with is ephemeral—with effects all too easily destroyed by the wrong light bulb, the misguided use of a rheostat, or the simple flip of a switch—Kelly obsessively documented his work and, indeed, his daily life. His archive, transferred to Yale in 2007 by his son Scott and daughter Addison, herself a lighting designer, is an invaluable resource for scholars and architecture preservationists alike.

I am very pleased that Dietrich Neumann, professor in the Department of History of Art and Architecture at Brown University, but for three consecutive spring semesters from 2007 through 2009 the Vincent J. Scully Visiting Professor of Architectural History at Yale, has undertaken to explore Kelly's career, and has taken full advantage of the Kelly archive, beautifully assisted by Seher Erdogan, a 2009 graduate who was one of the students in his seminar on the history of architectural lighting in the spring of 2009. Their work and that of the other scholars contributing to this book promises to pave the way for an expanding field of appreciation of the role deliberately and artistically designed light has in architecture. And I am delighted by Professor Neumann's decision, in organizing the symposium celebrating the Kelly exhibition and catalog, to complement the work of scholars with presentations by some of the most provocative professionals now working in the field.

Introduction

Dietrich Neumann

Students at the Yale School of Architecture in the early 1960s remember Richard Kelly as a dedicated and engaging teacher (fig. 1). He sporadically held courses in lighting design at the school and would sometimes invite a seminar class to dinner at his apartment at 1140 Fifth Avenue in New York (fig. 2). Alec Purves, one of Kelly's former students (and professor emeritus at the Architecture School today), vividly remembers one such evening. Kelly had vanished from the dinner table before dessert, and his wife, Betty, later motioned the group into the living room, closing the doors behind the students and leaving them standing in utter darkness. "The first light that came up was a pin spot which focused on a tiny sculpture of a silver phoenix which Calder had made as a pendant necklace for Kelly's wife. It was hanging within the fireplace (painted black). Then, SLOWLY, a curtain of tiny sparkling lights appeared, followed by wall washers which came up around the perimeter of the room lighting the walls which were covered — edge to edge — with woodcuts — pages from the Nürnberg Chronicle, and as the light came up, there was Kelly sitting on the floor behind the sofa manipulating a bunch of dials that were tucked under the table behind the sofa — eyes bright and grinning like a Cheshire cat — yes, the Wizard of Oz!"[1]

Fig. 1. Portrait of Richard Kelly, ca. 1958

Such a moment — unforgotten by all who witnessed it — made clear what Kelly loved about his work: he could use light to create theatricality and drama, change the mood and appearance of a space, make materials glow and contrast the play of brilliants with focal glow and ambient luminescence. His early fascination with the theater and his understanding of architectural space and materials remained strong qualities of his work throughout his career.

Richard Kelly became a lighting designer at a felicitous moment. A whole range of new technologies for lighting had been introduced, and a long period of prosperity emerged after the Great Depression and World War II, just as modern architecture became firmly established as the dominant style, bringing with it new challenges and opportunities. New building materials, structural approaches, and ideologies led to a shift in the role of the facade as the mediator between inside and outside. Floodlighting buildings from the outside — a common approach before World War II — became less applicable and instead, thanks to the ubiquitous glass facades, interior lighting could contribute to a building's exterior appearance by rendering its spatial depth visible outside.

Kelly was instrumental in formulating something that we might call a *nocturnal modernity* — a particular aesthetic vocabulary for the home, public spaces, and work environments at night that had a lasting impact on the appearance and reception of modern architecture. If carefully and consciously applied, the different appearance at night would reach beyond the mere fulfillment of functional needs, toward a particular interpretation, a mise-en-scène bringing qualities to a building it might not have shown during the daytime — and which were hardly considered part of the modernist mainstream—namely mood, theatricality, and drama. The complete control and flexibility of artificial light allowed a selective rendering of space and determination of use that was more specific than under daylight. Perhaps Kelly's most lasting contribution to modern architecture and its interpretation was his determination to make the light source itself invisible, and instead to plan for the reflective luminosity of materials and surfaces. A selective, purer image of a building would emerge, where certain walls would magically glow, large windows would be relieved of all reflections, outside landscapes would be theatrically enhanced. This meant that the lighting could not be established as an afterthought, but had to be planned from the very beginning, as the positions of recessed lights would need to be determined and the reflective qualities of certain materials chosen.

It is no wonder that many prominent midcentury architects were eager to work with Kelly, among them Eero Saarinen, Richard Neutra, Ludwig Mies van der Rohe, Wallace Harrison, Josep Lluís Sert, Paul Rudolph, and Louis Kahn. His by far most faithful client was Philip Johnson. Johnson called Kelly "my lighting man" and an "Architect of Light" and gave him full recognition and support. Kelly's list of works includes more than forty projects with Johnson, by far the largest number with a single designer. Johnson was less bothered with Kelly's costly fees (and sometimes idiosyncratic work habits) than other architects who had to adhere to a firm bottom line. Johnson's complex, rich, and independent oeuvre has often been overshadowed by the public interest in its colorful creator, but he was more prescient than most regarding the central importance of light early on in the design process.

Although lighting design has gained in recognition and acceptance in recent years--thanks in no small measure to Kelly's efforts—it is still far from being a natural part of the design process. Only a handful of architecture schools around the world offer courses in lighting design today. But an increasing number of buildings that treat light as an important aspect from the beginning serve as encouragement to teach students the potential of light in architecture early on.

When Kazuyo Sejima and Ryue Nishizawa created their tender and wistful homage to the essential dreams and visions of the modern movement in the form of a floating, curvilinear aluminum cloud at Hyde Park's Serpentine Gallery in the summer of 2009, the installation reached its apotheosis at night, with uplights in the paths turning the canopy into a luminous, reflective membrane, which in turn lit up the path underneath. Richard Kelly's vocabulary was at work here—the material itself began to glow (fig. 3). Similarly, the moabi wood panels surrounding the stage and auditorium in the reopened Alice Tully Hall (redesign in 2009 by Diller, Scofidio, and Renfro) emit a warm, mysterious glow, as a result of a resin backing with embedded LED lights (fig. 4). Kelly, I suspect, would have been delighted. His own experiments with tiny lights embedded

Fig. 2. Richard Kelly, Kelly Apartment, New York, 1958

Fig. 3. Kazuyo Sejima and Ryue Nishizawa (SANAA), Serpentine Gallery Pavilion, London, 2009. © 2009 James Newton.

Fig. 4. Diller, Scofidio, and Renfro, Alice Tully Hall, New York, 2009, interior view. Lighting designer: Arup Lighting. Photograph © Iwan Baan.

Fig. 5. Renzo Piano, New York Times Building, New York, 2007, view of lobby. Lighting design: Office for Visual Interaction, Inc. (OVI). Photograph by Frieder Blickle.

in a curtain, his interest in a luminous materiality, and his love for theater and theatricality, for moods and changeability, found a common ground here. Finally, the lobby of Renzo Piano's New York Times Building (2008) employs a wall-washing arrangement by OVI Lighting Design that consciously refers to Kelly's design for the Seagram Building (figs. 5 and 6).

The work of Richard Kelly can seem as elusive and ephemeral as the material he used. Most of his installations could be comprehended only at night, and they might suddenly vanish at the whim of a homeowner or building superintendent when one thoughtlessly changed light fixture would compromise a carefully calibrated arrangement. Indeed, many if not most of Kelly's lighting installations have been lost over the years.

The remaining evidence is fraught with uncertainties. Photographs, for example, turn out to be unreliable witnesses. Night photography had long been a genre in its own right and had acquired particular aesthetic conventions. Photographers might proudly apply a personal style to their interpretation of a building at night, through choice of location, film stock, and development techniques, or *in situ* through long exposures or even the help of portable lamps—placed, perhaps, behind a corner to send light up toward the brightly reflective ceiling. The resulting image might not coincide with Kelly's considerably more complex and perhaps less photogenic vision, where light applications engaged particular functions and spatial perceptions.

The fact that we can reconstruct Kelly's oeuvre to a reasonable degree at all is highly unusual, and entirely owed to Kelly himself. To this day the role of collaborators in architectural commissions is usually only poorly recorded, as both the architectural profession and the historians chronicling it lack an adequate model for the complexities of architectural production. Rather, the default approach is still that of a single author-architect, derived from fine arts and literature.

Kelly, however, had a clear sense of his place in posterity, the importance of his own work, and the need to establish a firm understanding of his profession's role in the design process. More than others, he published essays about his work, and tried to make sure that his name was mentioned in publications about a new building. (Not always with success: the unprecedented thirty-page spread in the *Architectural Forum* of July 1961 on Chase Manhattan Bank, for example, clearly one of Kelly's most important commissions, does not mention his contribution at all.) Most important, though, Kelly had a habit of keeping absolutely everything, from his earliest notes as a student at Columbia College to work files for most projects in which he was ever involved (fig. 7). Kelly was interested in documenting the process of design, and he kept sketches, bills, notes from meetings, the blueprints and lamp designs, even unflattering letters from clients frustrated with Kelly's somewhat unpredictable billing practices, but very rarely did he include photo-

Fig. 6. Renzo Piano, New York Times Building, New York, 2007, facade. Lighting design: Office for Visual Interaction, Inc. (OVI). Photograph by Frieder Blickle.

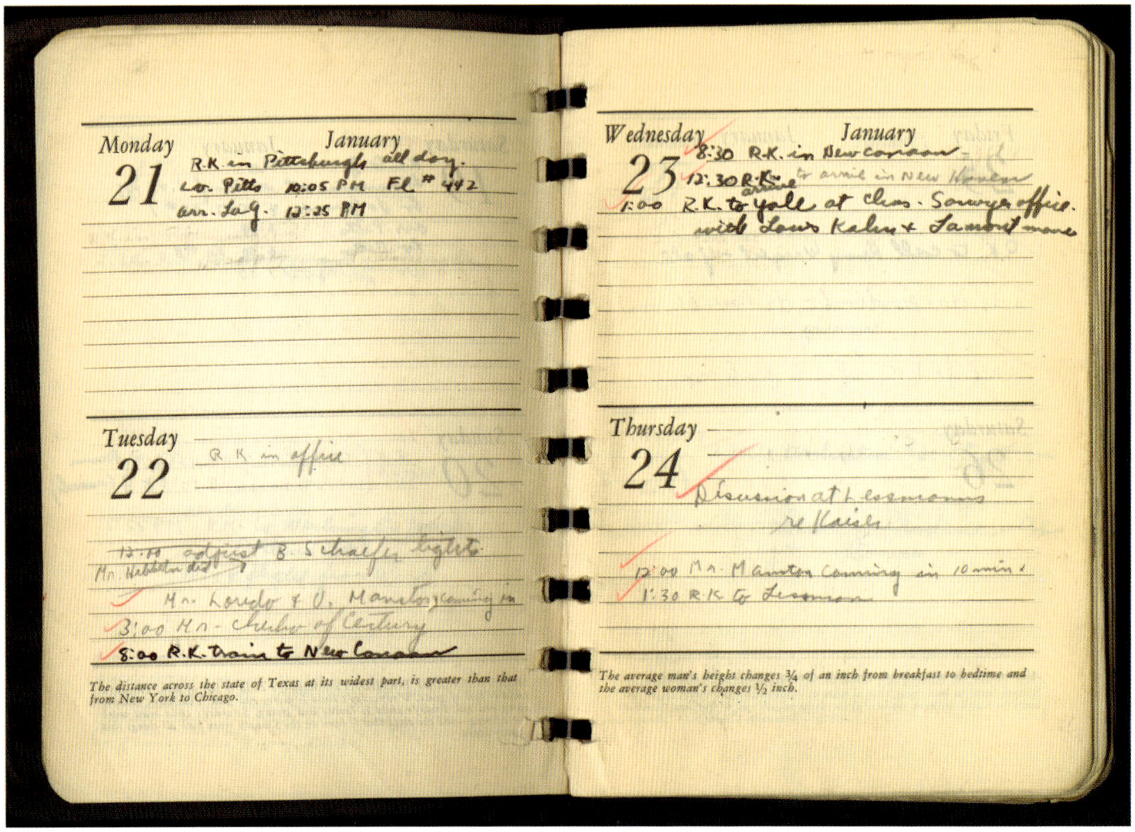

Fig. 7. Collage of archival material from the Richard Kelly Papers

Fig. 8. Pages from Richard Kelly's day planner

opposite

Fig. 9. Pages from Richard Kelly's pocket notes

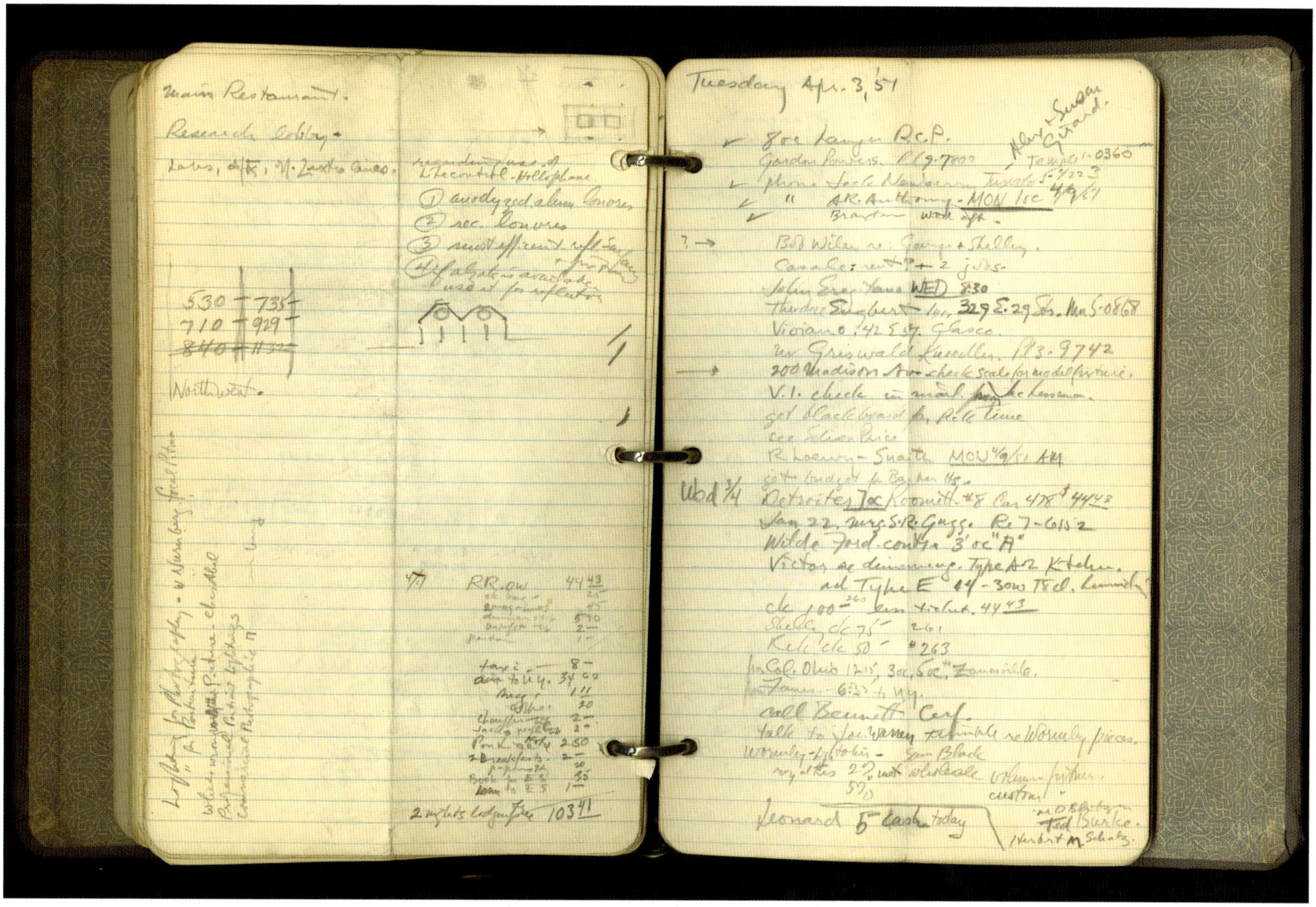

graphs of the finished building for further reference. Even this extensive archive is not complete, however. Records on several of his very early projects are missing, and Kelly's involvement among the hundreds of projects for which files exist varied greatly. The traces in the archive, and even Kelly's own recollections, are not always perfect indicators of his involvement or impact on a project. In some cases he might have only given advice to improve an existing lighting scheme; in others he was so deeply involved in the design process that the lighting he planned was not only integral to the building but made the nocturnal view the most frequently published image.

The most personally engaging and often touching parts of his papers are the appointment calendars and "pocket notes" that Kelly kept for every day of his career, giving us a clear sense of the—perhaps deliberately—frantic pace of his professional and private life (fig. 8). Probably intended to produce time sheets and bills, his daily note sheets record every phone call and every meeting he held (with a fascinating array of well-known architects and public figures), but they occasionally also contain fragments of conversations, insights and resolutions, lists of books he purchased and of things to do or to remember. These single leafs of six-by-nine-inch paper, filled to the edges with small pencil scribbles, always have a vertical crease where he had folded each one so it would fit into a shirt or jacket pocket during the day, and were ultimately assembled into three-hole ring binders (fig. 9). Their scholarly value extends far beyond the scope of this project.

Again and again, this enormous archive survived against all odds. In the 1960s, when his business temporarily saw hard times and Kelly had to move to a smaller space in Tudor City, the entire content of the office, including the archive, was impounded and put up for auction (a family member bought it back). It was then placed in storage, where a fire broke out and partially damaged it. Another storage location was found, but that flooded shortly after, again resulting in damage to the files. Finally, Philip Cialdella, a lighting designer, preserved the collection in his basement for several years, as he planned to write a book on Kelly. From there, it ended up with Kelly's daughter Addison in her office at U.S. Lighting Consultants in New York City and finally, in 2007, at Yale's Sterling Library, where it now resides.[2] The archive currently holds 765 individual project files in 92 boxes and 145 rolls for large drawings and blueprints, plus another 25 boxes containing Kelly's personal and professional papers.

Historical research began before the Kelly archive came to Yale. Cialdella made use of the material for his master's thesis on Kelly written for the Parsons School of Design in New York in 1992. Matthew Tanteri and Renee Cooley and a group of other New York lighting designers then turned a selection of his findings into a traveling exhibition, shown in a first version from 1993 onward at several venues.[3] A newer version began a European tour in 2007, which brought it to Stockholm, Berlin, Paris, Amsterdam, London, and Vienna, supported by ERCO Leuchten GmbH and the European Lighting Designers Association. Margaret Maile Petty, a senior lecturer at the School of Design at Victoria University in Wellington, New Zealand, was the first to publish a lengthy scholarly study of Kelly's work in the *Journal of the Society of Architectural Historians* in 2007.[4]

This volume is published on the occasion of an exhibition about Richard Kelly's work at the gallery of the Yale School of Architecture from August to October 2010 to celebrate the hundredth return of his birthday on September 22, 2010. It brings together scholars, architects, and lighting designers to assess Richard Kelly's history, legacy, and impact today. After a biographical essay introducing Kelly's career trajectory and work, Sandy Isenstadt of the University of Delaware examines Kelly's domestic interiors and landscape designs. Margaret Maile Petty of the University of Wellington, New Zealand, details Kelly's designs for corporate America through a number of examples from his collaborations with Ludwig Mies van der Rohe, Philip Johnson, and Eliot Noyes. Phyllis Lambert, former director of the Centre Canadien d'Architecture in Montreal and once a client of Richard Kelly's, presents his collaboration with Philip Johnson at the Glass House and the Seagram Building. D. Michelle Addington of Yale presents the technological context in which Kelly's work evolved. The lighting designer Matthew Tanteri looks at Kelly's daylighting work at Louis Kahn's museums in Fort Worth and New Haven. Also included here are Kelly's life notes, a list that he created in the early 1970s detailing his 125 most important commissions.

The American Institute of Architects (AIA) honored Kelly twice, first in 1964 with a Collaborative Achievement Award for his contributions to the Seagram Building and the Four Seasons Restaurant, and again in 1967 with a Gold Medal for his cumulative work on "light in architecture." The Illuminating Engineering Society awarded its Gold Medal to Kelly posthumously in 1979. Its New York section (IESNY) has been awarding an annual Richard Kelly Grant since 1980.

The title for this book came from handwritten notes in Kelly's archive—perhaps preparations for a lecture—where he was reflecting on his work. Other terms on that undated sheet read, "the architecture of light" and, boldly underlined, "visual truth lies in the structure of light"—revealing, perhaps, the influence of two of his most important clients, Louis Kahn and Ludwig Mies van der Rohe, and hinting at Kelly's deeply rooted belief in the interdependence of light, structure, and materials.

Notes

1. Alexander Purves, e-mail to the author, September 1, 2009.
2. Thanks to the efforts of Silas Montsieur and Richard Szary, then the Carrie S. Beinecke Director of Manuscripts and Archives and the university archivist at Yale University.
3. The others who organized the exhibition along with Tanteri and Cooley were Phil Cialdella, Jim Conte, Keesler Cronin, and Addison Kelly.
4. Margaret Maile Petty, "Illuminating the Glass Box: The Lighting Designs of Richard Kelly," *Journal of the Society of Architectural Historians* 66 (June 2007): 194–219.

CINEMA
ACTUALITÉS
PUBLICITÉ
FOX MOVIETONE
ECLAIR
PARAMOUNT
LIRE
Paris-Soir
LE PLUS FORT TIRAGE
EVIAN
LA CURE IDÉALE
COUTARD

Theater, Lights, and Architecture

The Career of Richard Kelly

Dietrich Neumann

"Thousands of years went by with their changes of style," the prominent architecture critic Douglas Haskell wrote in 1931, "but not until this century was there electric light, which, far, far more than the familiar triad of steel, glass, and concrete, has changed the basis of all architecture." Inspired by Hugh Ferriss's visionary drawings of the "Metropolis of Tomorrow," Haskell had identified a specifically American nocturnal modernism. "We get the night, the Europeans get the day. . . . [T]his is us . . . here is modernism indeed!" While Haskell had, for the sake of his argument, simplified the rather complex field of national identities and stylistic characteristics, he was correct in recognizing the rising importance of illumination in architecture. His essay came on the heels of a nationwide celebration of the fiftieth anniversary of Thomas Edison's invention of the light bulb and a general awareness of the epochal changes that it had already brought and promised for the future.[1]

For Richard Kelly, who arrived in New York City from Ohio in 1928, already fascinated with theater and lighting design, these changes were visible everywhere, and in particular on Broadway. The drama of a new generation of sophisticated stage lights in most theaters was matched by powerful new approaches to architectural illumination outside (fig. 1). Nowhere else in the world could one find a similar concentration of lighting designers, engineering firms, and manufacturers specializing in the development of new equipment. New York was the ideal environment for the emergence of the new craft of lighting design and became the fertile ground for Richard Kelly's remarkable career. He was neither the first nor the only lighting designer applying ideas and techniques to architectural illumination whose roots could be traced back to the theater, but his extremely active professional life, his ability to write with great clarity about his work, and his illumination concepts for buildings of major importance and visibility made him the most prominent member of his profession at midcentury. His own ideas as well as those he adopted and modified helped to shape and firmly define a particular vocabulary for the application of artificial light in modern architecture.

Lights in the City

In 1917 the theater critic Arthur Edwin Krows claimed in the *New York Times* that America's greatest gifts to the theater were the advances in "stage lighting." Krows's statement was more prescient than accurate at that point, as the major technical and creative developments in stage illumination were only just beginning. In the 1920s much-improved footlights, spotlights, dimmers, and lighting control panels appeared along with colored light, reflectors, and lighting effects to guide the audience's emotions. Convinced that "the story of a play may be told in light," Krows was one of the first to systematically discuss this newly emerging art.[2]

It is probably no coincidence that stagecraft innovation increased in the 1920s when the rising competition from movies threatened the survival of live drama. The new medium of film had obvious disadvantages—being black and white, silent, and two dimensional—but it could give an audience the illusion of movement, convincingly take it to faraway locations, and change scenes in an instant. The new theater lights increased flexibility, as the mood of a scene or the time of day could quickly change, the action could be focused on different parts of the stage, and glorious moving color effects became possible. Initially, set designers considered lighting part of their work and would engage the theater electrician to select and sometimes modify the lamps. Beginning in the early 1920s, however, more and more lighting designers for the theater were given individual credit in playbills and developed recognizable signature styles.[3]

Norman Bel Geddes, for example, a theater man, architect, and industrial designer, attracted considerable attention in 1921 when he published drawings for an imagined staging of Dante's *Divine Comedy*, in which the "lighting varies every moment of the performance."[4] The German director Max Reinhardt hired Geddes for his production of *The Miracle* in 1924, for which the Century Theatre in New York was transformed into a Gothic cathedral, illuminated differently for each scene with hidden floodlights and backlit stained glass windows.[5] Throughout the 1920s Geddes taught courses on scene design and lighting privately in New York City.[6]

Robert Edmond Jones was another pioneer of the field in the early 1920s, as both a stage set and lighting designer. According to his colleague Jo Mielziner, "Jones never developed a design without constant consideration of what light would do to form and to color. Shadow was no longer for him just the absence of light, but in itself something to be mastered and controlled and made expressive. . . . [T]he brilliance, the imaginative scope of Jones's designs, were enormously heightened by his sensitive control of the power and beauty of dramatic lighting."[7] The newly available lighting technologies brought greater control of the medium and greater freedom to apply it. This led for the first time to serious discussions about the artistic approach to stage lighting. The Illuminating Engineering Society hosted lectures by theatrical lighting designers, including Louis Hartmann, who had worked for several decades with David Belasco, and architect and lighting designer Claude Bragdon.[8] Soon a number of books appeared on the subject, such as *Stage Lighting* by Theodore Fuchs in 1929, *Theatre Lighting* by Louis Hartmann in 1930, and *A Method of Lighting the Stage* by Stanley McCandless in 1932.

McCandless held the first chair for theater lighting design in the country at Yale University, from whose Department of Drama much innovation in the field originated (fig. 2). It was the school's youngest department, funded in 1924 by Edward S. Harkness, who also helped underwrite the building of the University Theater, designed by James Gamble Rogers. Its first chairman, George Pierce Baker, had been a faculty member at Harvard's English Department for thirty-six years and was

Fig. 1. Times Square, New York, view at night, ca. 1930

above left

Fig. 2. Stanley McCandless, portrait

Fig. 3. Theatrical productions at Yale: *The Merchant* by Plautus *(above)*, setting by Donald Oenslager, lighting by Stanley R. McCandless; *Prometheus Bound* by Aeschylus *(left)*, setting by Donald Oenslager, lighting by Stanley R. McCandless. From *Bulletin of Yale University, School of the Fine Arts, for the Academic Year 1940–1941*, p. 87.

widely considered the foremost teacher of playwriting in the country. But he also had a keen eye for contemporary trends, and he turned the Yale theater into a leading center for innovative stage techniques. Baker had spotted the talents of two of his recent students at Harvard, Stanley McCandless and Donald Oenslager, and in 1925 he hired them. Both had participated in the Harvard Dramatic Club and graduated in 1923, Oenslager with an English degree and McCandless from the architecture school. After a year of traveling on a fellowship, McCandless worked for McKim, Mead, and White; he was twenty-eight when Baker asked him to join Yale's Drama Department as lighting consultant and technical instructor. Oenslager had traveled to Europe after graduation to study the stage designs of Edward Gordon Craig and Adolphe Appia, whose atmospheric and minimalist stage sets from beams of light influenced him deeply. After working as an actor in New York and landing his very first job as a set designer, he joined the Yale faculty in 1925. George Charles Izenour came to Yale's Drama Department in 1939, at twenty-seven, as head of the theater design workshop, where he worked on technically sophisticated stage lighting systems.

Stanley McCandless, who became an associate professor at Yale in 1933, is mostly remembered today for his publications on theater lighting, such as *A Syllabus of Stage Lighting* (1931) and *A Method of Lighting the Stage*, as well as for the "McCandless method" of lending intensity and definition to an actor's features with the help of additional colored spotlights from two directions. McCandless was an important educator for several generations of lighting designers at Yale, such as Jean Rosenthal, Claude Engle, Joe Rubin, and Thomas Skelton, and he produced the lighting for a number of plays at Yale, often collaborating with Oenslager, who became one of the most prominent set and lighting designers on Broadway (fig. 3). The archives at Yale hold hundreds of lantern slides from McCandless's lectures and careful drawings explaining the flow of light from different types of lamps and the reflective qualities of the projectors. McCandless was also the head of research and development at Century Lighting in New York, since 1929 one of the major developers of theater and architectural lighting equipment.

As a trained architect, McCandless early on suggested a transfer of ideas from theater lighting to the home, at a time when the electrification of middle-class houses had reached a saturation point. In 1930, he observed: "Light can influence our feelings in regard to a certain place, in other words, . . . as designers we can control the individual mood to some degree by means of light. . . . It involves the understanding of how light affects the individual and then providing the means for producing that light. The designer's job is the former, and he depends upon the engineer to supply the latter." In 1937 he wrote: "If we turn to the theatre to see how effectively light is used to produce mood, it gives us some hope that perhaps before long we can achieve the proper atmosphere in our

Fig. 4. Eero Saarinen, Kresge Chapel at Massachusetts Institute of Technology, Cambridge, Massachusetts, 1955, interior view. Lighting designer: Stanley McCandless. Photograph: Ezra Stoller © Esto.

Fig. 5. Skyscraper lighting model on stage at the Chicago Lighting Institute, 1930

houses, where it is even more important than in the theatre."[9] His recurring emphasis on the creation of "mood" could come only from someone not trained as an architect in the modernist tradition, and it would profoundly influence Richard Kelly, who adopted many of the positions and arguments found in the writings of McCandless when he became involved in lighting design for the middle-class home after the war.

Through his work for the Century Lighting Company, since the 1930s McCandless received several commissions for the illumination of theater spaces, such as Radio City Music Hall in New York and the Bushnell Center in Hartford. After the war, these were followed by Eero Saarinen's Kresge Auditorium and Chapel at MIT in 1955 (fig. 4), the TWA airport terminal in New York City (1956–1962), and, in 1958, Edward Durell Stone's United States Theatre at the Brussels World's Fair, where he collaborated with Donald Oenslager.[10]

The luminous drama on Broadway's stages seemed to continue outside, where New York was glowing in the new abundance of electric light. Times Square had become a brilliant display of colorful and luminous advertising, and tall buildings throughout the city were flooded with light, including the Woolworth Building, the Bush Terminal, the American Radiator Building, the Metropolitan Life Tower, and the Standard Oil Building. "There is a new Manhattan skyline—a new city of light and color rising above an old one," the *New York Times* proclaimed in 1925, recognizing this "fairyland of night" as the "forerunner of a new order . . . a huge city of illuminated castles in the air."[11] The electricity companies and the Illuminating Engineering Society had begun promoting collaborations with architects and advertising the beauty of nocturnal urban illumination through theatrical demonstrations and lectures (fig. 5). In 1929, Raymond Hood, Harvey Wiley Corbett, and George Rapp published a booklet under the title "Architecture of the Night" on behalf of General Electric in which they laid out a philosophy of nocturnal illumination for their still widely reluctant colleagues (fig. 6).

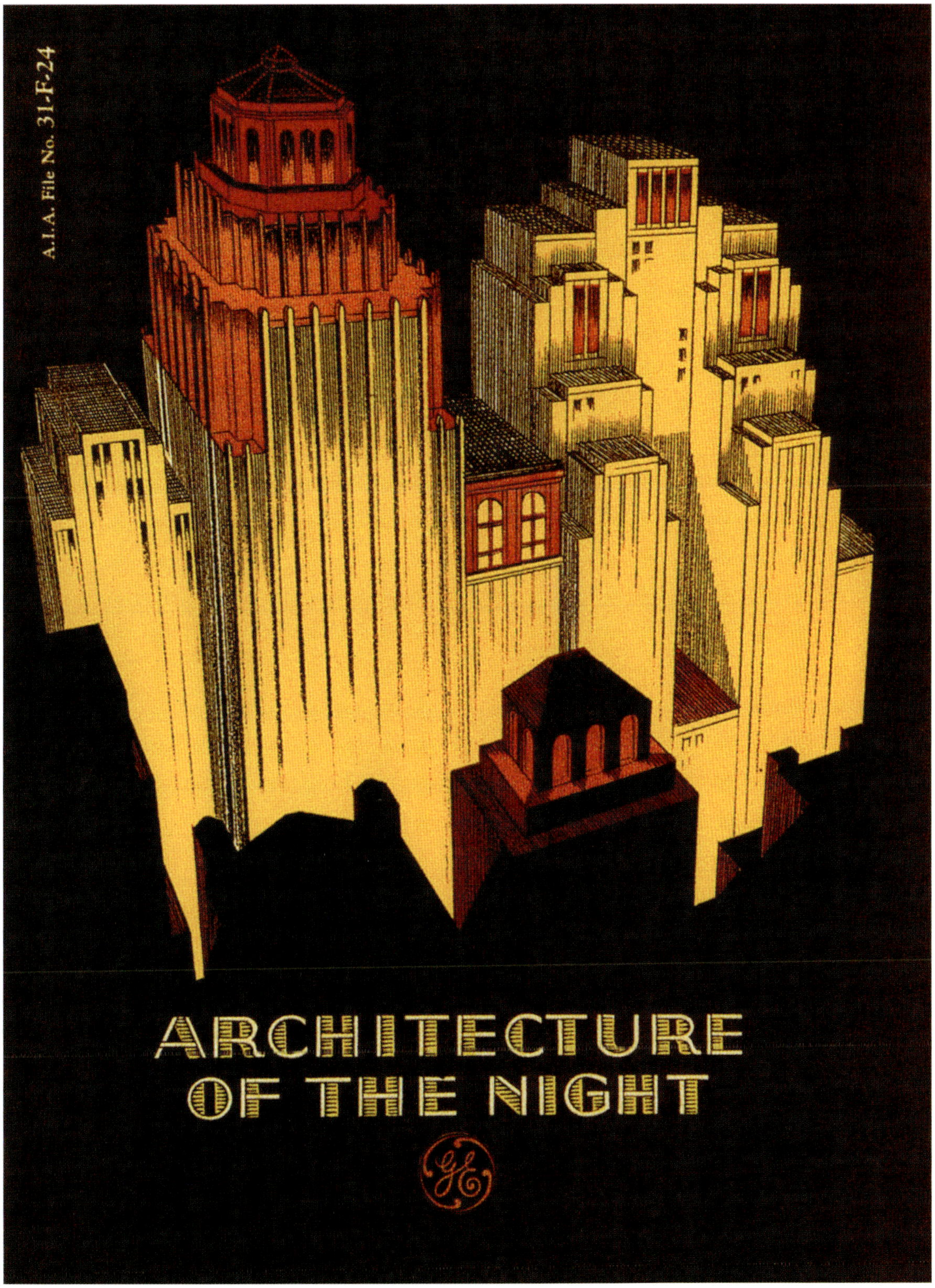

Fig. 6. "Architecture of the Night," General Electric company bulletin GED-375 (February 1930)

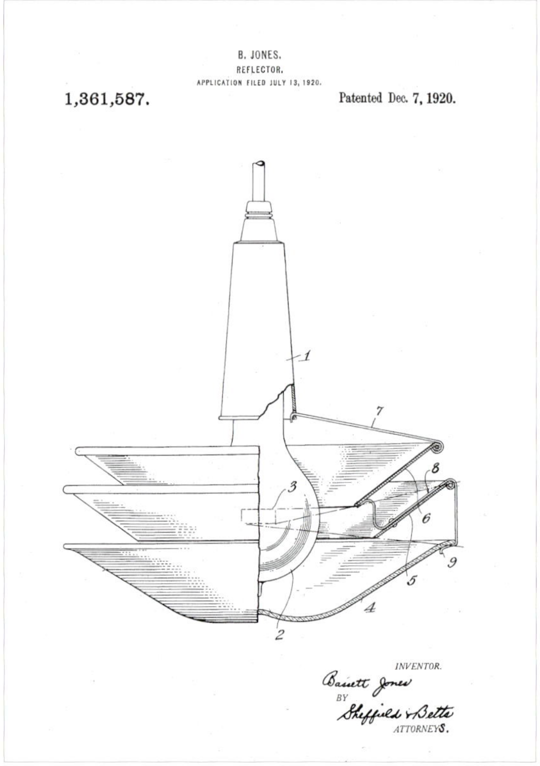

Fig. 7. Bassett Jones, portrait, ca. 1925

Fig. 8. Bassett Jones, patent application for lighting fixture, filed July 13, 1920

One of the key figures in architectural lighting in the 1920s and early 1930s was Bassett Jones, a multitalented engineer, economist, and lighting designer (fig. 7).[12] More than anyone else, he prepared the ground for the rising interest in architectural lighting in the 1920s and beyond. In many ways Richard Kelly's most immediate predecessor, Jones was a founding member of the Illuminating Engineering Society in 1908 and frequently a lecturer and writer about the application of artificial light to architecture.[13] Disappointed with the lukewarm response among architects, he told a convention of lighting engineers in 1919: "The architect is a very difficult man to handle," being part of "a cult looking back to ancestral conditions and not to the future" and failing to embrace modernity.[14] A case in point were architect-designed light fixtures that would typically look like candle holders, with bare, bright light bulbs producing unpleasant glare. In response Jones developed several modern glare-free lamp shades (fig. 8).[15] He made a number of significant lighting installations in architecture that paved the way for later applications. He was one of the first to develop a "luminous ceiling," in his Allegheny County Soldier's Memorial in Pittsburgh, from 1908, and he designed the unexecuted "Theatre in the Air" for Raymond Hood's Tribune Tower in Chicago from 1924, which contained several lighting ideas that would become part of Kelly's later vocabulary (fig. 9).[16] Here, Jones suggested the use of downlights to create a "pool of light" at the foot of the building, strip lights in window sills, opal glass lit from behind, and metallic colored curtains for light reflection.[17]

Jones also developed the lighting for the American Radiator Building, the Chrysler Building, and the Empire State Building, and at the 1939 World's Fair (his last work before his retirement), he dazzled visitors such as Lewis Mumford with buildings that at night had a "richness and a radiance that no ordinary architecture can boast." Trees were lit by floodlights in the ground, taking on "exciting depths of green one never sees in daylight."[18] The apparent climax of everyone's visit was the highly theatrical fountain lake display at night, which, according to the *New Yorker*, culminated in a "pageant of chaos" and "a combined Niagara and Vesuvius" (figs. 10–11).[19] Jones also pressured the lighting industry into introducing the newly developed fluorescent lamp at the fair, which created a sensation and led to its mass application afterward.[20]

Ideas from Europe

Modern European theater and its approach to lighting had been much discussed in the United States, in particular the work of Adolphe Appia and Gordon Craig, which brought an unprecedented degree of abstraction to stage design, and can be considered one of the key influences in the formation of modern architecture.

Less well known than Craig and Appia, the Spanish designer Mariano Fortuny is another particularly interesting figure in the history of European

Fig. 9. Howells and Hood, Tribune Tower, Chicago, 1925, contemporary postcard. Lighting designer: Bassett Jones.

stage lighting in the early twentieth century. A multitalented painter and lamp and fabric designer, he developed and patented a method of indirect illumination intended to faithfully render natural light. He would project light not directly onto the stage but onto colored silk fabric, which would in turn redirect the light on the stage. Fortuny later concentrated mostly on the production of fabrics, developing his own dyeing and printing techniques at his manufacturing plant in Venice. Their superb quality and success resulted from his understanding of how their surface reflected light. The effects were much discussed in Europe.[21] It was hardly coincidental that Richard Kelly and Philip Johnson selected Fortuny fabrics for the interior walls of the bedroom of Johnson's Brick House in New Canaan, Connecticut, as they were meant to reflect the artificial light grazing them from above with increasing or decreasing strength several times a day.

Fortuny also developed the cyclorama still in use in many theaters today. Flooded with colored light, it gave the impression of infinite space. A small European model of such a cyclorama had been shown in New York City in 1914, and it suggested to the young stage designer Robert Edmond Jones that a story could be "told by means of light alone."[22]

Just as new approaches to theater lighting in the United States had been inspired by earlier European developments, the foreign debates on architectural illumination and nocturnal images of modern buildings also had a palpable influence. Such images and ideas might have reached the young Richard Kelly directly, as they were widely published in lighting magazines and probably discussed with him by some of his clients, such as Philip Johnson and Ludwig Mies van der Rohe, or indirectly as they were adopted by others.[23] In the Weimar Republic, for example, numerous modern architects took part in widespread debates about artificial light in the architecture journals and—occasionally—in the mainstream press (among them Ernst May, Ludwig Hilberseimer, Hugo Häring, Marcel Breuer, Martin Wagner, and Arthur Korn), in addition to journalists and representatives of the lighting industry.

The lighting engineer Joachim Teichmüller, the chairman of Germany's first institute for lighting technology, at the University of Karlsruhe, presented "light as a new building material" at a large exposition in Düsseldorf in 1926.[24] He coined the term *Lichtarchitektur*, which he defined as "particular architectural effects . . . achieved exclusively with the help of

opposite

Fig. 10. New York World's Fair, 1939, Lagoon of Nations fountains, contemporary postcard. Lighting designers: Bassett Jones, J. S. Hamel, Richard C. Engelken.

above

Fig. 11. New York World's Fair, 1939, spectacle over the Lagoon of Nations, contemporary postcard. Lighting designers: Bassett Jones, J. S. Hamel, Richard C. Engelken. Courtesy of Lake County Discovery Museum/Curt Teich Postcard Archives.

Fig. 12. Erich Mendelsohn, Rudolf Petersdorff Department Store, Breslau, Germany, 1928, night view, contemporary photograph

Fig. 13. Luckhardt and Anker, office building conversion, Tauentzienstrasse 3, Berlin, 1924, night view, contemporary photograph the light." This applied to interior illumination, which Teichmüller was especially interested in, as well as to "painting" with projected light and the "luminous ornaments" of light bulbs lined up along cornices, known as "outline lighting," and luminous advertising, or *Lichtreklame*.[25] At the same time, the German Werkbund commissioned a publication about the emerging field of architectural illumination, which was obviously appealing to an organization intent on furthering the collaboration between artists and industry. The publication appeared in 1928 under the title *Licht und Beleuchtung* [Light and Illumination] and contained essays by a number of Werkbund members.

Walter Riezler and Ernst May emphasized the potential differences between the German and American efforts. May, for example, considered "luminous advertising on Broadway" a "classic counterexample" to how light should be sensibly used. "The eye is unable to read any letters, or distinguish individual form, it is blinded instead by the overbearing amount of glimmering lights, countless luminous elements that cancel out each other's effects." Floodlighting "on towers and skyscrapers" was also problematic, as "a building's mass will then, however, appear like a ghost against the night sky." Ideally, a building should be designed with the nocturnal illumination in mind and offer "bright, even, and large" surfaces, for the light to "develop its full potential" and to "calmly maintain its position in contrast to the liveliness of its surroundings."[26] May cited as concrete examples the "light cornices" in Erich Mendelsohn's and the Luckhardt Brothers' recent stores, which he found "discreet and artistically of excellent appearance" (figs. 12–13).[27] The next step—according to May, "more expensive, but highly effective"—was panels of translucent glass lit from behind.

For German architects in the 1920s, the new lighting technology seemed to provide an important tool for stylistic development, and the nocturnal city was envisioned as the stage for the final, liberating act in the project of modern architecture. The prominent critic Walter Riezler, among others, was tempted by the prospect that the "fantastic world" of light in the nocturnal city was about to offer a vibrant alternative to "the sobriety of functional life."[28] Other critics stressed the fact that only at night did the structure of the building behind its facade become fully comprehensible: "The nocturnal view shows clearly and unmistakably that the facade is only the skeleton for the inner distribution of spaces and that its design is determined by the spatial organism within" (fig. 14).[29] This quiet observation about night lighting for modern architecture can hardly be overestimated. The unprecedented window dimensions in modern facades would allow views deep into the building at night, when the rooms were lit. The dark, reflective glass that shielded the interior from the gaze of the passerby during daytime now turned it into part of the exterior, and good inside lighting could reveal the structure and spatial organization of a building. It is this aspect of modern architecture

Fig. 14. Erich Mendelsohn, Deukon Haus, Berlin, 1927, night view, contemporary photograph

that became of key importance for modern lighting in the 1950s and in particular for Richard Kelly's work.

Mies van der Rohe's ideas about the use of artificial light are particularly telling, given that his collaboration with Kelly in the 1950s produced some of the most significant results. In 1928, he had designed two visionary buildings — a department store and a bank — for Berlin and Stuttgart, entirely clad in translucent glass and lit from inside at night, imagining a "fairy-tale effect."[30] Luminous facades became so popular in the following years that Berlin's "display lighting [of] glass brick and opal glass" made it "the best-lighted city in Europe," according to the *New York Times*.[31]

While his traditional buildings before 1925 showed a conventional approach to domestic lighting, Mies had struggled to find a convincing lighting solution for the radical modern interiors of uninterrupted planes and polished marble of his Tugendhat House and the Barcelona Pavilion. The Tugendhat House had a few Poul Henningsen ceiling lamps, whose placement seemed unconvincing and halfhearted (fig. 15). The Barcelona Pavilion was notoriously dark at dusk and night, its only source of artificial light a luminous wall of opal glass, with the result, according to several reports, of numerous visitors tumbling into the water basins. Mies probably came closest to his ideal solution in the "Glasraum" (a product display space for the German glass industry) at the Stuttgart Werkbund Exhibition of 1927. He covered its cool modernist spaces divided by translucent and transparent glass walls with a white canvas ceiling, providing a diffuse, even light, thanks to suspended lamps above (fig. 16). Mies was probably inspired by solutions for the theater, like Heinrich Tessenow's reform stage in Hellerau near Dresden, where Adolphe Appia had clad the entire stage and auditorium in canvas with electric multicolored backlighting. Photo and film studios employed similar arrangements, and the occasional luminous ceiling with electric light had begun to appear at utilitarian buildings, such as gas stations, in Germany in 1929 (fig. 17). It took almost twenty years before similar luminous ceilings started being promoted in the United States by Lightolier and other firms in the late 1940s.

New lighting ideas were developed all over Europe. In Paris, Pierre Chareau worked with the brilliant lighting designer André Salomon on the illumination of his "Maison de Verre" in 1929. Glass tiles form the main facade of the building, allowing for its carefully planned diurnal and nocturnal effects. During the day, diffuse white light flooded in from outside, whereas at night the entire facade turned into a screen, as the lights inside and the shadowy movements of the inhabitants became visible to visitors or neighbors in the courtyard in front. Salomon provided

Fig. 15. Ludwig Mies van der Rohe, Tugendhat House, Brno, Czechoslovakia, 1928–1930, interior view, contemporary photograph

Fig. 16. Ludwig Mies van der Rohe, Glasraum, Stuttgart Building Exhibition, 1927

a third lighting alternative: five strong floodlight projectors, suspended from a metal scaffolding on the outside, would bathe the interior in diffuse artificial light at night. "The effect in the interior is quite curious for an artificial illumination, as it provided the impression of summer sunshine outside," Salomon observed.[32]

In the Netherlands, the Philips electronics corporation in 1924 had hired a young designer, Louis C. Kalff, fresh from art school, who soon steered the company toward better product design and the creation of a corporate identity. Kalff established Philips's first advertising studio in 1929 and, in the same year, an office for lighting advice (Lichtadviesbureau). He was responsible for the illumination of the Dutch pavilion at the Barcelona World's Fair (1929) and created light installations at the Colonial Exhibitions in Antwerp (1930) and Paris (1931). This work culminated in his close cooperation with Iannis Xenakis and Le Corbusier for the Philips Pavilion at the Brussels World's Fair in 1958. He was also a prolific lamp designer and published several articles and a book on architectural illumination.[33]

On the eve of the Great Depression, a distinct vision of architecture's future direction emerged from a debate that on occasion seemed to care little about earlier determining factors, such as space, structure, and function. The German design journal *Form* recognized the importance of this development for modernist architectural discourse: "Light provides us with a new formal element devoid of material firmness, stability, and organic definition. It seemingly stands in great contrast to the formal elements of our time. We have to ask if our traditional understanding of form, based as it is on material and measurable values, might not have to be replaced with a new, more comprehensive notion."[34]

Kelly at Columbia and Yale

Richard Kelly arrived in New York City from Zanesville, Ohio, in the summer of 1928 as a freshman at Columbia College. He chose English literature as his major and physics and mathematics as minor subjects. His greatest interest in those days, however, was the theater. "I didn't care whether the shows were good or bad," he recalled: "I wanted to see them all." The young Kelly was "dazzled by the brightness of the lights on Broadway," and he would recklessly buy theater tickets despite being hardly able to afford them—occasionally even slipping into a performance at the end of the first intermission among the guests returning from having a smoke at the curb outside.[35] In his second year he joined the Columbia Players Theatre Club.[36] A number of sketches among his papers from those years suggest that he was in charge of set and lighting design. Drawings for a scene in a "sandwich shop" are particularly interesting, as they clearly emphasize the interior lighting, particularly downlighting from the outside, which would become one of Kelly's signature applications (fig. 18).

While still in college Kelly worked for a number of interior designers and lamp manufacturers. In the hard times of the Depression, a lucrative job with designer Ruth Collins Allen and the prospect of a purchasing trip to Europe in 1931 lured him away from Columbia, which he left without a degree in August of that year.[37] For a while he seems to have taken his education into his own hands. Inspired by the Modern Architecture exhibition at the Museum of Modern Art in 1932, he undertook an investigation of his own, writing an eighty-page manuscript that he titled "A Concentrated Study of European Architectural Design, known as the International Style." The report paired his analysis of functionalism in architecture (containing an astonishing richness of detail about the latest European designs) with a manifesto about the qualities required of the modern home. Besides protection from heat and cold, dampness and dryness, Kelly's next priority was the "provision of a choice of any amount of light from darkness to maximum without glare at any spot in the home both day and night." Dimmers, lenses, and floor outlets would serve as the tools to solve this problem, he explained.[38]

By 1934 Kelly's letterhead identified him as a "Designer and Typographer," and in the summer of 1935 he started an independent lighting design company.[39] One of his earliest commissions was at General Electric's Future House exhibition, which opened at Rockefeller Center

Fig. 17. Unknown architect, gas station on Teltower Strasse, Berlin, ca. 1926–1929, night view, contemporary photograph

on October 2, 1935. The architectural firm of Walker and Gillette had designed a new, space-efficient prototype of an air-conditioned suburban home with "rooms . . . illuminated with sunken ceiling lights" by Richard Kelly.[40] (Much noticed at the time, this might have been the first application of the feature.) The "Future House" was one of many attempts in the years following the Modern Architecture exhibition at making modernist home design more accessible to the American mainstream, where the International Style had found little appeal. For *New York Times* critic H. I. Brock, it was America's answer to the type of "modern houses . . . that suggest to old-fashioned and artistically unreconstructed folk some ingenious arrangement of packing cases, cans, slabs and cages."[41] Many more model homes would follow in the coming years, such as the Vision House, Pace Setter House, and the House for Young Homemakers, and Kelly was usually asked to design the lighting.

In 1937 Kelly seems to have founded a short-lived "First School of American Dada," a loose gathering of friends and artists. Very little has survived in Kelly's archive about this, except invitations to receptions in October and November 1937 at its headquarters at 623 Lexington Avenue, and a photograph by Walker Evans showing Richard Kelly's hand with a sculptured luminous object, perhaps in response to the invitation to a pajama party on October 19, 1937, where every guest was asked to bring "something that will float" (fig. 19). The group's title might have been inspired by Lincoln Kirstein's First School of American Ballet.

Chauncey A. Thompson, a Cornell-trained architect, joined Kelly in 1938 as partner, but he assumed a lesser role as secretary and treasurer in 1942 when Kelly became president of the firm of Kelly and Thompson.[42] The company enjoyed considerable success with a sequence of small commissions—from the neon-lit clouds at the Stork Club to new lights at a Wheaton College dining hall, the Marine Historical Museum designed by James Gamble Rogers in Mystic, Connecticut, and Wallace K. Harrison's portion at the Industrial Designer's Exhibition at the Metropolitan Museum of Art.[43] Kelly designed numerous modern lamps in a style comparable to that of Kurt Versen, Walter von Nessen, Poul Henningsen, and others (fig. 20). Perhaps the most significant job in this period was the illumination of the Masterpieces of Art exhibition at the 1939 World's Fair. Kelly's involvement in the preparation of the fair offered him countless opportunities to observe the latest innovations in lighting and the most talked about luminous spectacle of its time.

In 1942, as a result of the United States entering World War II, "dim outs" and "black outs" were mandated in cities all across the country. In New York City restrictions applied to all "exterior lighting for advertising purposes . . . all upward beams of direct or reflected lights [and] lights above the fifteenth floor of buildings."[44] It seemed unlikely that lighting designers would be much in demand in the near future, and Kelly enrolled in the bachelor of arts program in architecture at Yale.

Fig. 18. Richard Kelly, sketch for set design in a theater class at Columbia, ca. 1930

Fig. 19. Walker Evans, photograph of Kelly's hand with an object for the First School of American Dada party, 1937

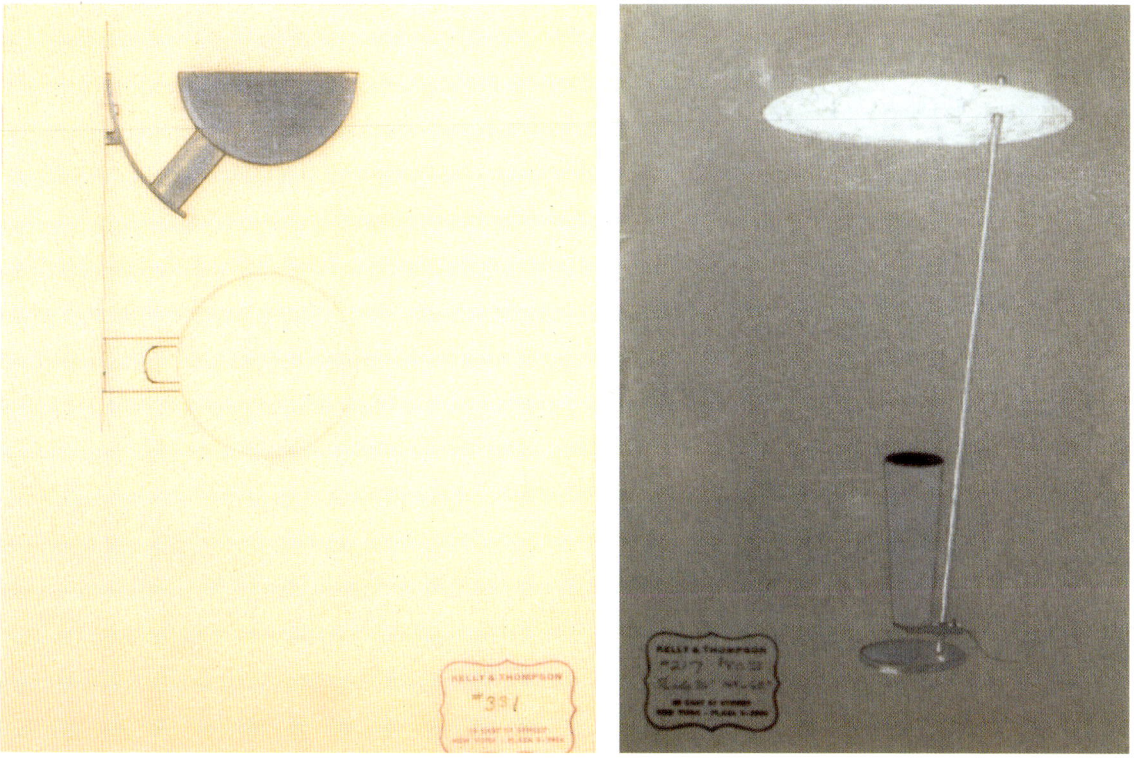

Fig. 20. Richard Kelly, drawings for lamp designs, ca. 1938–1942

Under Dean Everett Victor Meeks the Yale Architecture Department had recently transitioned from Beaux Arts training to modernism. In the academic year during which Kelly signed up, Wallace Harrison and Max Abramovitz were on the faculty, and Erich Mendelsohn and Sigfried Giedion had given guest lectures. Dean Meeks firmly believed in employing practicing architects and artists as teachers, and he founded the program of visiting faculty that has flourished ever since.[45]

Kelly's experience at Yale was severely affected by wartime. From January 1943 onward, three thousand cadets of the Army Air Force Technical Training Command moved in, taking over half of the residential and a third of Yale's academic facilities.[46] Yale offered a wartime "accelerated program" in 1942–1943 featuring additional summer terms that allowed a student to finish eight semesters of work in just two years and seven months.[47] Kelly received generous additional credits for his work at Columbia, shortening his stay further by another two terms.[48] He entered the school for the summer term on June 6, 1942, and graduated in October 1944, during which time he was not affiliated with any of Yale's residential colleges and lived off campus. Kelly immersed himself as much as possible in undergraduate life, becoming a member of the architecture fraternity Iktinos and Mory's lunch club.[49]

The Architecture Department at Yale's Weir Hall had to work with limited staff. Wallace Harrison was drafted and left in early 1942, and Max Abramovitz left half a year later.[50] Urban Design was taught by Maurice Rotival, the French town planner who had just developed the master plan for Venezuela's capital, Caracas.[51] Among Kelly's design teachers was Oscar Nitzchke, who was working in the office of Harrison and Abramovitz at the time, after an apprenticeship with Le Corbusier in Paris and after designing a much noticed visionary newspaper building (Maison de la Publicité), whose facade consisted of nothing but luminous advertising and a back projection screen for newsreels (fig. 21). Nitzchke and Kelly stayed in touch after the war, together completing an apartment restoration at 485 Park Avenue in 1946 while developing a manuscript and proposal for a "Home of Your Own."[52]

Kelly's final studio project and bachelor's thesis were supervised by William Wilson Wurster, the California modernist who had moved to the East Coast to pursue graduate studies in urban planning at Harvard and became dean of architecture at the Massachusetts Institute of Technology the next year. In 1949 Wurster returned to California as dean of Berkeley's architecture school. Kelly, for his final design project, selected a "Television Studio." He had to design the work in his final ten weeks and then present it to a jury. This thesis project was a rather bold choice at a time when television was only just beginning, but Kelly made use of a new course, Television Program Production, taught by Edward Cyrus Cole, assistant professor and technical director in the Drama Department, which was the only class Kelly took in that department. If Kelly had selected Yale's architecture school for its proximity to the theater department (both belonged to Yale's Department of Fine Arts) and its focus on innovative lighting, he must have been somewhat disappointed. The accelerated wartime program of studies did not leave him any time to pursue other interests, and Stanley McCandless was drafted into war services at the end of 1942 and stationed at Fort Belvoir, Virginia, with the camouflage division.[53]

Midcentury Modern

After the war and in the midst of an economic upswing and housing boom, Kelly returned to his practice as a lighting designer. He soon became one of the major protagonists in a lively campaign for home lighting that had begun in the 1930s and lasted through the 1950s.[54] The numerous articles in home decorating magazines, as well as advisory booklets by Westinghouse, General Electric, and others, hardly amount to a critical debate, as they all to varying degrees seemed to promote the same idea: that electric light should be used in any new home as a key element of its interior decoration. Some of the most conspicuous voices (among them Kelly and McCandless) suggested more: using electric light to help design and articulate patterns of life at home. Here, the transfer of stage lighting to the home had a substantial impact. In fact, it meant a revolution in the approach to interior lighting.

Of course, not the entire range of stage lighting was applicable to interior decoration. No lighting designer would seriously consider turning someone's living room into a foreboding, gloomy place ripe for the unfolding of tragedy. But one could establish different lighting moods for a dinner party with several guests, a romantic evening for a couple after the children went to bed, or simply enhancing everyone's skin color. Lamps designed for stage lighting would be used for installation in the home and regulated with dimmers, resulting in a higher degree of control and precision. Before, the emphasis had been on new lamps for the home, but now the need for a highly directional focused lighting was formulated, culminating in Kelly's efforts to hide the actual light source in favor of luminous spaces with glowing surfaces and materials, which was an entirely new approach.

Throughout the late 1940s and 1950s Kelly contributed a number of essays for interior design magazines, and his own apartment on Fifth Avenue served as a testing and demonstration workshop for new ideas. When designing lighting for *House Beautiful* magazine's "Pace-Setter House" in Orange, New Jersey, Kelly provided an astonishing, and somewhat overwrought, panoply of lighting applications: concealed spotlights, floor lamps, table lamps (all on dimmers), cove lights under the ceiling, and valance lights for the draperies. The garden and terrace were lit by concealed floodlights under the trees and on the roof.

The commission to design the lighting for Philip Johnson's guest house for Blanchette Rockefeller in 1949 represented an important breakthrough and shift in Kelly's career. He managed to limit his sometimes overly rich vocabulary for the application of light in the home to three precisely defined gestures: wall washers for the art, recessed downlights with a diffusing grate underneath, and a luminous canopy in the courtyard. Invitations to design the lighting for Philip Johnson's Glass House in New Canaan, Connecticut, as well as Mies van der Rohe's Chicago Art Club and then his Lake Shore Drive Apartments followed this commission and had a formative influence on Kelly's career.

The arrival of European immigrants who brought a particular sensibility to the design of spaces and their lighting was an important factor in the emergence of Kelly's mature style. Kelly must have observed with fascination the debates emerging from the lighting design in Marcel Breuer's model home in the garden of the Museum of Modern Art in 1949. Breuer's decision not to use any portable lamps touched off a debate in the lamp industry, and he was invited to defend his view in a public discussion with three lamp manufacturers (Yasha Heifetz, president of the Heifetz Company, Kurt Versen of Kurt Versen Lamps, Inc., and Mrs. Greta von Nessen of the Nessen studios). "Mr. Breuer likes a room to be well lighted without his being aware of the source of the glow, an effect usually achieved with built-in installations," the *New York Times* reported. "There are certain places, he conceded, where portable lamps are necessary, and where built-in lighting would be impractical and too costly."[55]

From Richard Neutra, whom Kelly had visited in 1947 and advised on the Kaufmann and Tremaine Houses, he adopted one of his signature gestures. Neutra had thought about the nocturnal impressions at his houses from inside and outside since the 1930s. A long, suspended light trough had already been a new and powerful (if not exactly cozy) illumination tool inside the Lovell House. In the following years, incandescent and later fluorescent lights were placed behind strips of translucent glass in the overhangs of flat roofs, just a few feet outside the large plate glass windows. According to Barbara Lamprecht, Neutra liked to call this an "optical curtain."[56] It softened the transition from inside to outside, and eliminated reflections of the interior and the black background beyond. Dion Neutra claimed that his father also maintained that on warm nights, when the sliding windows were open, the strip of light in the soffit kept mosquitoes from flying into the home. Early examples of this technique can be seen at the 1932 VDL Research House, the 1936 Douglas Plywood Model Demonstration House, and the Kun and Richter Houses in the same year. In the Grace Lewis Miller House of 1937 and the Lyndon House of 1943, the light trough continues from a screened veranda onto an open porch (fig. 22). Neutra seems to have been happy with this particular approach, as it resurfaces unchanged in his first residential commission after the war, the spectacular Edgar J. Kaufmann House in Palm Springs. Kelly wrote to Neutra about improving the downward light in these light troughs with the help of egg-crate louvers and recommended "high hat" lights for wall washing inside. It is not clear

Fig. 21. Oscar Nitzchke with Hugo Herdeg, Maison de la Publicité project, Paris, exterior perspective, 1936. Gouache, ink, and cut-and-pasted printed paper on photograph mounted on canvas, 28 ¼ x 20 inches. The Museum of Modern Art, New York; Gift of Lily Auchincloss, Barbara Jakobson, and Walter Randel, 424.1976.1 © The Museum of Modern Art/ Licensed by SCALA/Art Resource, N.Y.

Fig. 22. Richard Neutra, Lyndon House, Los Angeles, 1943, photograph by Julius Shulman. © J. Paul Getty Trust, used with permission, Julius Shulman Photograph Archive, Research Library at the Getty Research Institute (2004.R.10).

from Kelly's or Neutra's archives whether those recommendations were realized in the end.[57]

From 1948 until 1977 Richard Kelly kept meticulous notes for every day of his life. Several folders with undated scrap pieces of paper exist for the earlier years, beginning around 1928, and a few small "featherweight" notebooks from 1946–1948 have survived, but his personal recording system was established in 1948, when he resumed his professional practice after returning from Yale and the end of the war. The system remained basically unchanged for the next thirty years. Every morning, Kelly would take a six-by-nine-inch sheet of paper from a ring binder, fold it lengthwise to fit it into a pocket, and then jot down events, calls, and appointments throughout the day. At night, he would return it to the ring binder.

In this way Kelly produced about ten thousand pages with notes in a tiny pencil script, often densely filling both sides of each leaf. The pages take up twenty-nine ring binders, always running backward chronologically, with the last sheet of paper added at the top. Although these volumes are not a work of literary quality, they are perfect complements to the hundreds of office files for Kelly's projects, indicating the amount and length of his involvement in each.

The seemingly laconic lists of office appointments turn out to be a roll call of the major midcentury modern architects Kelly collaborated with. Philip Johnson (invariably labeled "P.c.J.") is perhaps most frequently mentioned, but Eliot Noyes, William Lescaze, Louis Kahn, Eero Saarinen, and many others make an appearance, as do colleagues in the field, such as Marie Nichols, the fabric designer, Billy Blitzer of Lightolier, and most importantly Edison Price, the lighting engineer and designer. Ellsworth Kelly, the painter and sculptor, became a close friend in the 1950s. During Richard Kelly's busiest period, from the late 1940s into the early 1960s, phone calls, meetings, and business trips followed each other in breathtaking sequence, recorded in quarter-hour increments (without much of a break on weekends). Countless weekend trips to Philip Johnson's Glass House are recorded, daily visits or phone calls with Marie Nichols, who collaborated on some early projects, and frequent visits with Lincoln Kirstein, the impresario and director of the New York City Ballet.

We learn a lot about the genesis of the Seagram Building, for example, as Kelly meticulously recorded the countless phone calls and meetings he had with Philip Johnson, Phyllis Lambert, and Edison Price from 1955 to 1958. From the many days Kelly spent with Lou Kahn in Philadelphia in the 1960s we can deduce the hours it took to develop appropriate exit signs or the perforated metal reflectors for the Kimbell Art Museum in Fort Worth. Precise records of the lighting equipment are kept as well.

Beyond and between those lists, personal notes and observations abound. While working with the young Robert Venturi on the Duke House renovation, he noted, "Bob Venturi says: San Carlo Opera, Naples: appliqué balls & glitter flood boxes; Weltenburg by Asam Bros" (October 30, 1958). In addition, one gets glimpses of the flow of Kelly's life and persona from small descriptive notes, ideas about his profession, new plans for projects, candid self-evaluations, touching remarks about his children, Scott and Addison, and his wife, Betty ("Betty wants electric toaster," December 16, 1954), and memories of their frequent theater visits, such as Noël Coward's comedy *Fallen Angels* at the Playhouse ("Noel Coward and Marlene Dietrich were there," January 18, 1956).

In the late 1940s and early 1950s, Kelly began to formulate a personal theory of light, probably intended as a way of distinguishing his work from that of the growing competition. He strove for a credo as simple as the Vitruvian "firmness, commodity, and delight." In an essay for *Interior Design and Decoration* in June 1949, Kelly listed "three distinct design functions" for light: emphasis, or the organization of visual design; comfort, the fulfillment of the needs of seeing; and character, or the feeling of a space. Kelly presented the lighting designer as an interpreter or even editor of architecture. "A common example of emphasis is the lighting of a good wall to make it important, while a bad one is left in shadow, to conceal necessarily bad interruptions or surfaces," he wrote. And even though the "character of a room is always the most intangible of its elements," Kelly managed to be very specific in his recommendations: "Successful lighting makes moods. A burst of warm light above and about you spreads a feeling of welcome. Soft diffuse light extending over large areas is soothing. Warm areas of light blending into one another are comforting. Concentration of the most strongly lighted areas near the floor is cozy; while concentration near the ceiling is formal. Lighted areas at eye level give a sense of security, defining the room and its contents. In other words, good lighting adds to good living."[58]

Three years later, Kelly formulated his often quoted credo about the three types of light—"focal glow," "ambient luminescence," and the "play of brilliants"—during a lecture at a joint meeting of the American Institute of Architects, the Society of Industrial Designers, and the Society of Illuminating Engineers in Cleveland on April 23, 1952.[59] In an essay for the *College Art Journal* based on his lecture, and on many other occasions afterward, Kelly explained each concept. Much of his thought about light had been formed by the theater: focal glow was "the follow spot on the modern stage," ambient luminescence "the full cyclorama of the open theatre," and the play of brilliants could be seen in "Times Square at night." In addition, he listed six qualities of light: intensity, brightness, diffusion, spectral color, direction, and movement. In later renditions of his credo Kelly might mix observations from nature during daytime and applications of artificial light at night. Focal glow, for example, could be both "the pool of light at your favorite reading chair" or "a flashlight's beam," but also the "shaft of sunshine" at the "end of a valley."

Ambient luminescence could be both a "fog light at sea in a small boat" and an art gallery's strip-lighted walls, a translucent ceiling and white floor. He saw the play of brilliants in the sunlight reflected off a brook.

No one before him had defined lighting with such abundant love for metaphor. The pairing of natural phenomena and the results of his work with artificial light rather ingeniously elevated the lighting designers' craft and revealed once again his affinity for the theater, where natural lighting conditions were imitated through spot and floodlights and changes in color. Kelly's three categories simplified the field's possibilities considerably, and his own best work certainly transcends such categorization. One might wonder if, for example, the illuminated trees outside Johnson's Glass House provide a play of brilliants, focal glow, or a luminous ambience. Similarly, the Seagram's luminous ceiling presents both ambient luminescence inside and a play of brilliants outside to the passersby on Park Avenue. If the secretaries working directly under it were indeed reminded of "a snowy morning in the open country" when they arrived at their desks, as Kelly suggested, is hard to tell.[60]

Technology

Lighting technology made enormous progress during Kelly's career from the mid-1930s to the 1970s (fig. 23). Following its introduction at the World's Fair of 1939, the fluorescent lamp surpassed the incandescent light bulb as the leading light source in the United States by the early 1950s. The light it produced was cheaper, and new starter technologies and color correction from an eerie green-yellow toward a warmer red made it more acceptable. High-intensity discharge lamps such as mercury vapor enjoyed growing success as streetlights, especially since their blue-green color could be corrected to a warmer hue.[61] In 1952 Kelly stated that "nine out of ten light sources, fixtures and equipment . . . did not exist twenty-five years ago," when he arrived in New York.[62] General Electric alone introduced more than 750 new lamps in the early 1950s. Westinghouse and Sylvania, its nearest rivals, were not far behind.

For a lighting consultant like Kelly, the importance of the actual source of light was matched by that of the other parts of the light fixture, or "luminaire," consisting of the reflector for directing the light, an aperture (with or without a lens), and the outer shell or housing for lamp alignment and protection. Especially the reflector would be custom made for a particular situation, to ensure that the light reached precisely the areas for which it was intended. The inner surface of these reflectors could range from an optimal degree of reflectivity to the opposite, a complete dulling effect, to eliminate glare. This led to countless experiments with materials, such as silverized glass and highly polished aluminum at one end of the spectrum to a black, roughened surface interrupted by baffle rings on the other. New York City became the American center of an industry producing these light fixtures that turned out to be astonishingly stable and unencumbered by recessions and political tides of the twentieth century. Most of these firms still exist today.

Kliegl Brothers, founded by two Bavarian immigrants in 1895, was the oldest firm specializing in theater lighting, and it was soon joined in New York by other companies, including Century Lighting, Gotham Lighting, Lightolier, Swivelier, and Rambusch Lighting. In their competition for market share, all of these firms submitted patent applications; Edward Rambusch was probably the first to patent a "recessed light" for use in architecture in 1936 (one year after Kelly had employed it at the "Future House" exhibition in Rockefeller Center), followed by Stanley McCandless on behalf of Century Lighting in 1946, Harry Gerstel of Gotham Lighting in 1954, and Edison Price and Isaac Goodbar in 1958 (fig. 24). Their patent applications reveal a keen awareness of the aesthetics of modern architecture. Rambusch was typical in emphasizing that his fixture was "hidden above the ceiling" so "the source of light cannot be seen by an occupant of the space to be illuminated."

The precise calculation of a flow of light from a source into space was greatly helped by General Electric's "sealed beam" lamps, developed for the automobile industry in the late 1930s. Combining the glowing filament, the reflector, and the lens in one unit, these lamps produced a focused

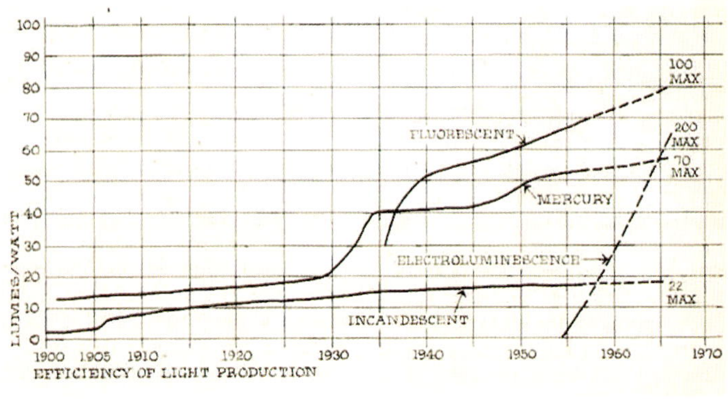

Fig. 23. Graph of light output efficiency for different types of light, published in *Architectural Forum*

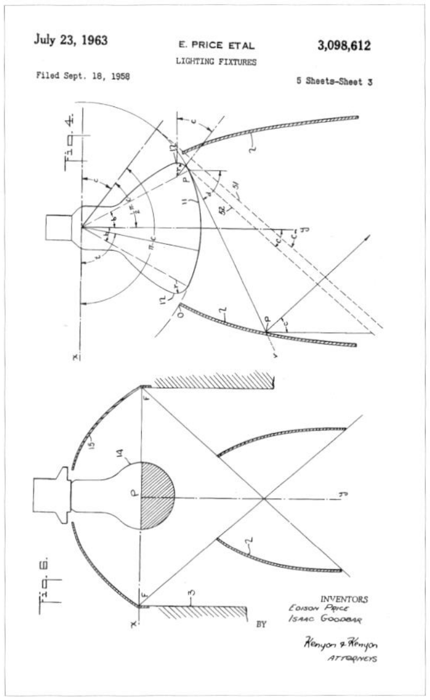

Fig. 24. Edison Price and Isaac Goodbar, patent application for lighting fixture, filed September 18, 1958

Fig. 25. Richard Kelly (*left*), with Edison Price and their model for the Barbizon Plaza chandelier, ca. 1953

oval pool of light. When aluminum plating was applied to the reflector surface in the early 1940s, the name Parabolic Aluminized Reflector (PAR) was introduced. Those focused beams simplified stage lighting significantly in the following years. McCandless, Kelly, and many others transferred this technology from the stage to the home, where PAR lamps became the favored choice for recessed can fixtures thanks to their tightly controlled beam.[63]

Kelly was particularly fortunate to work with Edison Price, a lighting designer, inventor, and mechanical engineer who was responsible for many of the fixtures Kelly used (fig. 25). Countless entries in Kelly's pocket notes document their almost daily interaction over the decades. After apprenticing in his parents' stage lighting company, Display Stage Lighting, Price became the—still widely unrecognized—genius of the profession. Called "a sensible mad inventor" (Philip Johnson) and "the dark horse in the lighting field" (*Industrial Design*), he was head of the Edison Price Lighting Company, which developed and manufactured light fixtures such as the recessed downlights in the soffits of the Seagram Building and the ceiling lights at the Four Seasons Restaurant there. He often worked with the Argentinian mathematician Isaac Goodbar, who developed highly complex formulas to determine the output of a particular lamp with the utmost precision, and early on used computers for his calculations.[64] Besides working with Kelly, Price had many independent lighting commissions from Skidmore, Owings, and Merrill, Alvar Aalto, Marcel Breuer, I. M. Pei, and others, at Yale's Beinecke Library, MIT's Baker House, and the Whitney Museum. Price often moved beyond the field of lighting—when Richard Kelly involved the artist Ellsworth Kelly in Philadelphia's Penn Center Transportation Building in 1957, it was Price who actually manufactured Ellsworth Kelly's abstract metal sculptures. For Buckminster Fuller's 1959 exhibition at the Museum of Modern Art he built a tensegrity mast, and he worked extensively with Isamu Noguchi on sculptures and stage sets for Martha Graham.[65] With Kelly he developed and built the chandelier for the Barbizon Plaza Hotel, and with Kelly and Johnson the three- and four-legged versions of a floor lamp.

The quantity of light used in the United States in 1957 was six times that of 1940. The main cause for this increase was the rapid rise of the fluorescent lamp following its introduction at the 1939 World's Fair, to the top of the list of light sources used nationwide. Kelly's colleague Bertha Schaefer, a designer of furniture and interiors, was one of the first, in 1945, to suggest using fluorescent lights in the home, an idea that Kelly employed often.[66] Both the glass and lamp industries had begun to promote the idea of a luminous ceiling in publications and sales exhibitions in order to sell newly developed materials, such as "vitrolux"—colored, translucent glass as a new application area for fluorescent lamps—from the late 1930s onward. But the general breakthrough came with the frequent publication of nocturnal images of the Manufacturers Trust Building on Fifth Avenue, designed by Skidmore, Owings, and Merrill in 1953.

"An important factor in the rise of the fluorescent is the development since 1945 of the luminous ceiling," wrote *Architectural Forum* in 1957: "banks of fluorescent fixtures screened by diffusers. No lighting idea in recent years caught on so firmly, for it offered an opportunity to integrate lighting with architectural design. The ultimate expression of this, so far visible in only a few buildings, is the ceiling integrating all four elements of lighting, air conditioning, acoustical control and sprinklers into a single system. But architects soon learned that luminous ceilings had three shortcomings: too monotonous, if uncritically used; too glaring, unless shielded; too diffuse a light for sharp perception. Despite many improvements in one or another of these factors, the luminous ceiling is still a problem requiring carefully studied treatment."[67] Kelly provided a perfect example. For the office of fellow lighting designer Douglas Leigh, famous for his spectacular luminous advertisements on Times Square, Kelly had designed a particularly elegant translucent ceiling, which employed glass instead of the plastic offered by Lightolier and left the light sources above vaguely visible (fig. 26). Although Kelly managed to get the installation published, the papers in the archive tell of a dramatic failure. Kelly's "shimmering ceiling plane," developed with the architect Landis Gores, in charge of the remodeling of the office, ended up causing "high operating costs, . . . box-overheating and fuse- and switch-blowing, and . . . excessive heat output." In the end, the entire installation had to be removed and Kelly and Gores lost a subsequent job as a result. Gores tried to console Kelly: "I still feel your idea was both brilliant and sound."[68]

Fig. 26. Landis Gores, Douglas Leigh Office, New York, 1953. Lighting designer: Richard Kelly.

Night Photography and the Mise-en-Scène

Lighting and nighttime photography have long engaged in dialogues with architecture, sometimes pursuing parallel or identical goals, sometimes opposite approaches to the nocturnal aesthetics of architecture. In the 1920s, in the context of debates about a new "architecture of the night," architects, lighting designers, and producers of lighting equipment began requesting images of illuminated buildings, and photographers developed strategies to present them as attractively as possible in darkness. Hardly ever could a photograph be taken without substantial intervention by the photographer, and the resulting images usually had little resemblance to the often rather unheroic impression most buildings gave after dark.

Long exposures allowed photographers to make a building's lights appear brighter, and manipulation during the developing process could emphasize or downplay certain areas and effects, or achieve the appearance of even illumination, even if there was none. On the night of a photo shoot, for example, often all the rooms on every floor would be lit—an otherwise rare occurrence after hours. Making two or more exposures on the same negative allowed areas with differing luminosity to be combined in one photograph. Julius Shulman's famous image of Neutra's Kaufmann House was the result of three different exposures on the same negative (fig. 27). For each shot different light sources in the house were turned on or off, and the exposure time and aperture were adjusted accordingly.[69] The first exposure was for the overall exterior illumination and some of the house lights; the second recorded the exterior soffit lighting and other interior lights. For the third exposure, Shulman asked

Fig. 27. Richard Neutra, Edgar Kaufmann House, Palm Springs, California, 1946–1947, photograph by Julius Shulman. © J. Paul Getty Trust, used with permission, Julius Shulman Photograph Archive, Research Library at the Getty Research Institute (2004.R.10).

Mr. Kaufmann to turn on the pool light, and posed Mrs. Kaufmann to block the glare. The image looks convincing in spite of its artifice, as the photograph mimics the adjustment that the eye would make over time as it focused sequentially on areas of different luminosity.

The most powerful of the photographer's tools directly intersected with the work of the lighting designer. Since the 1920s, portable light sources had become affordable for the average photographer, who would usually bring several for both daytime and nighttime photography.[70] If not enough light sources were available, a cheaper method would be applied: while the camera's shutter remained open, assistants would walk through the building with electric floodlights or gas lamps and, for example, sequentially illuminate all the ceiling areas visible from the street below. The German language actually has a term for this method, *Wanderlicht*—wandering light.[71] The finished photograph would show the sum of these partial and temporary illuminations as a brightly glowing ceiling. The illusion of a perfectly luminous structure was created, which might have represented the photographer's vision, perhaps even the architect's intentions, but actually never existed. In many professional photos of interiors at night, one finds shadows and bursts of light or evenly glowing ceilings without a light source to be seen.

With the appearance of new architectural journals in the 1920s with plenty of photographs and the simultaneous interest in nocturnal imagery, such staged photos began to shape an aesthetic of luminous modern architecture, at a time when it could be achieved only through the photographer's intervention. Of course, architects and interior designers would often welcome the photographer's ability to lend drama and intensity to their creations.[72] By the 1950s, when buildings could actually look as brightly and evenly luminous as they had in photographs before, lighting designers might either succumb to an aesthetic established by another craft and to another end, or find themselves at odds with some photographers' intentions.

Richard Kelly's work easily fell victim to such constellations. The house designed by Gregory Ain and exhibited in the garden of the Museum of Modern Art in 1950, for example, was presented to millions of readers of the *New York Times* and *House and Home* in Ezra Stoller's dramatic nocturnal photograph from the outside in (see Isenstadt fig. 5). Stoller switched off Kelly's signature downlights in the outside soffits (visible in the foreground upper left), took down all the curtains, rearranged the furniture, and brightly illuminated the space and ceiling with hidden light sources casting stark horizontal shadows throughout. While this photograph rendered the spatial depth and organization with a clarity that no daytime view could have provided, it was a pure fabrication, reminiscent, indeed, of a stage set. Kelly's concept was diametrically opposed: the downlights would have mellowed the contrast between inside and out, his baffle lamp and David Wooster's floor lamp created focal glow, and the ceiling would have been comparatively dark—according to Kelly a precondition for feeling comfortable in small residential spaces.

Similarly, Lionel Freedman's photograph of the courtyard facade of Louis Kahn's Yale Art Gallery suggests some photographic manipulation. The back walls of the galleries with their washes of light provided brightness in the lower floors; in the uppermost floor, though, the back walls have become invisible and more of the dramatic ceiling has become visible. As the lights hidden in its open tetrahedral ceiling were carefully designed by Edison Price to not blind visitors, the ceiling itself remained comparatively dark. On closer inspection of Freedman's iconic photograph of the nocturnal facade, the third-floor ceiling seems astonishingly light compared with its counterpart in other floors. It is likely that the photographer brought in additional, temporary light sources when he took the photo, or he exposed the upper floor longer in developing it.

The Later Years

Throughout the 1950s and most of the 1960s, Kelly kept very busy, regularly working on twenty or more lighting commissions per year, and more than thirty in some years. But in the late 1960s work for Kelly dried up considerably; from 1968 on the jobs dwindled to only a handful, often fewer than five. The reasons might have included the general economic situation, the growing success of his competitors, and perhaps also his sometimes erratic work habits. Many clients complained about surprisingly high additional bills coming in long after a job was done, and others about the work not being executed in time.

And, indeed, the field had changed. Kelly had been a pioneer as a lighting consultant in the 1940s, but now there was strong competition. Probably the closest contender was Abe Feder, who had begun his career on Broadway and later gained major architectural commissions, working closely with electrical firms on the development of new lamps. There was also Edison Price, who would often take on lighting commissions independently, and William Richardson, who made a name for himself with particularly successful color illuminations.[73]

Kelly's notebooks in these years reflect the resilience of his daily recording routine—the lack of work did not lead to shorter appointment lists, but rather gave way to an almost obsessive jotting down of the minutiae of every day's progress. Private matters claim a larger role—appointments at the barber, his wife Betty's comings and goings, every newspaper purchase is recorded (and its price duly noted), and little vignettes appear, sometimes gems of an almost literary quality. "1:00: walk to town in new orange shoes," he noted on Sunday, July 27, 1968, while staying for an extended sojourn at his parents' house in Zanesville, Ohio. "On west Main Str. little cloud bursts began 11 am; RcK [Richard C. Kelly] in doorway, then another doorway, then across bridge, more rain just before Z News on 5th Street. Rushed inside and took off raingear. Met Lucille Tuttle Holmes of San Diego. Bought NY Times. Rain stopped. Walked Lucille T.H. from 5th to Library. Closed." The style of his handwriting, casual at first, gained urgency in those later years, often nervously retracing entries for emphasis, changing direction in midpage. There are touching notes of frequent calls to his answering service in hope of a message and his delight in people complimenting his work. Occasionally there are inspirational messages to himself about new business ideas. At the same time, there are recurring problems with the Internal Revenue Service. On October 15, 1967, he noted darkly, in red pencil: "Had apocalyptic insight."

Increased financial worries in the 1970s led to even more obsessive bookkeeping, with each day's bills clipped to the page, the ring binders swelling with added pieces of paper. Always a voracious reader, Kelly seems to have bought piles of mostly used books on almost any subject on a daily basis (fig. 28).

In the late 1960s and early 1970s Kelly spent a considerable amount of time researching and promoting the growth of plants under artificial light, something that had interested him for a long time and that he had occasionally applied, as in the small grove of trees under the main staircase in the Bankers Trust Building on Park Avenue.

The two largest projects in those years were commissions to design the lighting for Louis Kahn's Kimbell Art Museum in Fort Worth and the Yale Center for British Art in New Haven. Although most of his projects dealt with the application of artificial light, throughout his career Kelly had emphasized the importance of daylight.[74] His "primary interest in lighting is to use the best source of light—day light—to its maximum possibility and to use artificial light only to the extent necessary to augment daylight," he explained to potential clients and their architects in 1962.[75] Kelly had combined light sources in many projects, such as when he installed incandescent lamps inside the skylights of the courtyard of the Davis House in Wayzata, Minnesota, and the Munson-Williams-Proctor Arts Institute in Utica, New York. Kelly's diaries show his deep involvement in the development of the daylight reflector beneath the vaulted gallery roofs at the Kimbell Art Museum. His understanding of light distribution and reflection in fixtures such as recessed downlights was surprisingly applicable to the large-scale section of the skylights at the Yale Center for British Art, where a similar sequence of devices on a larger scale, some of them movable, achieved a comparable goal.

Kelly and Louis Kahn developed a friendship in the late 1960s and early 1970s, when Kahn's name shows up regularly in Kelly's diaries. Among the most gripping pages are the breathless and desperate entries written on March 19, 1974, when Kelly expected to meet with him following Kahn's return from a trip to India. Kelly was the first to learn over the course of the day the details of Kahn's death from a heart attack at Pennsylvania Station in New York two days before.

Richard Kelly's work displays an astonishing breadth of applications, a large vocabulary, and impressive range of scale. His aesthetic vision has become a central element in our understanding of modern architecture, and several of the buildings he illuminated are presented preferably at night. By adopting the conceptual and technical progress made on Broadway theater stages from the 1920s onward, Kelly introduced considerations and formal elements that had been absent from the mainstream modernist discourse. The precision and control of light developed for the theater helped to create a set of tools for both home lighting and larger urban commissions. As in the theater, light sources were invisible, and the intensity and color of the light itself, as well as the surfaces reflecting it, occupied the center of attention.

On the other hand, Kelly carefully stayed away from the use of color, stark contrasts of light and shadow, and theatrical effects in general. He emphasized the changing visual moods in spaces for different functions, but he never produced atmospheric drawings of the envisioned results of his work like the ones made by Robert Edmond Jones, Donald Oenslager, and Stanley McCandless. While he was a passionate theater lover all his life, and happily embraced the use of focused spotlights and dimmers that had been developed for the stage, he was also keenly aware of the differences. His installations had to work in space, to be seen from all directions, not just for the limited view of a seated audience, with actors on stage suffering the glare of the floodlights.

For the historian, the work of figures like Kelly, McCandless, and Edison Price offers a broader and more complex view of the conditions of architectural production. Details of their involvement not only complicate established notions of authorship in architecture, they also show in more subtle ways the undercurrents of activity that accompany and sometimes enable stylistic change.

Critics often compared the nocturnal and diurnal view of a building to the negative and positive prints of a photograph. Kelly's nocturnal modernity went far beyond the merely visual level of such comparisons and introduced measures of time and change, by scripting sequential narratives for certain spaces and providing varied lighting concepts for particular functional situations and specific moods. In addition, and perhaps most important, at night the reflective sheen of windows during the day was replaced with the visibility of a building's spatial depth, internal organization, and structure. Often, a modern building's most important qualities became fully comprehensible only at night. Such a nocturnal interpretation of a building added richness and complexity to the architect's vision and ultimately challenged the scope of modern architecture itself.

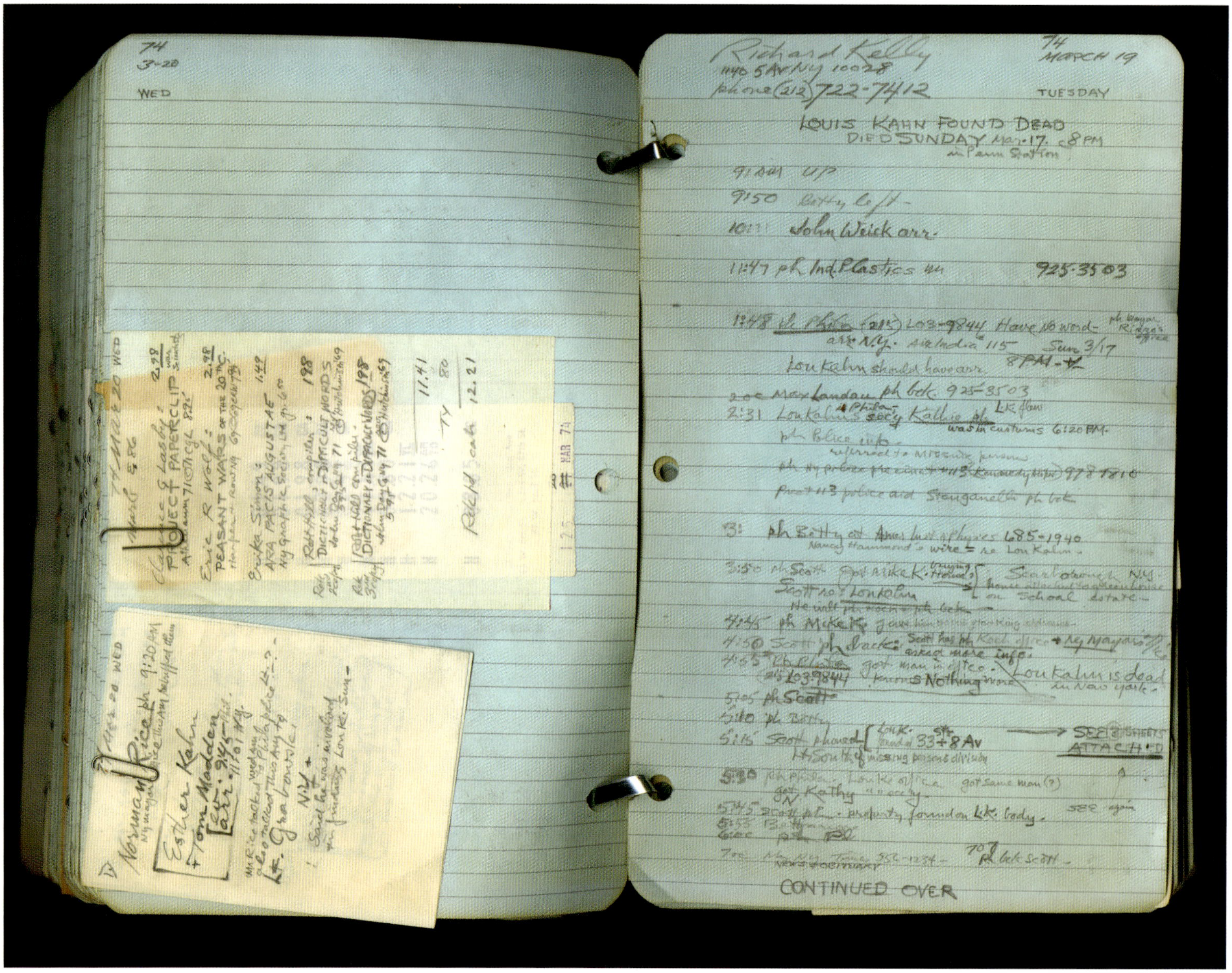

Fig. 28. Pages from Richard Kelly's pocket notes written on the day that Louis Kahn's death was discovered

Notes

1. Douglas Haskell, "Architecture: The Bright Lights," *Nation* 132, no. 3419 (January 14, 1931): 55–56.
2. Arthur Edwin Krows, "The Theatre's Debt to America," *New York Times*, December 2, 1917; Bobbi Owen, *Lighting Design on Broadway: Designers and Their Credits* (New York: Greenwood, 1991), ix; Arthur Edwin Krows, *Play Production in America* (New York: Henry Holt, 1916), 217.
3. By 1944 one quarter of all Broadway productions listed a lighting designer, and in 1962 the United Scenic Artists recognized lighting design as a separate category. Owen, *Lighting Design on Broadway*, xi.
4. Norman Bel Geddes, *A Project for a Theatrical Presentation of the Divine Comedy of Dante Alighieri* (New York: Theatre Arts, 1924), 13. See also Claude Bragdon, "A Project for a Theatrical Representation of the Divine Comedy of Dante Alighieri by Norman Bel Geddes," *Architectural Record* 56 (July 1924): 95–96; Robert A. M. Stern, Gregory Gilmartin, and Thomas Mellins, *New York, 1930: Architecture and Urbanism Between the Two World Wars* (New York: Rizzoli, 1987), 232–234.
5. John Corbin, "'The Miracle': Fine Spectacle Shown," *New York Times* January 16, 1924. George E. Bogusch mentions that the lighting for *The Miracle* required 440 one-thousand-watt spotlights, 500 electric candles, and 1,500 miniature "star" lights, not to mention the less specific lighting on the cyclorama and behind the more than 70 "stained-glass" windows of the setting. George E. Bogusch, "Norman Bel Geddes and the Art of Modern Theatre Lighting," *Educational Theatre Journal* 24, no. 4 (December 1972): 415–429.
6. Bogusch, "Norman Bel Geddes and the Art," 415.
7. Jo Mielziner, "Practical Dreams," in *The Theatre of Robert Edmond Jones*, ed. Ralph Pendleton (Middletown, Conn.: Wesleyan University Press, 1958), 24.
8. See Louis Hartmann, "Lighting Effects on the Stage," a paper presented to the Illuminating Engineering Society (IES), January 11, 1923, and Claude Bragdon, "Theatrical Lighting," a paper presented to the IES October 29, 1924, reprinted in Theodore Fuchs, *Stage Lighting* (1929; reprint, New York: Benjamin Blom, 1963), 461–474.
9. Stanley R. McCandless, "The Problem of Lighting and Illumination: With the Aid of the Illuminating Engineer and Designer, Lighting Is Gradually Assuming an Artistic Quality," *Yale Scientific Magazine* (January 1930): 13–14, 44; Stanley McCandless, "I Light My House" (1937), typescript written for *Architectural Forum*, Stanley McCandless Papers, Yale Manuscripts and Archives, Box 4, Folder "1937."
10. Baldwin MacDonald, "M.I.T. Chapel, Auditorium, Lighting as Striking as Building's Exteriors," *New England Electrical News* (October 1956).
11. Hollister Noble, "New York's Crown of Light," *New York Times*, February 8, 1925.
12. Jones supervised the lighting for the shows of his friend Maude Adams with the Washington Square Players on Broadway (including *Peter Pan*) and introduced the first floodlights to the theater stage in 1912, as well as one of the first dimmer switchboards at the Artist's Guild Theatre in St. Louis. Russell Flinchum, "Broadway Lights," *2wice*, vol. 6, no. 2: 33–41; Irving Pichel, "Stage Machinery and Lighting Equipment for Small Theatres and Community Buildings," *Theatre Arts Magazine: An Illustrated Quarterly* 4 (1920): 145.
13. Some of the key essays by Bassett Jones are: "Some Artistic Requirements of Artificial Illumination," *Electrical Review* (September 14, 1904); "The Relation of Architectural Principles to Illuminating Engineering Practice," *Transactions of the Illuminating Engineering Society* 3, no. 1 (1908): 9–66; "Indirect Lighting," *American Architect* 96, no. 1772 (December 8, 1909): 245–249; "The Lighting of Churches," *American Architect* 96, no. 1761 (September 22, 1909): 105–111; "The Lighting of 'Period' Interiors," *American Architect* 97, no. 1788 (March 30, 1910): 133; "Mobile Color and Stage Lighting," *Electrical World* 66, nos. 5–9 (July 31–August 28, 1915): 245–249, 294–297, 346–349, 407–409, 454–456; and "Colors for Hospitals," *New York Times*, December 12, 1920.
14. National Electric Light Association, 42nd Convention, Commercial Section Sessions, Papers, Reports, and Discussions, Atlantic City, New Jersey, May 19–22, 1919, p. 237.
15. "Lecture to Architectural Students," appearing in two parts in the *Journal of the American Institute of Architects*, May and June 1919.
16. Edgar H. Bostock, "Sheet Glass in Lighting," *American Architect* (December 29, 1915): 417.
17. For special occasions Jones had more ideas, all derived from his theatrical experience: "The whole effect will be that of Walhalla burning in the skies, bringing to mind, perhaps, the finale of the Götterdämmerung. With manual control, smoke boxes added and mortars firing bombs from the tank roof, a most gorgeous display can be produced. . . . There lies in the future a development even more fantastic than anything that has ever been accomplished on the stage. Eventually, the night lighting of buildings is going to be studied exactly as Gordon Craig and Norman Bel Geddes have studied stage lighting." Bassett Jones, "Structures in Light," *Light* (April 1924): 4–7.
18. Lewis Mumford, "The Sky Line in Flushing: West Is East," *New Yorker*, June 17, 1939, reprinted in *Sidewalk Critic: Lewis Mumford's Writings on New York*, ed. Robert Wojtowicz (New York: Princeton Architectural Press, 1998), 236–237.
19. Geoffrey T. Hellman, "Profiles: Day-Before-Yesterday Man," *New Yorker*, April 29, 1939, 24–30.
20. Ibid., 30; Harland Manchester, *New World of Machines* (New York: Random House, 1945), 75. For Bassett Jones, lighting design was just one of many generally unrelated areas of interest that he unfailingly managed to be very good at. He improved the speed of elevators in New York City; with Clarence Birdseye, another lighting designer and inventor in many different fields, he developed a method for freezing freshly caught fish; and he successfully introduced the hardy black Japanese pine tree to the windy shores of Nantucket, where he spent most of his time. He developed a new theory of economics as a co-founder of the "technocracy" movement, which continues to have its followers today. H. Scott, "Toward Technocracy," *Living Age* (December 1932): 292. His only unsuccessful venture was an initiative to gain independence for the island of Nantucket from the State of Massachusetts—due to an apparent lack of interest on the mainland. "Want Nantucket to End Ties with Massachusetts," *New York Times*, November 13, 1935.
21. Fuchs, *Stage Lighting*, 50.
22. Robert Edmond Jones, "Stage Lighting: Its Interpretative Power in the Theatre Illustrated," *New York Times*, November 21, 1914.
23. For a more extensive discussion of the flow of ideas among European and American lighting designers, see Dietrich Neumann, *Architecture of the Night* (Munich: Prestel, 2002), 36–64.
24. Joachim Teichmüller, *Moderne Lichttechnik in Wissenschaft und Praxis, dargestellt an den Darbietungen der Lichttechnischen Ausstellung auf der Gesolei in Düsseldorf* (Berlin: Union Deutsche Verlagsgesellschaft), 1928. The exhibition was called *Gesolei*, which stood for "Gesundheit, soziale Fürsorge, und Leibesübungen" [Health, Social Care, and Exercise of the Body]. See also Joachim Teichmüller, "Lichtarchitektur," *Licht und Lampe*, nos. 13–14 (1927): 421–422, 449–458.

25. In the fall of 1928 Teichmüller traveled to the United States and enthusiastically described the "abundance of light" in New York City in his travel diary. Teichmüller estate, Studienreise in die USA 8.8.-8.11.1928, manuskript, Universitätsarchiv Karlsruhe 10/60/583, p. 108.
26. Walter Riezler, "Licht und Architektur," in *Licht und Beleuchtung*, ed. Wilhelm Lotz (Berlin, 1928), 42–43.
27. See also Michael Stoeneberg, "Arthur Köster, Architekturfotografie, 1926–1933" (Berlin: Gebr. Mann Verlag, 2009); Ernst May, "Städtebau und Lichtreklame," in *Licht und Beleuchtung*, ed. Lotz, 44–47.
28. Walter Riezler, "Umgestaltung der Fassaden," *Die Form*, no. 2 (February 1927): 33–40.
29. "Das Deukonhaus von Erich Mendelsohn," *Die Form*, no. 2 (February 1928): 43–48.
30. Ludwig Mies van der Rohe, "The Adam Building," in *The Artless Word: Mies van der Rohe on the Building Art*, ed. Fritz Neumeyer (Cambridge: MIT Press, 1991), 305.
31. Mildred Adams, "In Their Lights the Cities Are Revealed," *New York Times*, December 11, 1932.
32. Delphine Jacob, "André Salomon, éclairagiste de l'architecture moderne," *Cahiers du Musée national d'art moderne*, no. 90 (December 2004): 93–102, 147–148, 163–164.
33. Iannis Xenakis, "The Architectural Design of Corbusier and Xenakis," *Philips Technical Review* 20, no. 1 (1958–1959): 2–8; L. C. Kalff, "Illumination and Architecture," *Philips Technology Review* 2, no. 1 (1937): 8–12; L. C. Kalff, *Kunstlicht und Architektur* (Eindhoven: N. V. Philips' Gloeilampenfabrieken, 1943); L. C. Kalff, Michel Butor, Jean Petit, et al., *Le Poème électronique Le Corbusier* (Paris: Editions de Minuit, 1958); L. C. Kalff, "The 'Electronic Poem' Performed in the Philips Pavilion at the 1958 Brussels World Fair: The Light Effects," *Philips Technical Review* 20, no. 2–3 (October 23, 1958): 37–42.
34. Ernst Reinhardt, "Gestaltung der Lichtreklame," *Die Form* 4, no. 4 (February 15, 1929): 73–84.
35. Richard Kelly, "Theatre Crashing," "Show Crashing," typescripts, probably writing exercises for his English classes at Columbia College, undated, ca. 1930, Richard Kelly Papers, Manuscripts and Archives, Yale University Library.
36. Richard Kelly, "Lighting Starts with Daylight," *Progressive Architecture* 54 (September 1973): 82–85, and handwritten biographical note in the Richard Kelly Papers. Kelly also joined the Delta Upsilon fraternity, was the editor for the student yearbook, *The Columbian*, and art editor for the *Jester*, a student humor publication.
37. I would like to thank Catherine N. Carson, processing archivist at Columbia's Rare Book and Manuscript Library, for this information, as well as for retrieving additional information from the registrar's office at Columbia University. The architect Der Scutt, who knew Kelly well, claimed that the fact that physical education was a mandatory course at Columbia made Kelly leave the college. Der Scutt, "Richard Kelly, 1910–1977: A Personal Memento," *Lighting Design and Application* (October 1979): 56–58.

According to a handwritten note in Kelly's papers, he worked as "chief designer" for Crucet Lamp Company (the interior designer and lamp manufacturer Joseph M. Crucet), 226 Fifth Avenue, from June 1, 1928, to July 6, 1929; then for Ruth Collins Allen, an interior designer (and author of the popular 1928 book *How to Make Lampshades*), from July 12, 1929, to April 1, 1933; and at Macy's as a salesman in the lamp department from August 4, 1933, to March 31, 1934.
38. Handwritten manuscript, no date, Richard Kelly Papers.
39. Kelly produced several book designs, among them the decorative vignettes in the 1933 edition of Noël Coward's *Play Parade* (New York: Doubleday, 1933).
40. "Art: Future House," *Time*, October 14, 1935; "Shows Trend in Homes," *New York Times*, September 29, 1935; "'New American' Home Is Put on View Here; Hailed by Leaders as Step to Prosperity," *New York Times*, October 2, 1935.
41. H. I. Brock, "Small House, New Style," *New York Times*, October 20, 1935.
42. Chauncey A. Thompson had graduated from Cornell in 1926 and moved to New York to practice architecture. *Cornell Alumni News* 28, no. 40 (August 1926): 498; Yale Alumni File, Special Collections, Yale University Library.
43. Chauncey A. Thompson, letter to LeRoy Ward, August 6, 1940 (Richard Kelly Papers, Folder: Stork Club New York).
44. "Drastic Dimout of All City Lights Effective Tonight," *New York Times*, May 18, 1942.
45. C. H. Sawyer, "Obituary: Everett Victor Meeks, 1879–1954," *College Art Journal* 14, no. 3 (Spring 1955): 295.
46. Judith Ann Schiff, "When Yale Schooled for War," *Yale Alumni Magazine*, December 2002 (retrieved online: www.yalealumnimagazine.com/issues/02_12/old_yale.html).
47. *Bulletin of Yale University for the Academic Year 1943–1944*, Series 39, no. 16 (August 15, 1943): 7–9.
48. Kelly received two course credits each for Drawing, Construction, Design Theory, and Mathematics. Richard Kelly Papers, Student File.
49. Kelly was also twelve years older than the average freshman. During his first term he lived at 337 George Street, then at 95 Cottage Street.
50. *Bulletin of Yale University, . . . for the Academic Year, 1942–1943*, Series 38, no. 8 (April 15, 1942): 8–9.
51. Arturo Almandoz Marte, ed., *Planning Latin America's Capital Cities, 1850–1950* (London: Routledge, 2002), 233.
52. Dr. R. A. Kling project folder and Richard Kelly and Oscar Nitzchke, "A Home of Your Own for Perfect Living," unpublished proposal (ca. 1946), Richard Kelly Papers.
53. McCandless's work regarding deceptive uses of light and shadow was included in an exhibition about the art of camouflage at New York's Advertising Club on Park Avenue in December 1941. Edward Alden Jewell, "Art in a Practical Service to War," *New York Times*, December 14, 1941.
54. See, for instance, Mary Roche, "A Lift from Lighting," *New York Times*, January 14, 1945; "Model Home Shows Lighting Advances," *New York Times*, November 13, 1945; Faith Corrigan, "Book by Experts Sheds New Light on Home Lamps," *New York Times*, August 16, 1956.
55. "Home Lighting Debated," *New York Times*, September 15, 1949.
56. Barbara Lamprecht, *Richard Neutra: Complete Works* (Taschen, 2000), 58.
57. I would like to thank Barbara Lamprecht, Los Angeles, for this information.
58. "Design Journal: Richard Kelly, Lighting Design Consultant, Notes Some Problems Involving Public Lighting," *Interior Design and Decoration* (June 1949): 42–47.
59. Richard Kelly, "Lighting as an Integral Part of Architecture," *College Art Journal* 12, no. 1 (Autumn 1952): 24–30. See also Richard Kelly, "Good Lighting Is Part of Good Living," *House and Garden* 101, no. 3 (March 1952): 138–141, 191, 192.
60. Richard Kelly, "Lighting's Role in Architecture," *Architectural Forum* 102 (February 1955): 152, 168.
61. Ibid., 152, 168.
62. Kelly, "Lighting as an Integral Part of Architecture."

63. The numbers in their product name indicate their size in increments of one-eighth inch. A PAR 64 is eight inches wide, a PAR 20 is two and a half inches wide.

64. In the early 1970s Goodbar promoted a package of five programs under the name "Light" that could compute room illumination from data about a lamp's brightness, position, and direction together with the room size and the brightness and reflectivity of its surfaces. Kaiman Lee and Jacqueline Masloff, "Energy-Oriented Computer Programs for the Design and Monitoring of Buildings" (Environmental Design and Research Center, Newtonville, Mass., 1979), 239–244.

65. Michael Quint, "Bringing Light (and Fixtures) to the World," *New York Times*, December 5, 1988; Maude Dorr, "Edison Price," *Industrial Design* 6 (June 1963): 45; Stanley Abercrombie, "Edison Price: His Name Is No Accident," *Architecture Plus* (August 1973): 34–43.

66. Roche, "Lift from Lighting."

67. "New Progress in Light," *Architectural Forum* 106 (February 1957): 152–155.

68. Landis Gores, letter to Richard Kelly, March 4, 1953.

69. Simon Niedenthal, "Glamourized Houses: Neutra, Photography, and the Kaufmann House," *Journal of Architectural Education* 47, no. 2 (November 1993): 101–112.

70. Julius Shulman recalls many instances of how he would use electric lights in buildings by Richard Neutra, for example, to counterbalance the glare from the Palm Springs desert, which would make a soffit or ceiling appear too dark. He was responding to lighting differences on behalf of film's sensitivities in a similar fashion to Richard Kelly's intervention with additional ceiling lights near the glare of window openings. Peter Gössel, ed., *Julius Shulman: Architecture and Its Photography* (Cologne: Taschen, 1998), 15.

71. For a rare description of the technique of *Wanderlicht*, see Heinrich Heidersberger, "Moderne Architektur im Lichtbild," in *Angewandte Fotografie*, ed. Nikolaus Karpf (Munich: Verlag Großbildtechnik, 1960), 34–54. I would like to thank Professor Rolf Sachsse, Saarbrücken, for this reference.

72. "A prominent decorator once told us that early in her career she was often disappointed with some of the finished interiors she had labored over. One day when photographers came to make pictures of one of her completed jobs she suddenly found the missing ingredient clear—lights. Anyone who has ever been around when the photofloods are turned on can appreciate her sudden awakening to the way in which dramatic lighting brings to life the color and texture of even well-worn fabrics and makes one newly conscious of the graceful lines of beautiful furniture." Roche, "Lift from Lighting."

73. Maude Dorr, "Lighting Consultants," *Industrial Design* 6 (June 1963): 40–47; Abe H. Feder, "Light as an Architectural Material," *Progressive Architecture* 39, no. 9 (September 1958): 124–131.

74. For example, in Kelly, "Lighting as an Integral Part of Architecture."

75. Folder on St. Michael's College Chapel, Colchester, Vermont, Richard Kelly Papers.

The Invention of Modern Light

Richard Kelly and Home Lighting

Sandy Isenstadt

Almost any use of artificial light is basically dramatic. It is beyond nature, it is man made and under his control.

Stanley McCandless

As late as 1957, an article in *House and Home*, a magazine for building professionals, could still ask whether architects and builders were planning domestic lighting as if they were "just wiring gas jets." Too often, the article ran, designers would simply place "a spot of light here and there," as if following the path of all but forgotten piping. If so, they ignored important developments in lighting design. Lighting equipment had improved vastly in recent years: fluorescents, commercially available only twenty years earlier, were more reliable and sold in a range of sizes and tints; dimming controls were rare twenty years before but they had since become more sophisticated, cheaper, and easier to use; and incandescent lighting was available in an ever-wider range of colors, intensities, and fixtures, with new options coming to market regularly. In regard to design, the article noted, architects and builders needed to escape their fixation with fixtures and think more abstractly, in terms of luminous points, lines, planes, and volumes. Artificial light was a vital building material: able to direct attention or distract it, expand a room or shrink it, facilitate labor or frustrate it, make a home seem more varied or more monotonous; it could turn night into day or, more imaginatively, conjure effects alien to the day. A good scheme could even increase sales. A number of photographs followed the opening text to illustrate the wide range of options in the age of modern lighting that *House and Home* trumpeted. Only one lighting designer was named, however: Richard Kelly, the person who did more than any other individual to change professional and public attitudes toward the possibilities of light in the home and who, in many ways, made domestic lighting modern.[1]

Fig. 1. The tools and moods of home lighting around 1920, from Matthew Luckiesh, *Artificial Light*, 1920

Fixtures and Functions

At the turn of the twentieth century, electric lighting in the home was rare. But after World War I, it began to spread rapidly. Where progress in lighting had once been measured in centuries, it was visibly improving year to year in the 1920s. Even in the dark days of the Depression, the completion of regional power grids and New Deal endorsement of electrification spread electric light across the country, making it appear the fruit of egalitarian virtues more than mere prosperity. Better lighting improved safety and facilitated cleaning and personal hygiene; it lessened eye strain, aided education; it was even said to improve posture; and, for many, it made the home more beautiful.

Despite the rapid acceptance of electric lighting, domestic lighting design had not changed much since the era of the gas lamp. In many installations, electric lights did, in fact, simply replace gas lamps, with existing piping a convenient conduit for wires. With gas lighting competitive through the early 1920s, most manufacturers made fixtures that worked with either system: brackets turned upright for gas chimneys or downward for electric bulbs. Even fixtures intended for electrical use were made from gas-pipe fittings. Whereas artificial light sparked numerous changes in home life, the art of lighting itself changed rather slowly.

Lighting design was split between the illuminating engineer, who tried to match lighting levels with the purpose at hand, and architects, who worried about a fixture's stylistic fit in any given room. Their concerns overlapped in discussions regarding the way light could change a room's atmosphere or mood, which usually ranged narrowly between formal and restful, but light itself played no independent aesthetic role beyond this.[2] Design advice was conditioned by underlying assumptions of the home as a compound of cellular spaces and so, in any guide, would always proceed room by room. In any case, fixtures were limited to overhead lights, brackets or wall-mounted lights, and portable lamps. Several beliefs, however, that would remain important in later practice were already becoming evident: general or ambient lighting should be balanced with local or task lighting; utility and beauty were often at odds; and a controlled choreography of light and motion, achieved by strategies such as path lighting or consolidated panels of switches, might be the foundation for new forms of luminous space (fig. 1).

By the 1930s, lighting at home was seen to have more directly decorative possibilities on its own terms. Walter Kantack, for instance, one of the best known lighting designers of the period, pointed out new factors of control, such as reflectors and prismatic lenses, that allowed light to be shaped in many different ways (fig. 2). Lighting was no longer inert, he wrote in 1932: "*light can be made to do things.*"[3] Designers experimented with new sources, including luminous boxes, panels, and coffers, tubular lighting concealed in coves or atop columns, "spot lights" reengineered and miniaturized from stage lighting practice, and more. Architects were being freed "from the past domination of the light fixture as a major element" and, finally, were invited to "design in light."[4]

Correspondingly, thinking on the subject shifted from a focus on the fixture's style to manipulation of the sources of light, generally described as direct, indirect, or semi-indirect; as Kantack, who added a fourth, "directed indirect" lighting, put it, "we are beginning to think of *methods of illumination.*"[5] Nevertheless, Kantack and others such as Walter von Nessen, Kurt Versen, Egmont Ahrens, and Donald Deskey, along with a young Richard Kelly, concentrated their talents on the design of individual fixtures, often inspired by Art Deco motifs. At the time, then, that Kelly began designing and selling fixtures, lighting design was conceptually dominated, as Ely Jacques Kahn said approvingly in 1930, by the "intelligent arrangement of lighting sources."[6] Putting it more prospectively some years later, Walter Rendell Storey, design reporter for the *New York Times*, said that interior decorators should learn to work more closely with "that latest of technological experts, the lighting engineer," to learn psychological causes as well as artistic effects: "Here is a tremendously undeveloped field."[7]

Fig. 2. Effects of bad and good domestic lighting, from *Transactions of the Illuminating Engineering Society*, 1929

Outside the Glass Wall

Soon after he had taken his degree in architecture Kelly was being described "as a man 'who can do anything with light.'" Domestic lighting was the subject of his first published article, "The Better to See," in 1946.[8] Although he took several more years to arrive at his terse formulation of lighting as an amalgam of ambient, focal, and sparkling light and thus finally fuse the engineer's standards with the designer's vision, he very quickly solved one of the most vexing problems facing modern domestic architecture: the big, uncurtained window after sundown, or, as it was sometimes described, "the black square of night."

Windows had gotten dramatically cheaper in the twentieth century and had begun taking up a larger proportion of wall area in homes. Clients, it seems, liked them, so much so that a number of architects began to warn of a "craze for windows unduly large," and drew attention to "the hideousness of an unbroken expanse of glass."[9] Large windows disrupted domestic character and introduced black voids at night or disturbing reflections. They also threatened privacy by opening up interiors to neighbors. Regardless, an increasingly middle-class clientele seemed to like large windows because they created a sense of spaciousness, even in a small house. Difficult to reconcile with revival styles, large windows came to be associated with modernism, an aesthetic program already featuring large expanses of glass. Indeed, a number of émigré architects in the 1930s abandoned the technological imperatives that had earlier legitimated their use of glass walls and emphasized instead their ability to enhance a sense of space. Large windows soon became modernism's defining characteristic. As George Nelson and Henry Wright wrote in their popular 1945 guide, *Tomorrow's House:* "Big, well designed windows are the trademark of modern architecture."[10]

Warnings regarding lost privacy persisted.[11] Whereas living in a "goldfish bowl" was a nineteenth-century phrase applied to elected officials, it was literalized at midcentury to include anyone with a large window and curious neighbors. At night, again, the effect was all the more threatening. The big-windowed house became a transparent lantern at night, and the viewer of the outdoors became herself something to be viewed. In the single-family home, the throne of privacy, only one thing was more distressing than seeing someone look in while you looked out: not knowing whether someone was out there, looking in. The gaze of the modern house, it turned out, was reversible.

The common remedy was to recommend curtains, but many modern architects repudiated such domestic paraphernalia even as they struggled with the effects of glass walls at night. The archetype of the problem was Philip Johnson's Glass House of 1949, discussed elsewhere in more detail in this book. Kelly's solution—to illuminate the interior with exterior lights—made the entire house a two-thousand-square-foot light fixture. The impression, Kelly said, left one "almost floating, on a sea of light." The immediate outside was brighter than the inside, so the spaciousness-inducing view was no longer stunted by darkness. Lighting particular trees then drew the eye even deeper into the view. Kelly brightened the interior lights during the day, too, and put them on dimmers to lessen the difference in brightness between inside and out, removing a potential source of glare and, again, easing the occupant's vision through the glass wall (fig. 3).

As the glass wall extended the home's visual reach into the landscape, so had Kelly extended its reach into the darkness. He understood transparency less as a material like glass than in terms of having a modern eye, that is, conditioned by what was "most important in our seeing habits." Modern architecture, he realized, was less a style than a set of visual patterns, and seeing through glass to the outdoors was one of them. But the presumed continuity of the modern home from indoors to out was temporally discontinuous; glass walls "worked" for only half of the diurnal cycle. He had translated an architectural objective that was forceful by day but hobbled at night into a single and continuous visual experience.

Kelly generalized the solution and would thenceforth light large windows and glass walls from outside and call out some "significant object" in the glass wall's landscape theater. For his part, Johnson took a keen interest in "indirect lighting effects," so much so that he was considering a "structure with no windows at all." That was reported in 1952, the year before he remodeled his Brick House to have a windowless bedroom with concealed lights timed to imitate the effect of sunrise, eventually rising to the brightness of outdoor light, only indoors.[12] Kelly was Johnson's consultant on the project.

Three Houses: Ain House, Hechinger Residence, Morosani Residence

As director of the Department of Architecture and Design at the Museum of Modern Art, Johnson commissioned a series of three houses to be displayed in the museum garden, intended to introduce Americans to modern architecture. The first, designed by Marcel Breuer, won positive reviews but, built in its final, "expanded" phase and imagined for a one-acre site, it was criticized for being out of reach for most Americans. Johnson subsequently turned to Gregory Ain, a Los Angeles architect interested in low-cost housing who had worked for Rudolf Schindler and Richard Neutra. MoMA announced that Ain was "one of the few modern architects" so inclined. The budget for the house was modest and the site was said to be only a fifth of an acre, in order to validate the use of modernism for speculative housing.[13] With speculative houses criticized as monotonous and cramped, Ain created a varied streetscape from the outside, even were it repeated in a subdivision, and on the inside conjured a generous sense of space despite limited dimensions.

Sliding panels dominated the use and aesthetics of the interior, as

Fig. 3. Philip Johnson, Glass House, New Canaan, Connecticut, 1949, view at night

Fig. 4. Gregory Ain, Ain House, Museum of Modern Art, New York, 1950, including the "reel lamp," a thin valance along the wall and across a window, and the split bamboo sliding curtains. Photograph: Ezra Stoller © Esto.

Fig. 5. Ain House at night from the outdoor terrace. To emphasize the interior volume, the soffit lights, the primary source for interior ambient light, have been switched off. Sliding panels are visible in their open position. Photograph: Ezra Stoller © Esto.

well as the press coverage. When open, the panels gave way to a single expanse lined by a thirty-two-foot-long wall of glass. Panels also divided two children's bedrooms, which could likewise be parted to make one big playroom. Spaciousness was the end result: sliding open the panels extended sight lines within the interior and out through the glass wall. But the panels also enhanced the sense of space functionally as well as visually. By virtue of their flexibility, the panels allowed a smaller area of multifunctional modern space to substitute for separate compartments of traditional space, each dedicated to a single function (figs. 4–5).

Kelly interpreted just these aspects of Ain's design with what came to be called the "reel lamp," a lamp hung from a pulley attached to the ceiling. The design was forthright: a source was shielded from direct view by a truncated cone baffle, which was open at the bottom to shine light directly downward onto a surface and open at the top to shine light onto a shallow saucer that added to the direct light below a wider ring of reflected light. But the fixture's most important aspect was its mobility. A polished metal handle, like a sliver of sparkle, emerges from inside the baffle so the entire assembly can be moved up or down as needed. Kelly himself referred to it as a "flying saucer," no doubt for its aerial changeability as well as for the hovering profile of its shallow dome.[14]

Like the panels, the reel light afforded, in Kelly's words, "more freedom" for the occupants and thus reinforced the panels' premise of multifunctionality. The lights, found in the dining area and all three bedrooms, could be pulled down for intimate pools of light, lifted up and out of the way for large gatherings, and everything in between. Kelly designed the lamps to hold a three-way bulb, a product relatively new to the domestic market, making the lamps that much more variable. In other words, the reel lamp was an analog of the sliding panel: a moving part that by virtue of its accommodation of different uses contributed to a sense of varied and expanded space. Also like the panels, the mechanisms of movement, handle and pulley, were visually prominent, thereby emphasizing processes of change as well as effects.

Other lighting features further reinforced Ain's principles. As at Johnson's house, Kelly put lights outside the glass wall, in the exterior soffit, to illuminate the terrace, which became the brightest surface visible inside and provided most of the interior ambient lighting. Secondary in terms of quantity of light was an extremely thin valance, less than three inches wide, and positioned less than two inches from a solid wall or, where it crossed a window, doubling the fixed transom sash it was aligned with. Opaque at the front and back, the valance cast light up and down, raking the surfaces it hung in front of. With this, Kelly had found a fixture that either echoed an architectural line directly or visually reinforced the surface it raked. The emphasis on surface would have been apparent at the windows, too, since the curtains would likely be closed at night on an actual fifth-acre lot and the light would brush across them to pick out the slightest variation in texture. To this end, the curtains were carefully chosen. In the playroom, they were split-bamboo, a common material then as now, but installed perpendicular to the normal setup so that they would slide horizontally rather than roll up vertically. The arrangement eliminated cluttering hardware, such as pulleys and cords, and echoed the panels, similarly sliding along a recessed track.

Along the glass wall hung a curtain of yellow and white Osnaburg, a heavy fabric noted for its coarse weave. To create a sense of depth at the glass wall even with the curtain drawn, it was designed as two layers, separate, rather than sewn. The light bounced from the terrace outside would then meet the raking light from the valance inside on the rolling billows of curtain, which would alternately brighten and darken as the two layers moved independently of one another. The well-known British decorator Arundell Clarke had specified the curtains, but Kelly had been kept apprised of Clarke's progress and at one point had advocated a separate sliding panel of curtain for use above the transom.[15] Kelly clearly understood the modernist conception of enclosure as a configuration of planes in varying phases of transparency and opacity, rather than walls punctured by an occasional opening, and he rearticulated that conception for nighttime.

A similar sensitivity on Kelly's part to the aims and precepts of modern architecture is evident at the Hechinger Residence, also from 1951 but more than double the fourteen hundred square feet of the Ain House, with a real client and built on a definite site. It was designed by The Architects Collaborative, in Cambridge, with both Walter Gropius and Robert McMillan, Gropius's associate, credited with the design. Located in rugged terrain in the northwest corner of Washington, D.C., where a number of modern houses had already been built, it was commissioned by John W. Hechinger, the owner of hardware stores that rode the do-it-yourself trend to become a large regional home-improvement chain. Hechinger, in fact, acted as his own contractor for his home. In addition, The Architects Collaborative designed and built another house on the same lot for Hechinger's sister and her husband, Richard England, an executive at Hechinger Company. Designed as a pair, the houses were less than twenty feet apart but were planned to be both private and open.

The plan is a shallow "T" shape, with entry, stair, and study in the short leg, and kitchen, dining area, and living room spread along the arms. The living room is lightly defined by level changes at the open stair hall and the adjoining dining area, and by the wall of the study, with a large sliding panel atop a broad sill holding a swiveling television. The exterior edge of the continuous living-dining room is a thirty-nine-foot south-facing glass wall, immediately visible from the entry and overlooking a deck and the yard below. "As with most modern houses," reported the Washington, D.C., *Evening Star*, "the glass wall faces the garden."[16] Only one living room wall is solid, the western wall, and even that is broken by a projecting hearth.

Kelly's lighting scheme centers on the glass wall. Two banks of downlights, one inside and one outside, shine onto it. The exterior lights are recessed into the underside of the second-floor overhang to shine on the deck, which is painted a pale gray to catapult light inside. Interior downlights are similarly recessed and aligned with those in the soffit, which is coplanar with the ceiling and finished in redwood matching the interior walnut veneer. "Tree lights," as noted on the plans—pairs of spotlights mounted on movable planks located on each gardenside corner of the roof—pick out patches of foliage and summon the eye outdoors.

While visual continuity from inside to out is clearly at stake, Kelly subtly alters the repetition. Exterior lights with parabolic reflectors to focus their light point straight down to the deck, whereas the interior lights, labeled "washlights" on the plan for their angled, concave lens, are aimed diagonally, toward the window mullions, throwing them into strong relief. The emphasis on these vertical elements reappears when the curtains are drawn and the mullions are covered, as bright elongated scallops carved onto the repeating folds of the curtain, which would be brighter from the western side of the room than from the eastern side. The asymmetry is understated but clearly intentional, as Kelly indicates a similar shift in the lighting over the hearth, where he echoes that wall's tripartite design with three recessed downlights that are placed just off-center, biased toward the glass wall (fig. 6).

Hechinger wrote to Kelly in July 1951 to register his excitement with the lighting, even though he had not yet moved in: "stark white . . . it does look sensational." He was so interested, in fact, that he asked Kelly for "some reading material as to the theory behind the lighting," for himself as well as for Mr. England. It would have been fascinating had Kelly responded in kind, but he offered Hechinger only a utilitarian response, saying the request "threw me for a loss. It was designed as part of the architecture of the house and of your comfort, convenience, and, I hope, delight."[17]

Although he sidestepped stating his theoretical background to Hechinger, he soon afterward published his enduring characterization of three types of light: ambient, focal, and sparkling. In essence, Kelly had reconfigured earlier categories of direct, indirect, and semi-indirect lighting, which had described only the eye's relation to a light source. With his new typology, as well as his evocative analogies—the shadowless light of a foggy day, "the campfire of all time," candles and diamonds—Kelly had fused function with feeling. Often closely involved in detailing fixtures to achieve his design goals, Kelly had, in bridging the gap between engineer and architect, distinguished the lighting designer from either.

As admirable an encapsulation as are Kelly's three types of light, and as important as his resolution of glass wall lighting proved to be, his

Fig. 6. The Architects Collaborative, Hechinger House, Washington, D.C., 1952, interior from the raised dining area looking west, showing luminous scallops on living-room curtains from recessed downlights

residential practice went well beyond these accomplishments. His sheer inventiveness in lighting is drawn out to perhaps its widest scope in a house Kelly worked on in 1953. It was designed starting in 1949 by Edward Durell Stone for Remy and Virginia Morosani in Litchfield, Connecticut, a town whose aesthetically progressive residents seemed no less fond of modernism than those in New Canaan, where Johnson built his Glass House.

The house has an L-shaped plan, with four bedrooms and private baths composing the long leg, capped by a thirty-foot-long playroom, and a short, almost square leg containing a master bedroom suite, living room, kitchen and dining room, and an indoor patio with a sunken pool. The patio is separated from the living room by a masonry fireplace wall and from the dining room by a wide overhead shelf topped with foliage. The clients were particularly excited by the decorative possibilities of light, calling for a "glistening, sparkling, fairy-tale effect" in the living room, including "changeable colored lights" for parties, a "Zodiac motif" in the dressing area, and dramatic effects throughout the house. Kelly came up with more than twenty different types of lights to meet their ambitions, with a total energy consumption of more than forty-five thousand watts, a figure that included only interior fixtures.[18]

The living room, of course, received great attention and was given luminous form with four distinct types of lighting. Ambient lighting was generated by the outdoor eave lights, which could be turned on from a dimmer panel near the kitchen and turned off at evening's end from a switch in the master bedroom. Downlights rendered a focal glow at various niches in the fireplace wall and along the interior wall separating the master bedroom from the living room. These were supplemented by two different brightnesses of Lumiline lamps mounted above shelves in the niches at the interior wall. Rather than align interior and exterior downlights to reinforce a sense of transparency, here Kelly specified the same fixture at the exterior eaves for use at the fireplace niches, thus assuring that whether inside or out, masonry received the same illumination. The lights, made by Kliegl Brothers, founded in 1896 to fabricate stage lighting and one of several manufacturers Kelly frequently turned to, were deeply recessed with multiple interior ring baffles to concentrate the light beam and to minimize surface glare (fig. 7). Kliegl's catalog of architectural lighting, first printed in 1955, suggested that these fixtures were effective lights for "restaurants, night clubs, cocktail lounges, etc."[19]

Along the room's perimeter, just above the curtains, ran the "L" fixture, as it is designated on the lighting plan: a recessed, downturned metal trough containing thirty-nine alternating pink and blue tinted forty-watt bulbs. It was sealed in a custom-designed lens angled to push light toward the curtains and consisting of clear glass, ribbed diffusing glass, a colored filter, and a layer of Koolshade, a wire fabric that would have further helped to diffuse and enliven the light. Kelly designed the fixture to provide "general luminous surfaces inside" in tandem with the light reflected from exterior soffit lights. Accents and some night lighting were afforded by a pair of wall-mounted lights, switched from the main entry as well as the living-room entry. Finally, several angled downlights with reflective rather than matte louvers focused on various "objets d'art" mounted on brick portions of the exterior walls. These picture lights were operated by the same control as the room's central crystal chandelier so that decorative objects became a species of sparkle and the entire space achieved, as expressed in Kelly's notes, a "shiny ball-room look." The owners also had the option of automatic controls that gradually brought up interior lighting levels at twilight, guided by photoelectric sensors outside.[20] That was just the living room (figs. 8–10).

Other rooms received equal consideration. The patio, for instance, had banks of downlights aimed at the masonry wall, the "L" fixture along the glass wall, uplights mounted in the pool, "spot lighting on plants," and "lighting up through plants to cast shadows and glow on wood ceilings," an effect he envisioned for at least four other rooms. The playroom featured cove lights, fed by exposed raceways, to illuminate the pitched, trussed roof, as well as spotlights for the fireplace and niches. Backlit glass ceilings were specified for most bathrooms, while the master bath and dressing area, which measured some sixteen by twenty feet, was ringed by a luminous duct, roughly triangular in section, to cast light down onto counters through a composite panel of frosted glass, Koolshade, and clear glass, and to cast light sideways, through a "transparent mirror," into a central coffer, providing what Kelly described in his notes as a "continuous sparkling fascia around bath." In addition, of course, every room could accommodate portable lamps with switched or unswitched outlets.

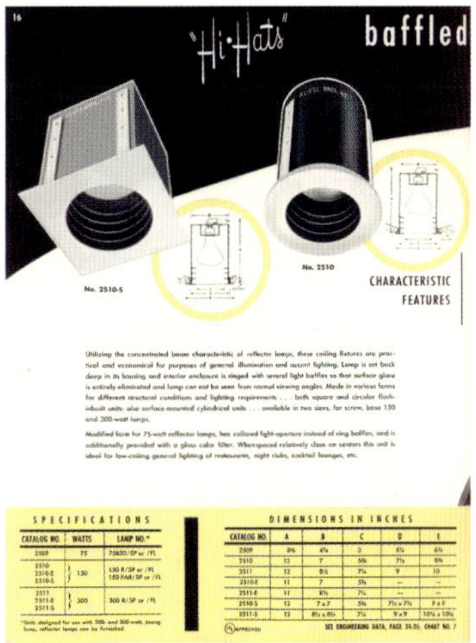

Fig. 7. Catalog page for Kliegl "Hi-Hats," recessed downlights with interior baffles. Kelly specified the lights for the living room of the Morosani House, designed by Edward Durell Stone, in Litchfield, Connecticut.

The master bedroom was nothing less than a private stage set, studied closely by Kelly in sketch form. The bed rested under an angled, fabric-veiled skylight, from which Kelly hung long curtains. Custom boxes framed "pinhole" reading lights at the skylight while "2 Gothic chandeliers sparkle in encirclement," hanging on either side of the bed. (These were first described in Kelly's client notes as "Venetian . . . in pink white & blue.") Beyond the bed area, solid walls, windows, and curtains were washed by the "L" fixture, picked out by angled downlights, and further animated by wall-mounted crystal fixtures planned to "match bed chandelier in feeling." The entire ensemble was controlled by its own bank of dimmers and switches and served by pairs of quad-plex outlets. In addition, a panel with tiny red indicator lights allowed the owners, from their bedroom, to see who was still awake and, if necessary, to switch off their bedroom reading light remotely.[21] The Morosanis had at their fingertips a range of lighting conditions and controls for any bedtime scenario: staying up late by light reflected from the page of a book, falling asleep encircled by the soft glitter of low-hanging chandeliers, or waking to daylight seeping in from above to filter down long, falling folds of fabric.

For the exterior, Kelly specified three different lights: fixed 150-watt recessed downlights set into the eaves along the house's long side, angled 150-watt downlights set into the eave along the narrow ends, which, as the roof rose higher and more glazing was introduced, were increased to 200-watt bulbs. In the landscape beyond the perimeter, Kelly called for "extensive lighting of trees and gardens" in order to "dramatize garden features and planting," an effect he had discussed with the clients and in any case was a signature feature of his lighting designs.[22]

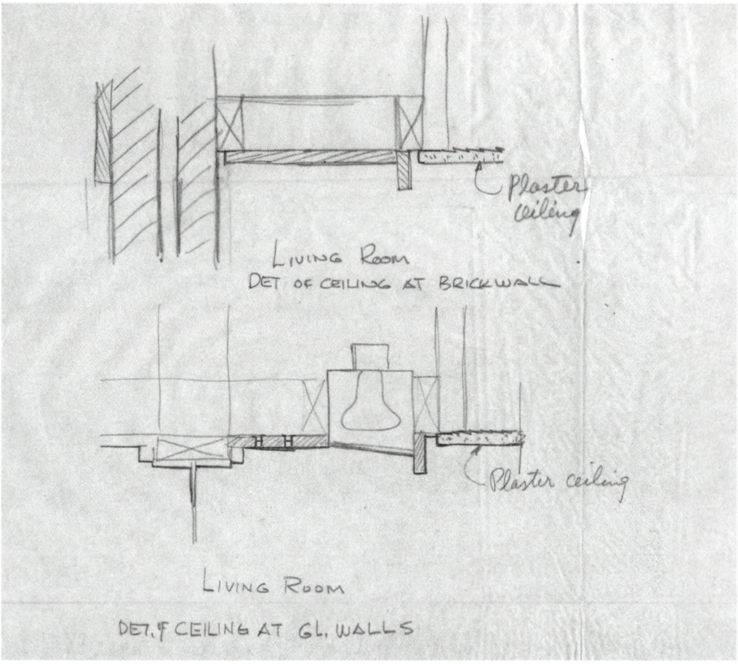

below left

Fig. 8. A hand-colored sketch by Kelly for Stone's Morosani House. Drawings like this are uncommon in his archive; this one gives some sense of his vision for the patio and adjoining dining room. The curtains are doubly lit, once from inside by the "L" fixture and then from outside by the eave lights. Similarly, the eave lights appear in two registers, muffled through the curtains and directly visible through the clear glass in the glazed gable end. The ceiling in the sketch is illuminated by an upward facing bank of lamps hidden in the overhead light shelf and, though not apparent in the sketch, would be unevenly shadowed by foliage also set into the shelf. An angled downlight centers the visual attention on a painting, appearing all the brighter for the relatively dark location beneath the shelf, while the source remains hidden, recessed into the shelf.

above

Fig. 9. Sketch by Kelly of the "L" fixture for the Morosani House: in relation to the glass wall and detail showing the custom composition of the layered lens, angled toward the glass wall

Fig. 10. King and Murphy, Architects, Van Meter House, Springfield, Illinois, 1962–1963, bathroom. The luminous bathroom ceiling, similar to that at the Morosani House, provides bright but dispersed general lighting. The later Van Meter House also features a recessed uplighting strip along the bottom of the mirror to balance light from above and eliminate shadows on the face.

Fig. 11. Gordon Powers, Graef House, Summit, New Jersey, 1951, view of landscape through the glass wall

Lighting Home Grounds

As Kelly well knew, the modern house was conceptually complete only when the landscape outside was visually present inside. Lighting the outdoor periphery was therefore central, literally, to his domestic lighting schemes. In many of his projects, especially smaller houses, trees outside are the most assertively three-dimensional, sculptural presence inside the house. To feed the "seeing habits" of modern homeowners, Kelly reignited the landscape, pushed back the blanket of night, and returned the sense of space that darkness had stolen.

The Graef House, from 1951, is representative of Kelly's integration of indoor and outdoor lighting. Robert Graef, an in-house publications editor for the marketing wing of Esso, the forerunner of Exxon, owned a sloping suburban site, no more than one hundred feet wide by two hundred feet deep, in Summit, New Jersey. He interviewed several architects to design his house, finally choosing Gordon Powers, who was then working for William Lescaze; Huson Jackson came in a close second. But Graef also contacted Kelly directly, for he was apparently on familiar terms with him already, saying he was eager to have "some little fancy work in the living room and exterior in your medium." He was all the more convinced after visiting the Rockefeller Guest House (1949–1950), designed by Johnson for the Rockefeller family, on Kelly's recommendation. Once Kelly agreed to take the job, Graef sent him a wish list. "Outdoor lighting," "tree lighting," and "pilot lights for most all outdoor lighting"—that is, low-level outdoor path lighting—topped the list (fig. 11).

In response, Kelly created a graded procession and culminating spectacle on the rather modest site, with six distinct exterior lighting conditions. A visitor arriving at the house at night would have encountered them in the following sequence. Right before the garage door, recessed into the underside of the overhanging main floor and about as far apart as automobile headlights, two lights threw down two bright circles to terminate the driveway. Leading away from the driveway, up and alongside the house, was a string of muted ten- to twenty-five-watt lights, held hip-high and mounted on rigid conduit. Shielded from direct view, the lights reflected off the brick wall of the ground floor. Ahead, toward the projecting front entry and main stair, the visitor would have seen two luminous horizontal planes where Kelly had butted thin tubular fixtures against glazed openings at the ceiling and landing. While the visitor's lower body moved through a furrow filled with subdued light modulated by bricks on one side and shrubs on the other, his or her eyes would be engaged by the sharper geometry of destination. Upon entering, the visitor would see twin strings of seventy-five-watt downlights, both fascia-mounted above but on either side of the living room's long glass wall. Although aligned and shedding the same light, the living-room floor is higher than the ground outside, so that the lights inside form a line of luminous pools while outside they spread far enough to make a continuous band. Further, the interior lights aim at the edge formed by the floor and the glass wall so that what might have been visually a strong line of containment is broken apart by a rhythm of light. Still more, Kelly called for a row of floor outlets at the glass wall to be separately switched so that a series of portable lamps could further syncopate this otherwise unseen transparent wall. With such design focus on the transparent plane and with the inside-to-outside succession of luminous pools and the continuous band of light, adjacent in plan but separate in section, Kelly had subtly but effectively called attention to the distinguishing attribute of the site, its slope.

Finally, he mounted adjustable pairs of three-hundred-watt "tree lights" on the roof corners and aimed each light at successive features in the yard, including a small stand of paper birch and a young specimen hemlock. Taken together they create a receding line angled away from the house to move deeper into the surrounding trees. Overall, the visitor traveled from the softest light up close and spread over a brick surface, toward a brighter light concentrated into regular shapes, to the parallel pools and band and, finally, a receding line of spotlit organic forms. Kelly, keenly aware of the time it took for the eye to adjust to new lighting conditions, had in addition calibrated this passage as a progressive exposure to increasingly higher levels of contrast. The path from driveway to entry to living room to landscape weaves inside with out in terms of both body and vision. It is an astonishingly rich sequence for what amounts to a progression of at most fifty feet.[23]

Landscapes even more constrained appear to have only inspired Kelly. The Davis House, designed by Philip Johnson in 1951 for the senior curator at the Minneapolis Art Museum, has at its center a skylit, glass-walled courtyard about twenty feet square, bringing daylight deep inside the nearly sixty-feet-square plan. Kelly introduced five types of lamp into the courtyard ceiling, each with a different brightness, color, and pattern of distribution, and put them on different circuits so that the Davis family could asymmetrically mix warm and cool tints, visually emphasize particular plants, and generally create a subtle, free-form pattern to gently veil the rigid grid above. Kelly explicitly noted his interest in creating "alternative possibilities" to daylight. Remaining sympathetic to an architecture conceived in daylight, Kelly's scheme visually reconfigures relations between interior volumes "rather than duplicates daylight effects."[24] In fact, daylight itself wasn't exactly daylight at the Davis House, since the deep louver, installed, one presumes, to Kelly's specifications, strips downward-streaming daylight of its glare, warms up its tone, and projects it sideways to radiate throughout the house as a bright but softened light (figs. 12–13).

The interior courtyard at the McIntosh residence, in Bedford, New York, designed by Raymond and Rado, the firm established by Antonin

Raymond and Ladislav Rado in New York in 1945, was larger than that at the Davis House, much simpler in design, but possibly more spectacular (fig. 14). It centered on a single large tree, with a narrow pool along one edge as the only other feature. Kelly installed fascia-mounted downlights all along the edge of the court, two lights in the pool, and a pair of two-hundred-watt uplights, buried on either side of the tree. The gallery entirely surrounding the court contained only six "shovel lights"—recessed downlights with shovel-shaped covers to direct light onto paintings hanging along one interior wall. The gallery dimmer allowed attention to be directed toward the court at the heart of the house. There, the tree's naturally irregular branches would be raised above eye level to reveal their brightly lit undersides, which would contrast sharply with the paving below. The result would have been a visual experience unique to the night: bright light projected from two opposite directions, each acting on divergent geometries; a glass-boxed spectacle that at night must have engulfed onlookers standing inside.[25]

Home Theater

To be effective, Kelly's lighting schemes had to be elaborately switched to manage the varied effects he planned, and indeed throughout his work webs of wires blossomed from multiple banks of dimmer controls and panels of three, four, or more toggle switches, all within any single project. The Hechingers, for example, modulated their living-room light with anywhere from one to more than two dozen fixtures in various combinations. From a single spot they could set the mood in their own living room from quiet reading to gala evening and just as easily blanch the terrace and yard beyond. At the Morosani Residence Kelly set a dimmer bank at the dining room so the family could vary the lighting at the table, inside the room, and along the exterior eave outside the room. The master bedroom, recall, had dimmer panels at each side of the bed to control a small theater of lighting effects, as well as manage lights throughout the house. In fact, sophisticated control systems were integral to all of Kelly's designs and he was a pioneer in their domestic use.

When Kelly began his career, however, elaborate lighting controls were known mostly from the theater, where they were a sine qua non of modern stagecraft. The acknowledged expert in the field was Stanley McCandless. By the early 1930s, McCandless had codified a method to pull apart facets of light and then to differentially recombine them to suit the action of a play. He manipulated the color, angle, and direction of stage lights to bring exceptional presence to actors or to create unprecedented scenic effects. Control was central to this process, and McCandless led the way in developing theater lighting switchboards with preset as well as variable configurations operated by "virtually frictionless" controls through the use of vacuum tubes. In 1932, he published *A Method of Lighting the Stage*, an outline of the courses he had been teaching at Yale, wherein he described his system of stage lighting, and with several collaborators that same year also filed his first patent for a theater lighting control apparatus. He went on to write a number of technical articles on the subject of theater controls, in addition to consulting on the subject for a number of theaters.

McCandless was also interested in lighting for homes but found the problem vexing. In an article illustrated with images of his own home, he argued that "the greatest responsibility of the architect" was to create atmosphere, although, he granted, it was a vague aim and led most architects to yield to historical styles that usually compromised lighting. Modern architecture promised better lighting since it was premised on efficiency rather than on style, but that goal conflicted, he thought, with good atmosphere. To conclude, he recommended that architects look to the theater for inspiration for further progress: "If we turn to the theater to see how effectively light is used to produce mood, it gives us some hope that perhaps before long we can achieve the proper atmosphere in our homes, where it is even more important than in the theater."[26]

McCandless may have had dimmers in mind, but they were impractical for home use at the time since they worked on the principle of variable resistance, which meant that electricity diverted from the lamp turned to heat that subsequently had to be dissipated. In fact, where McCandless sought variations in lighting in his own home, such as over the dining table, he had lights switched on separate circuits. But several new dimming technologies were introduced in the 1940s, with the result that lighting controls began to be made smaller and more cheaply. These technologies prevailed in the postwar era until the introduction of solid-state controls in the 1960s. Thus, in an article from 1951 on downlights, for which McCandless had been issued a rather broad patent just two years before, he included a separate discussion on controls to alter brightness, color, and even the profile of the light beam. Although he was primarily concerned with public spaces, his most elaborate suggestion was for a dining table, where he described the use of "remote control" to alter the shutter geometry and control the size, shape, and distribution of the light passing through it. It is a minor detail, but it indicates his point of reference since remote control—using low-voltage signals to a remote mechanism to operate a device, instead of manipulating the full operating current directly at a switchboard—was a recent development in the theater.[27]

Still, control systems for the home were a novelty when Kelly began his design career. But, just as lighting controls were essential to the theater, Kelly was committed to them. His low-voltage dimmer relays at the Morosani Residence, for instance, required rheostats that were enormous for a domestic installation, nearly a foot in diameter and perhaps fourteen to sixteen inches deep.[28] For the Ault House, designed by Eliot Noyes in 1951, in New Canaan, Connecticut, Kelly detailed four different

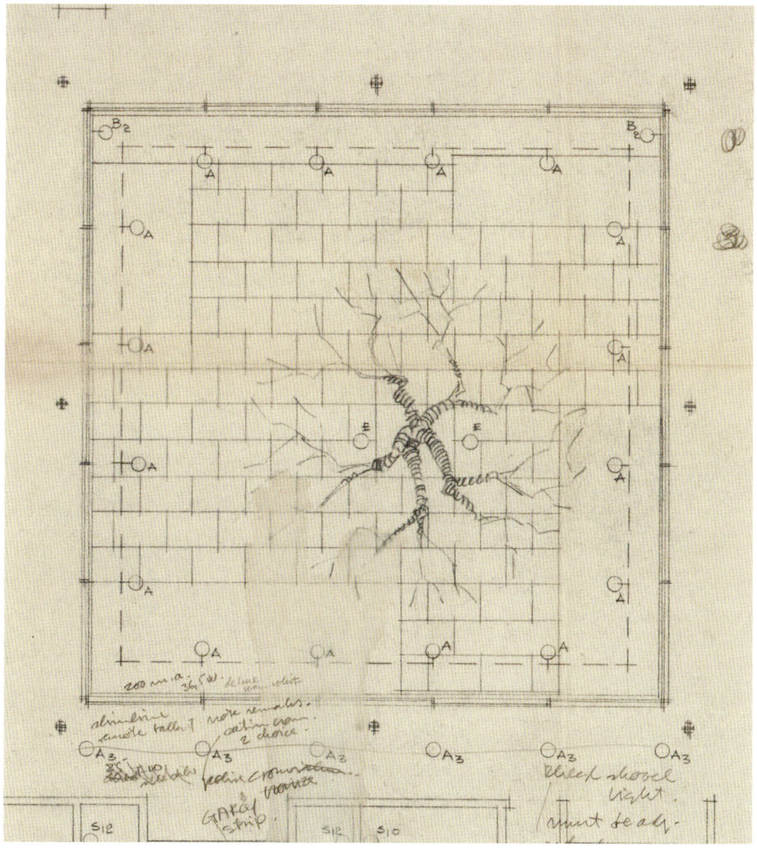

Fig. 12. Philip Johnson, Davis House, Wayzata, Minnesota, 1954, courtyard

Fig. 13. The courtyard of the Davis House in another of its luminous moods reiterates the staccato rhythm of serial downlights along the gallery wall

left

Fig. 14. Antonin Raymond and L. L. Rado, McIntosh House, Bedford, New York, 1955, courtyard plan

Fig. 15. Advertisement for Luxtrol dimmers, highlighting their ability to change the appearance of a room at will

combination dimmer and switch panels to control the twenty fixture types he indicated. At the Boissonnas House, a Johnson-designed project, also in New Canaan, Kelly specified "ebonite" (a shiny hard rubber) knobs for the lighting controls, and designed control panels for the curtains and exterior awnings.[29] In some instances he worked out the internal gearing to guarantee that his clients would have the variability and smooth operation he envisioned for them, along with a panel layout that corresponded intuitively to the fixture layout.[30]

Although Kelly had been custom designing dimmers for years, the Luxtrol, introduced at a lighting show in 1953, was probably the first home dimmer readily available through commercial outlets (fig. 15). An article in the *New York Times* noted that although they were new to home lighting, dimmers "have long been in use in theatrical lighting," leading the author to suggest, "Think of your home like a stage set," an idea illustrated with several installations, including one from Kelly.[31] *House and Garden* printed a thirteen-page primer on dimmers in 1961, explaining what they were, where to buy them, and how to use them. Kelly's own apartment was described in the piece as a "breathtaking spectacle": a burlap curtain to catch highlights from the raking light of hundreds of bulbs woven into it; sidelights grazing an open medieval manuscript to raise otherwise hidden textures; a table lamp slowly brightening like the rising sun, and more—each effect administered by Kelly from a switch box beneath the dining table (fig. 16). The article also features what might well be the first photograph in a popular periodical of a "battery of dimmers" (fig. 17).[32]

To the extent that modernity entails the progressive mastery and reconfiguration of nature to human ends, whether by technological or social means, control systems are a necessary if often overlooked factor in that process. When the object of historical or cultural analyses, they are usually taken at the largest scale, the technical and political regulation of power networks, say, or the biopolitics of Foucault, to name only two. But providing controls for individuals to instantly remake their domestic realm was an equally important development: countless controls installed for convenience or charm can accumulate to produce a qualitative change not only in the visual environment but in broader social terms as well. For one, ready-to-hand environmental controls that affect the house and yard can shift the general understanding of private property from a territory articulated by fences and walls to a sphere of influence subject to individual will, a volitional space, so to speak. Controls also give new meaning to one of the period's best known clichés: to bring the outside inside. The phrase usually described the glass wall's ambition to enfold within a single view dimensions greater than those of the interior and, by extension, to suggest possession in excess of actual ownership. Indeed, this was an explicit aim of landscape views in eighteenth-century picturesque theory, which, writ small, underpin twentieth-century residential landscape aes-

Fig. 16. Richard Kelly, Kelly Apartment, New York, 1958, library, from *House and Garden* (September 1961)

Fig. 17. A "battery of dimmers," as seen in *House and Garden* (September 1961). The picture showed dimmers in a house in Houston designed by architects who had consulted with Kelly on earlier projects.

thetics. But the formula could also imply that nature itself was domesticated, brought into the circle of the domus. Lighting controls (at their simplest, a switch) made one of the most transcendent patterns governing human inhabitation—the alternation of night and day—provisional, subject to convenience or amusement. The outside, in other words, that part of the world imagined to be forever outside human control, was inside, subject to the whims of everyday routine or occasional distraction.[33]

The Invention of Modern Light

Where earlier designers had imagined a kind of radiant ornament, Kelly realized an entirely new conception of domestic light that hewed more closely to prevailing ideals of modernism. He understood light geometrically, as points and planes, vectors and volumes, augmenting the modern architect's abstract forms with light. At the same time, Kelly went beyond and even against the grain of modernism in some of his designs. Where the architect indicated a single taut surface to conform to an aesthetic ideal that connoted, say, industrial production, Kelly's lighting might bring out a decorative texture or superimpose rhythmic pools atop otherwise unmarked planes. While a room such as the Van Meter House dining room in Springfield, Illinois, designed by architects Charles Erwin King and Robert Lowdon Murphy, and detailed by Kelly in 1963, was sharply defined by four walls, Kelly's hidden troffer lighting, similar to what he created for Johnson at his Brick House, made the walls recede and the room feel as if it were the ephemeral interval created by limited visibility on a foggy day, rather than a finite enclosed space (fig. 18).

Kelly exploited one of the defining tensions of modern domestic architecture: an ideal of spatial continuity at odds with the reality of fixed functions. A signal achievement of modernism was to replace the combinatory logic of nineteenth-century houses with an ideal of flowing space, epitomized, perhaps literalized, by the glass wall. Technologies such as central heating and electric lighting lubricated formal changes by loosening the tie between one or another function or criterion of comfort and the infrastructure needed to support it. Staying warm, for instance, could be invisibly assured anywhere in the home with radiant heating, rather than locally, at the hearth. Electric lighting—instantaneous, bright, and ubiquitous—similarly unmoored functions formerly dependent on a few fixed sources. In this sense, by retaining the idea of the house as a series of rooms with fixed services rather than a set of functions with indeterminate distribution due to ubiquitous services, the room-by-room format of home lighting advice in the 1920s and '30s failed to grasp the spatial potential of the subject it treated. In contrast, the modern architect's call for flexibility was a summons to this freedom. In other words, form would follow function only after function itself was free to roam.

Yet, having opened the home in spatial terms by removing interior walls and consolidating at least some functions into a larger single space, modern architects searched for new, non-mural means to articulate space since, after all, some functions are more fixed than others. To this end architects experimented with low walls and partial definitions, level changes at ceilings and floors, sliding panels, and so on. Kelly, more than any lighting designer before him, used artificial light similarly, as a way to subdivide large, open spaces into functional zones. Or, where the architect had differentiated spaces, Kelly's lighting could unite them. That such spatial definitions and functional zones were not only temporary but almost effortlessly brought about only enhanced flexibility. In short, by developing a powerful new tool to suggest form, Kelly helped modern architects advance a two-point program of functional flexibility and spatial continuity in the modern house. Transparency in this context was less about see-through materials or continuous space. Rather, it was an effect that resulted from the extension of visual control over one's property and the creation of volitional space, where the homeowner was witness to his or her power to spontaneously manage appearances. Bridging the long-standing divide between engineers and architects—internalizing the technical knowledge of the former, abandoning the stylistic blinders of the latter—Kelly had made of light a plastic, modern medium.

Fig. 18. Van Meter House, dining room with "troffer lights" to wash walls with progressively brighter light, similar to the lighting at Johnson's Brick House

Notes

1. "Lighting," *House and Home* (March 1957): 148–156.
2. See, for example, the seven-part series by Arthur Williams, "Electricity in the House," *American Architect and Architectural Review* (March 1, 15, 29, April 12, May 10, June 7, July 5, 1922).
3. Walter W. Kantack, "A Study of Fine Lighting Today," *Arts and Decoration* 35, no. 4 (August 1931): 48. Discussed in Kristina Wilson, "The Avant-Garde and the Conservative in Lighting Design: The Modernism of Walter W. Kantack," *Studies in the Decorative Arts* (Spring–Summer 2007): 124–125.
4. "Modern Interior Lighting," *American Architect* (November 1934): 59.
5. Kantack, "Study of Fine Lighting," 49.
6. Ely Jacques Kahn, "Modern Lighting Departs Radically from the Methods of the Past," *House and Garden* 58, no. 2 (August 1930): 43.
7. Walter Rendell Storey, "Illuminating the Modern Interior," *New York Times*, June 6, 1937.
8. Richard Kelly, "The Better to See," *House and Garden* (December 1946): 152–155, 191.
9. Walter Shaw Sparrow, *Our Homes and How to Make the Best of Them* (London: Hodder and Stoughton, 1909), 70, and Ruby Ross Goodnow, *The Honest House* (New York: Century, 1914), 84–92.
10. George Nelson and Henry Wright, *Tomorrow's House: A Complete Guide for the Home-Builder* (New York: Simon and Schuster, 1946), 151.
11. "House and Site United," Construction Aid 3, *Housing and Home Finance Agency* (1952), 20–22.
12. "New Directions: Philip Johnson," *Perspecta* 1 (Summer 1952): 26–27.
13. "Exhibition House with Sliding Walls," Press release #500515, Museum of Modern Art, New York, May 1950, Box 46, Folder 2, "Museum of Modern Art, Ain House," Richard Kelly Papers, Manuscripts and Archives, Yale University Library.
14. Richard Kelly, letter to MoMA, dated March 31, 1950, Richard Kelly Papers.
15. Kelly interview with Barbara Baer, typescript, Richard Kelly Papers; "About the House," *New Yorker* (July 22, 1950): 50.
16. Robert J. Lewis, "Gropius-Designed House Is 'Composition in Cubes,'" Washington *Evening Star*, December 15, 1951, Box 27, Folder 4, "Hechinger Residence," Richard Kelly Papers.
17. John Hechinger, letter to Richard Kelly, July 19, 1951, and Kelly's reply, dated August 29, 1951, Box 27, Folder 4, "Hechinger Residence," Richard Kelly Papers.
18. "Lighting for Mrs. Remy E. Morosani," notes dated March 17, 1953, Box 44, Folder 6, "Morosani Residence," Richard Kelly Papers.
19. Kliegl Bros., Kliegl Architectural Lighting, catalog (New York: Kliegl Bros., 1955), 16.
20. John Morosani, Remy and Virginia's son, who grew up in the house, interview with the author, October 23, 2009.
21. Morosani interview.
22. Lighting plans and schedules, Box 44, Folders 5–6, "Morosani Residence," Richard Kelly Papers.
23. Lighting plans and schedules, Box 23, Folder 10, "Graef, Robert," Richard Kelly Papers.
24. Richard Kelly, "Brightness in All the Various Living Areas Must Be Planned Relative to One Another in the Contemporary Architecture of Open Planning," typescript, n.d. Box 15, Folder 2, "Davis, Richard, Residence," Richard Kelly Papers.
25. Lighting plans and schedules, Box 42, Folder 18, "McIntosh Residence," Richard Kelly Papers.
26. Stanley McCandless, "Lighting the Small House," *Architectural Forum*, Box 4, Folder "1937," Stanley McCandless Papers, Manuscripts and Archives, Yale University Library.
27. Stanley McCandless, "Characteristics of Downlighting," *Architectural Record* 109, no. 2 (February 1951): 144–145.
28. Morosani interview.
29. Box 5, Folder 10, "Boissonnas Residence," Richard Kelly Papers.
30. Kelly later taught courses on environmental controls at the University of Pennsylvania; Box 34, Folder 10, "Kirstein," Richard Kelly Papers.
31. Rita Reif, "Dimmer Controls Put Additional Focus on Home Lights," *New York Times*, March 3, 1959. See also Bernard Gladstone, "Modern Switches," *New York Times*, May 4, 1958.
32. "Background Lighting—Instant Magic," *House and Garden* (September 1961): 122. The dimmers depicted were installed in the Frame House, designed by the Houston architects Neuhaus and Taylor. Kelly is not named as the lighting designer but Hugo Neuhaus Jr. sought him out two years earlier to consult on another project; Box 42, Folder 6, "Maher, John R., Residence," Richard Kelly Papers.
33. The instantaneousness of such controls was central to their magic. Indeed, the phrase "at the turn of a switch" earlier denoted the power to harness tremendous energy and have it act at a distance to serve the pleasure of mankind. Switching lights from hundreds of miles away was a feat that once made headlines. That such an ability has become routine, part of our "seeing habits," demonstrates the degree to which world-changing technologies can be assimilated to daily life.

Corporate America and the New Luminous Environment

Kelly's Work with Johnson, Mies, and Noyes

Margaret Maile Petty

Richard Kelly's contribution to the development of modern corporate architecture in the United States can be traced through his collaborations with Philip Johnson, Ludwig Mies van der Rohe, and Eliot Noyes during the 1940s and 1950s. Although there seems to be an increasing closeness between Kelly's approach to lighting design and the ideological and aesthetic goals of modernism, his most successful installations complement the rationalized aesthetic of modern architecture through emotive and decorative effects. His key projects, from Johnson's Glass House in New Canaan, Connecticut, to Mies's 860–880 and 900–910 Lake Shore Drive in Chicago, as well as the Seagram Building in New York City with both Mies and Johnson, show the evolution and solidification of Kelly's vision and experience as a lighting designer, both of which he would bring into partnerships with Eliot Noyes in the years to follow.

The Glass House

Within five years of graduating from Yale's architecture school in 1944, Kelly had completed more than thirty commercial projects and designed lighting for at least as many private residences. It was during this productive period that Kelly first collaborated with Philip Johnson on the Glass House in New Canaan (1949), in response to Johnson's desire to improve the livability of the glass pavilion at night. "Having used transparent walls to enclose myself within a decorative landscape, instead of hiding behind conventional walls, I wanted to enjoy that environment at night, I didn't want to clutter the place with drapes and shut myself in," Johnson said. "Neither did I want to live in a gold fish bowl."[1]

Based on these conditions, Kelly suggested that the house be lit from "the outside in," so that the interior would be illuminated indirectly, allowing the glass to maintain its desired transparency. Moreover, after dark the glass walls would serve as frames for planned compositions made visible through illumination of the surrounding landscape. The external lighting program then would serve a twofold purpose, one of fitness, allowing continued transparency of the glass at night, and one of aesthetics, creating decorative scenery out of the surrounding luminous landscape. As Kelly explained,

> There have been a great many more glass houses . . . where the indoors mean nothing after twilight without careful planning of artificial light. The entire idea of the use of glass to this extent was to relate the outside with the inside, and we have found by experiment that when we do not have the outside lighted properly the inside is a bleak, separated hole. On the other hand, when you at evening try to use the glass as it was intended to be used, as the cushion between the outdoors and the indoors it is very easily possible to make the surrounding scenery the wallpaper of the home.[2]

In Johnson's original plans there were no permanent lighting fixtures to interrupt the interior architectural volume or the transparency of the glass walls. To achieve the desired effects without marring Johnson's pure planes, Kelly positioned downlights in regular intervals along the cornice, illuminating a section of lawn around the perimeter of the building. After dark these lights created a soft layer

Fig. 1. Philip Johnson, Glass House, New Canaan, Connecticut, 1949, exterior view at night

of light surrounding the structure (fig. 1). The intensity of the illumination directed on the lawn also created the illusion that the darker floor of the pavilion was levitating above the ground. Five light cans inside aimed strong beams of light up onto the interior ceiling, providing soft diffused illumination that served as the principal lighting for the interior.

To create "wallpaper" for the Glass House, Kelly utilized "five different levels of illumination" in the surrounding landscape, placing individual spots and floodlights at the base of selected trees in the near and far ground, and mounting spotlights on the roof to accent certain trees from a higher vantage point."[3] Developing lighting design sensitive to the unique properties of modern glass architecture, Kelly provided control of the interior visual environment of the house, as well as a measured imaging and ordering of the landscape after dark.[4]

Mies's Early Light Experiments: "Publicity and More Publicity"

At approximately the same time as the Glass House project, Kelly began working with Mies van der Rohe on the 860–880 Lake Shore Drive Apartments (1948–1951). These glass and steel apartment towers were a long-sought opportunity for Mies to realize his ideal of the modern glass skyscraper. Throughout Mies's early career unfavorable economic and political circumstances in Europe limited much of his work to hypothetical projects and publications. In a number of these early proposals Mies addressed the role of light in modern architecture—particularly in relation to the performance and transparency of glass. His early interest in architectural lighting design is evident in his concept for the Adam department store on the Leipziger Strasse in Berlin, in which he placed considerable emphasis on the role of lighting in the overall function and success of this project:

> A building has nothing to do with taste but must be the logical result of all requirements that result from its purpose. . . . You need layered floor levels with clear uncluttered spaces. Furthermore you need much light. You need publicity and more publicity. . . . I therefore suggest to you making the skin of your building of glass and stainless steel, with the bottom floor of transparent glass, the others of opaque glass. Walls of opaque glass give the rooms a wonderfully mild but bright and even illumination. In the evening it represents a powerful body of light and you have no difficulties in affixing advertising. . . . [S]uch brightly lit advertising on an evenly illuminated background will have a fairytale effect.[5]

In this letter Mies gives special consideration to the complex interrelations of glass, light, and luminosity, both within the department store and from the vantage point of Leipziger Strasse. He discusses the use of translucent glass in order to diffuse daylight throughout the interior space of the building, as well as to create a "powerful" backdrop for advertisements when illuminated from within. It is the transformation of modern architectural materials into luminous planes, therefore, that provides the background for Mies's "publicity and more publicity." In his later projects these same luminous surfaces would provide the setting for the promotion of his own architectural message of grid, core, and column.

An early example of Mies's use of light to bring focus and clarity to his architectural compositions is the German Pavilion for the Barcelona World's Fair of 1929. Here, he incorporated an illuminated double screen of translucent glass that served as the only source of light for the structure after dark (fig. 2).[6] This glowing volume provided a gravitational center for the pavilion and a counterpoint to the colored light and illuminated fountains featured across the fairgrounds after dark. Mies's glowing white wall also visually embodied the fluidity and weightlessness of the building's composition, transcribing it onto the nighttime experience of the German Pavilion. This early suggestion of an illuminated core is more fully realized in two of Mies's later projects: 860–880 Lake Shore Drive Apartments and the Seagram Building.

860–880 Lake Shore Drive and the Luminous Core

Mies had immigrated to the United States shortly before the outbreak of World War II, and by 1946, after approximately ten years in America and as director of the Architecture Department at the Illinois Institute of Technology, he was commissioned by the Chicago real estate developer Herbert Greenwald to develop two residential towers on a plot of land facing the Lake Michigan shoreline.[7]

Fig. 2. Ludwig Mies van der Rohe, German Pavilion, Barcelona World's Fair, Barcelona, 1929

The 860–880 Lake Shore Drive apartment buildings are raised on columns and situated on a shared travertine plinth, creating an open terrace with a canopied space beneath each building (figs. 3–4).[8] Similar to the technique employed for the German Pavilion in Barcelona, Mies used translucent glass to partially enclose the recessed core of the ground and mezzanine floors of the Lake Shore Apartments. At night, this evenly and brightly illuminated base preserved the optical and volumetric integrity of the tower's structural center, sharply foregrounding the surrounding load-bearing columns and making the upper floors appear to be held aloft by a block of light. The correspondence between Mies and Richard Kelly in early 1950 offers insight into their working relationship and the design of the illuminated core and plaza.[9]

At a meeting in Chicago in early 1950, Mies and Kelly had worked out the details of the backlit translucent glass for the core, and the recessed downlights under the soffits. The core was to be lit from inside by fluorescent lamps under the ceiling with a curved aluminum projector, and four spotlights in each of the three bays at the shorter side of the building created pools of light on the travertine plinth. In a letter to Mies written on February 20, 1950, Kelly confessed to having second thoughts about this very simple arrangement, and urged Mies (unsuccessfully) to install stronger and more lights in the soffits, namely "linear highly concentrated down lights . . . instead of the row of individual recessed spotlights I suggested in Chicago."[10] Clearly, he felt that the glowing core needed a stronger luminous balance surrounding of it. As an alternative, the brilliance of the core could be toned down by a "smooth exterior wash of light," reflected off a finely ribbed glass surface for better diffusion. Kelly was developing ideas here that he would put into practice soon after in subsequent projects with Mies van der Rohe. He could not help seeing the need to balance the ambient luminescence inside the lobby with focused and brilliant spots of light. He suggested to Mies light fixtures "integrated with door lintels" and a two-foot-wide "pierced metal sphere," suspended from above or attached to a column throwing "pools of light" to floor and ceiling.[11] It is hardly surprising that such ideas ran afoul of Mies's cool minimalism, in which the lobby of an apartment building claimed the same degree of abstraction and disengagement as that of a corporate office tower.

Additional downlights and wall washers were used by Kelly and Mies shortly afterward at the residential towers next door at 900–910 Lake Shore Drive, called Esplanade Apartments (1953–1956). The auxiliary spaces at the core were again surrounded by white translucent glass lit from inside, and the adjacent elevator lobby by clear glass panels. Additional downlights in the soffits provided increased brightness on the travertine plinth. The elevator core, however, was clad in polished green marble and illuminated by wall washers recessed in the ceiling in front of it. This arrangement turned out to be problematic: the stone's color

Fig. 3. Ludwig Mies van der Rohe, 860–880 Lake Shore Drive Apartments, Chicago, 1948–1951, night view of towers from the city. Photograph: Chicago History Museum/Hedrich-Blessing.

Fig. 4. 860–880 Lake Shore Drive Apartments, night view of glowing core and lobby made the lobby appear darker and less inviting, and its highly reflective surface rendered the recessed ceiling lights visible in the lobby, thus undermining their intended effect.

Seagram's "Tower of Light"

In 1954, Ludwig Mies van der Rohe was selected by Phyllis Lambert to design the Seagram Building in New York City, and he chose Philip Johnson as his associate and Kelly as the lighting designer. This was a prestigious commission from its inception, and the new thirty-eight-story headquarters for the Seagram Corporation on Park Avenue in New York became the most expensive office tower built to that date, due to the use of unusual materials, customized fittings, and the building's extensive illumination.

In the margins of a personal photograph of the Seagram Building illuminated at night, Kelly scribbled, "A tower of light, but the lobby predominates," casually observing what most critics overlooked in their fascination with the glowing tower above.[12] Both Mies and Kelly had been certain that "the ground floor had to be much brighter than the upper floors; otherwise, design effect would be lost."[13]

Kelly was finally able to realize the vision he had formulated for 860–880 Lake Shore Drive in 1950. A continuous band of downlights in the soffits along the perimeter created a luminous pool around the recessed lobby, and two rows of downlights in the building's canopy emphasized the entrance. A similarly increased illumination marked the transition toward the Four Seasons restaurant in the back. Another line of downlights on the inside of the frontal glass walls ensured their transparency at night. Initially Mies had specified dark green marble as cladding for the massive elevator banks at the core of the building, just like at 900–910 Lake Shore Drive. Although this material would have lent a somber opulence to the lobby, the Esplanade Apartments had demonstrated its significant disadvantages. Kelly recommended returning to the smooth, unpolished surface of light travertine that had been used at the elevator banks of 860–880 Lake Shore Drive, and Mies agreed. Recessed wall washers were installed in front of every wall of the massive elevator towers and evenly flooded the length and breadth of the travertine-clad walls with warm incandescent light. In partnership with lighting engineer and fixture manufacturer Edison Price, Kelly designed a tailored wall-washing system using newly engineered darklights recessed in troffers along the ceiling perimeter of the elevator banks. ("Darklights" are usually recessed ceiling lights constructed in such a way that light reaches the wall or objects to be illuminated, but not the eyes of the passerby.) Kelly and Price's wall-washing system articulated the drama of the building's proportions, emphasizing both the soaring elevation of the twenty-four-foot-high lobby walls and the solidity of the bronze-sheathed support columns (fig. 5). Four times the level of brightness of

Fig. 5. Ludwig Mies van der Rohe and Philip Johnson, Seagram Building, New York, 1954–1957, illuminated elevator banks in the lobby. Photograph: Ezra Stoller © Esto.

the upper floors, the combined illumination of the core and the perimeter downlighting visually illustrated the building's "free-plan" construction and defied expectations of gravity and mass.[14]

Above, a luminous ceiling on each floor traced the perimeter of the building in a twenty-foot-wide band, illuminating the office spaces inside and serving as an aesthetic device for the benefit of viewers on the street (fig. 6). The ceiling was illuminated throughout the day—ostensibly to counterbalance the effects of glare inside—but its full aesthetic impact was most apparent after dusk, when it provided unifying lighting throughout the elevation of the tower. This effect was widely exploited in promotion of the Seagram Building, as exemplified in the "tower of light" rendering that accompanied an article on the new headquarters in *Architectural Forum* from February 1957 as well as a variety of other marketing materials (figs. 7–8).

The technical precision and aesthetic unity of this luminous ceiling received much attention from contemporary popular and trade publications. An article in the *International Lighting Review* praised the "specially designed and engineered luminous ceiling system . . . which glows at night as well as during the day."[15] The article also detailed several "new concepts in architectural lighting," including the ceiling's fifty-two-inch square translucent vinyl diffuser panels set in an anodized aluminum-trimmed modular grid and configured to correspond exactly with that of the building's facade modules of fifty-five and a half inches. Seagram's luminous ceiling panels, custom designed and manufactured, were the largest flat diffusers manufactured to that date, specially engineered to emit a nondirectional, diffuse light pattern (fig. 9).[16]

Great lengths were taken to maintain the aesthetic simplicity of the luminous ceiling. The diffuser frames were designed to fit cleanly inside the skeleton of the ceiling grid to avoid the "clutter of a frame within a frame."[17] Similarly, to avoid visible latches or hinges, portions of the grid were designed to drop down a short distance with a hidden spring device

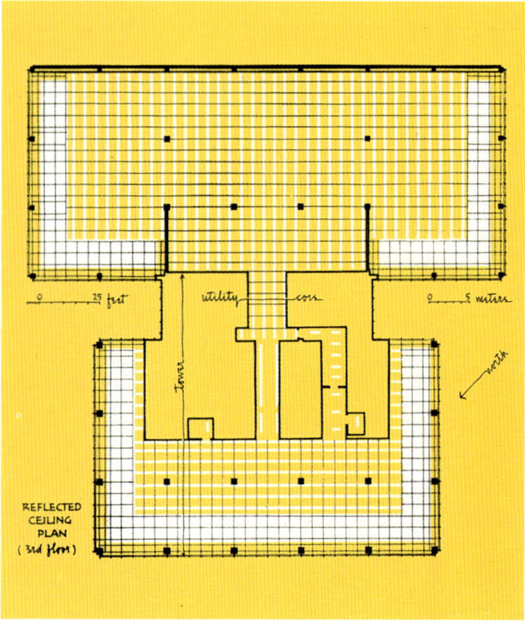

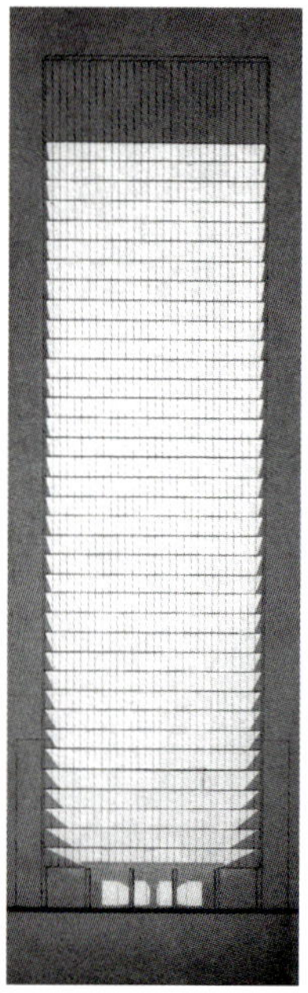

left

Fig. 6. Plan of the luminous ceiling for the Seagram Building, from *Progressive Architecture*, September 1958

Fig. 7. Lighting diagram for the Seagram Building's "tower of light," from *Architectural Forum*, February 1957

above

Fig. 8. Promotional brochure from Lightolier, produced for a special Seagram section of the *New York Times*, Sunday, April 7, 1957 that permitted insertion or removal of diffusers and access to services. To reduce sound spill, a common problem with open plenum ceiling systems, Kelly and the engineers at Lightolier developed a system of sound-insulating modular sheet metal boxes as the reflecting cavity for the lamps and ceiling grid support. In addition to helping reflect and diffuse light, the modular boxes shielded the ducts, pipes, and beams passing above, creating a closed plenum system and eliminating any shadows that might interrupt the uniform glow of the luminous panels.

Although one can trace Mies's interest in luminous glass walls and ceilings back to his unexecuted Adam department store in Berlin and the Stuttgart Bank Project of 1928, as well as his Stuttgart Glasraum from 1927 and the Barcelona Pavilion of 1929, the actual application and general availability of prefabricated, large-scale luminous ceilings in the United States seems to go back only to 1948, when Lightolier presented the first example.[18]

The Manufacturers Trust Building (1952–1954) designed by Gordon Bunshaft for Skidmore, Owings, and Merrill is perhaps the most direct precedent for the illumination of the Seagram tower. Uncharacteristic for bank construction at the time, Manufacturers Trust was distinguished by the openness and transparency of its glass and aluminum curtain wall, qualities that were emphasized both visually and symbolically by the lighting program for the building.[19] Bunshaft developed a luminous ceiling for the five-story building in collaboration with the mechanical engineers, Syska and Hennessy, and the electrical contractor, Fischbach and Moore, to counteract glare during daytime hours and to maintain the building's transparency after dark.[20] Bunshaft's luminous ceilings were installed throughout the second floor and in an L-shape bordering the curtain wall along Fifth Avenue and Forty-third Street on the third and fourth floors (fig. 10). The luminous ceilings were central to the identification of Manufacturers Trust with modern banking, and their striking effect was remarked upon by numerous reviewers, including Lewis Mumford, who described the building as a "crystal lantern," and Ada Louise Huxtable, who credited the building's illumination with the ability to make "material walls disappear."[21]

From the 1920s to the 1950s, facade illumination in the United States had typically taken the form of floodlighting, often making use of the setbacks for America's iconic skyscrapers, as for example at the American Radiator Building (1924), Empire State Building (1931), and Rockefeller Center (1931). In the 1950s, new and powerful mercury vapor lamps allowed designers to illuminate a tower as tall as Carson, Lundin, and Shaw's thirty-nine-story aluminum and glass Tishman Building (1957) in New York City with a continuous wash of light (fig. 11).[22] Richard Kelly himself had designed floodlighting for the upper twelve floors of William Lescaze's 711 Third Avenue less than a year before his work on the Seagram Building. He used the new "General Electric 500 Watt

Fig. 9. Seagram Building, corner executive office with luminous ceiling. Photograph: Ezra Stoller © Esto.

Fig. 10. Gordon Bunshaft for Skidmore, Owings, and Merrill, Manufacturers Trust Building, New York, 1952–1954. Lighting designer: Gordon Bunshaft with Syska and Hennessy, Fischbach and Moore.

PAR-64 flood lamp" to illuminate the entire shaft of blue glazed brick from the roof of the lower part of the building.

All of these buildings had a reflective surface of stone or brick. Large expanses of glass, however, as in the Manufacturers Trust and the Seagram Building, were impossible to floodlight from underneath, as the polished surface would reflect light upward without diffusion, and thus deprive it of any visible effect. Interior lights, in contrast, exploited and emphasized the spatial depth of a building. According to Phyllis Lambert, Mies originally recommended that lights be placed in pots on the floor along the interior window walls with their beams directed upward to create an indirect lighting scheme.[23] This would have kept the ceilings free of lighting fixtures but would have interrupted the floor plane and potentially presented issues of glare.

The luminous ceiling system was the ideal solution to Mies's vision. Kelly specified a secondary lighting circuit within the main ceiling system. During office hours, the primary circuit produced illumination of roughly eighty-five foot-candles. At night, the system was switched to the secondary circuit, which used separate lamps running at one-quarter maximum output to produce light levels near twenty foot-candles. Kelly specified the use of warm white fluorescent lamps rather than standard cool white, ensuring a soft light complimentary to the bronze-tinted glass of the curtain wall.[24] These warm lamps, when illuminated at quarter power, rendered a temperature and quality of light more closely approximating the color of the incandescent lamps used in the building's lobby, thereby providing greater continuity between the illuminated tower and the core. When lit at night by the luminous ceiling, the special fluorescent lamps and the custom amber-tinted glass transformed the building's dark, impenetrable daytime facade into a warm, glowing tower that served as an opulent symbol for the House of Seagram (fig. 12).

In his 1962 overview of office design in the United States, the German critic Jürgen Joedicke singled out the Seagram Building for its lighting program: "The external effect of the lighting at night was deliberately utilized by the architects as an aesthetic feature, thus giving artificial light an entirely new significance as an element of architectural design. . . . [L]ighting by 'luminous ceilings' is provided on all floors which strikingly reveals the building's structural pattern at night."[25]

The magazine *Progressive Architecture* delivered one of the few dissenting voices among the overwhelmingly positive response to the Seagram Building in the press. Its editor, Thomas H. Creighton ("T.H.C."), acknowledged that one of "its glories as a spectacle is its floating-above-the-street quality at night," but he was disturbed that virtually all other reviewers, in particular William H. Jordy and Lewis Mumford, had only appreciated the building's bold stand on Park Avenue and its elegant lobby and plaza, ignoring its interior spaces on the upper floors. "Here

Fig. 11. Carson, Lundin, and Shaw, Tishman Building, New York, 1957, night view of floodlighting. Lighting designer: Abe Feder.

Fig. 12. Ludwig Mies van der Rohe and Philip Johnson, Seagram Building, New York, 1954–1957, "tower of light" illumination, night view. Photograph: Ezra Stoller © Esto.

the results are not so happy," he claimed; while the executive offices on the perimeter might induce vertigo in some of their occupants, the interior spaces, of which there are many in an essentially square building, are—"no matter how well lighted"—still "inferior, claustrophobic space."[26] His objection was strengthened by the fact that the central offices did not bask in the glow of the luminous ceiling, which stopped twenty feet away from the perimeter, but instead had to contend with rather ordinary office lighting—making plainly visible the substantial drop in prestige in the corporate landscape from periphery to center (figs. 13–15).

Creighton was the only one who, rightly, asked if the "problem of glare had been countered by the increased artificial lighting, called for by the lighting consultants, at the perimeter."[27] After all, that had been the rational explanation for the installation of the luminous ceiling so close to the edge. And, indeed, the need of additional bright ceiling lights right next to a window to counter glare would only be justifiable when the room was exposed to direct, horizontal sunlight (in the afternoon on the western facade), and if the room's occupant refused to make use of the curtains that would otherwise solve the problem. Clearly, the luminous ceiling, which was visible from the street in each floor day and night at two distinct light levels, had a more substantial role to play for the outside appearance of the building than for its inside illumination. As Kelly later candidly remarked: "The night lighting of the building is a purely promotional use."[28] The cost, both financial and environmental, of that kind of promotion was significant, and the tower illumination was discontinued after the 1973 energy crisis.

As most critics were preoccupied with the exterior of the building, again it was also only Creighton who mentioned the disproportionate width-height ratio in the Seagram Company's multipurpose conference rooms on the fourth floor. These had a standard nine-foot ceiling, but the rooms were very large, at thirty-six by sixty-nine feet, a size that "cries for the greater height that two stories would have provided," Creighton wrote. In fact, Kelly and Edison Price were clearly aware of the fact that those rooms needed as much help from the lighting systems as they could get. They provided for luminous, light-washed walls from recessed sources in the ceiling. As *Progressive Architecture* noted, "This background lighting, diffuse and indirect, creates 'space' in a windowless room."[29] In addition, the tables could receive focused light from above, and adjustable spotlights for demonstrations or exhibitions provided a third option. These spotlights could be dimmed, and were built into troughs behind motorized hinged ceiling panels, which opened only when needed, just like disappearing footlights in the theater.

Shortly after the completion of the Seagram Building, the *New York Times* stated: "Lighting, once mere utility, has become an important element of design." Featured in the article were photographs of the General Motors Technical Center and the Seagram Building (both with lighting

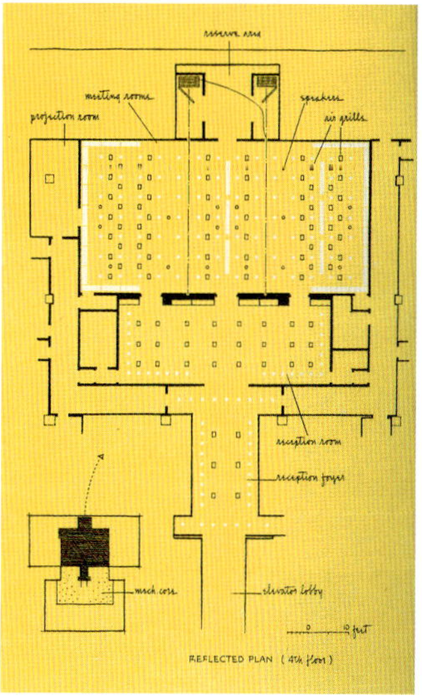

top to bottom

Fig. 13. Interior office space in the Seagram Building, showing the perimeter's luminous ceiling where it meets the regular ceiling. Photograph: Ezra Stoller © Esto.

Fig. 14. A conference room in the central part of the Seagram Building, away from the perimeter. Photograph: Ezra Stoller © Esto.

Fig. 15. A lighting plan for the Seagram Building, *Progressive Architecture*, September 1958 by Kelly) as well as the Tishman Building and Bankers Trust at Thirty-ninth Street (both with lighting by Abe Feder). The author, Thomas Ennis, explained: "Often regarded as a utility, lighting is now an art that combines function and decoration. Nowhere is this more apparent than in new skyscrapers, stores and bank buildings, in which lighting is an integral design element."[30] Ennis's article hints at the growing interest in the commercial sector of incorporating luminous architectural elements in an organization's visual identity program. In an era of substantial expansion across corporate America and the concomitant proliferation of prestigious new headquarters and research campuses built almost without variation following the minimal palette of the International Style, integrated lighting design became a principal means of controlling the visual presentation of these environments and identifying the corporate brands they represented.

IBM: Ambient Luminescence and the Aesthetics of Information

One of the most interesting if perhaps least often discussed examples of the synthesis of lighting design with corporate architecture and ideology can be found in Richard Kelly's collaborations with the architect and industrial designer Eliot Noyes beginning at midcentury.[31] Noyes developed a substantial collaborative relationship with the International Business Machines Corporation (IBM), starting with Thomas Watson Jr.'s preparations to take over the company chairmanship from his father, the longtime president Thomas Watson Sr., in 1952.[32] Working in close partnership, Noyes and Watson Jr. developed plans for both the strategic and the aesthetic reorganization of the company. Central to Watson Jr.'s vision of a modernized IBM was the horizontal integration of the company's management structure and, importantly, a new and unified "look" for the organization.[33]

The younger Watson had been inspired by the cohesive, colorful, and modern design program employed by the Italian office machines company Olivetti. The clear visual unity across the diversity of Olivetti products, environments, and promotional materials served as a model for the new IBM. With these objectives at the fore, in 1956 Watson persuaded Noyes to join the company as consultant design director for the new design program, which embraced the full breadth of corporate image development, including architecture, industrial design, interiors, exhibits, and graphic design.

The remodeling of IBM World Headquarters' ground-floor showroom on the busy corner of Madison Avenue and Fifty-seventh Street in New York in 1955 served as an important precedent for Noyes's role as design director for the company. Watson Jr. asked Noyes to bring what was a very dowdy and traditional showroom into step with contemporary modern design (figs. 16–17).[34] Among the first of the sweeping changes made to the IBM World Headquarters was the renaming of the Madison Avenue showroom as the "Data Processing Center"—a symbolic gesture expressing the refocusing of the showroom on the production and processing of information. With this initial remodeling project Noyes's vision for modernizing IBM began to take shape; importantly, architectural lighting took a primary and integrated role in the design and visual control of the IBM brand.

For Noyes, however, defining a new "image" for IBM was problematic. As he explained in an interview for *Industrial Design* in 1966, "I don't believe in corporate images. This image game is very superficial, using design as a sort of slipcover. . . . But I do believe in corporate character,

Fig. 16. IBM World Headquarters, interior showroom, Madison Avenue and Fifty-seventh Street, New York, ca. 1949

Fig. 17. IBM World Headquarters, exterior, Madison Avenue and Fifty-seventh Street, New York, ca. 1949

and that design programs can both identify and express that character."[35] The remodeled Madison Avenue showroom was intended to demonstrate the "character" of IBM as a modern company engaged in the production and exchange of information.

The lighting program Kelly developed for the remodeled showroom was a central aspect in the presentation and aesthetic regulation of the IBM "character." With no trace remaining of the original coffered ceiling or traditional decorative elements, the new showroom was wrapped in the vocabulary of midcentury International Style architecture (fig. 18). The predominately horizontal orientation of the open-plan space was divided into crisp volumes by a floor-to-ceiling glass wall, one side of which was a reception and display area for new IBM typewriters and business machines. The other side of the glass wall was reserved for the "heart" of the Data Processing Center—the new IBM 702 mainframe (fig. 19).

Three years before he began working on the IBM Data Processing Center, Kelly had published an article in the *College Art Journal* titled "Lighting as an Integral Part of Architecture," in which he introduced his "three elemental kinds of light effect."[36] These effects, "focal glow," "ambient luminescence," and the "play of brilliants," were all required for the perception of "visual beauty," according to Kelly, but he also suggested that, generally, one of the three would dominate any given composition. Identifying the principal light effect, according to Kelly, resulted from consideration of several key factors, including how the space was to be used, for whom it was intended, and the desired mood or "personality" of the environment.[37] Kelly's attention to defining the unique personality of an environment finds resonance in Noyes's desire to articulate the "character" of IBM as a modern American corporation, suggesting a shared approach to the design of an appropriate aesthetic for expressing the company's new identity.

Throughout the Data Processing Center, ambient luminescence played a significant role in defining both visual hierarchies and a unique environmental identity for IBM's showroom. In the business machines area the light-washed white wall anchoring the space provided a unifying monumentality that balanced the diminutive size of much of the displayed office equipment, which was individuated by focused downlighting. The prominent expression of ambient luminescence, which according to Kelly is what one would find in "any art gallery," thereby provided a cultural reference for the retail display of IBM's products (fig. 20).[38] In the data processing room, however, ambient luminescence played a much more dominant role. Intense light values radiating downward from the suspended ceiling were reflected back again from the white linoleum-tiled floor, creating a distinctly luminous volume in which IBM's latest technology and data processing services could be presented. Seen from Madison Avenue, the brightly illuminated data processing room appeared as a twenty-four-hour spectacle of IBM's customer service and commit-

Fig. 18. Eliot Noyes, IBM Data Processing Center, interior showroom, Madison Avenue and Fifty-seventh Street, New York, ca. 1956. Photograph: Ezra Stoller © Esto.

Fig. 19. Electronic data processing machine, IBM Data Processing Center. Photograph: Ezra Stoller © Esto.

Fig. 20. An exhibition at the Museum of Modern Art in the 1940s curated by Eliot Noyes

ment to the development of the information age (fig. 21).[39] As Watson described it: "The Data Processing Center generated enormous excitement . . . the 702 was actually a working machine. Customers who wanted to rent computer time would simply bring their data in, and we kept the computer running around the clock. If you went by on Madison Avenue in the middle of the night you would see it behind the big plate-glass windows, tended by well-dressed technicians in its brightly lit room."[40]

The highly regulated visual environment Noyes and Kelly created to house the IBM 702 became a central element in the imaging of IBM and its products. Despite Noyes's claim that he was not interested in crafting a corporate image for IBM, the Data Processing Center and the luminous space of the 702 mainframes, which later would be fully realized in the Poughkeepsie "white room," provided one of the most important visual elements in the articulation of IBM's corporate character in the second half of the twentieth century. The first "white room" built for IBM, at the Poughkeepsie research campus (1956–1959), designed by Noyes with lighting by Kelly, consisted of an internally sealed environment of white walls, floor, and ceiling illuminated under high light levels (figs. 22–23). A refinement of the Madison Avenue data processing room program, the undifferentiated wall-to-wall white surfaces and the high and even levels of ambient light in the white room created an intensely luminous and indeterminate space. Inside the room, Noyes and select design consultants critiqued all new IBM products, and from the latter 1950s forward it is also where all IBM products were photographed for advertisements, catalogs, and exhibitions. Throughout the 1960s and 1970s, the "white room" served as the conceptual and promotional backdrop for the company, establishing Kelly's ambient luminescence as a principal aesthetic condition for the information age.

Beyond the White Room

Noyes and Kelly's efforts to define a modern visual expression for IBM was translated to other corporate projects, soon becoming part of the vocabulary of corporate modernism and losing its specificity to IBM. The "white room" aesthetic is clearly recognizable in Noyes and Kelly's concept for the New York City Xerox showroom in 1963 (fig. 24). Here Noyes and Kelly created a set of white boxes suspended in a black volume. The contrast between the glowing white boxes, in which the Xerox

above left
Fig. 21. Exterior of the IBM World Headquarters looking in. Photograph: Ezra Stoller © Esto.

above right
Fig. 22. "White room" in the IBM Design Center, Poughkeepsie, N.Y., designed by Eliot Noyes, with the IBM 360 computer, ca. 1964

lower right
Fig. 23. The IBM Design Center's "white room" featuring the IBM DCS 370 Model 145 mainframe computer, ca. 1970

products were displayed, and the surrounding dark areas emphasizes the frozen, hygienic, space-age quality of both the white spatial envelope and the products inside it. Scale models for the project suggest that even in the conceptual stage the Xerox showrooms were designed to be viewed from the street (fig. 25). For both the IBM and Xerox projects, the pedestrian gaze plays a central role in the organization and presentation of the corporate space.

In the second half of the twentieth century the increasingly widespread use of the luminous ceiling transformed both the typical corporate office and the image of corporate America as expressed in showrooms and commercial spaces, such as those Noyes and Kelly created for IBM and Xerox. In a number of Kelly's corporate projects from this period, we find fascinating variations on the expression of ambient luminescence. Skidmore, Owings, and Merrill's Chase Manhattan Bank (1961) in many aspects responds to the paradigm set by the Seagram Building. The lighting of the lobby's elevator cores, for example, is very similar, although the image of a glowing tower of light at night, which the luminous ceiling at Seagram had made possible, was not pursued here. The Chase Manhattan Bank established its significant presence downtown during daytime through its light, shimmering aluminum skin. The ceilings in most offices were equipped with more economical individual Lightolier units, or in the less bright executive areas with a series of recessed downlights. The only area where Kelly specified a brightly luminous ceiling was the computer department, where he employed eighty thousand square feet of Smithcraft Integrated Lighting, consisting of open coffers with fluorescent tubes (fig. 26).[41]

Two years later, at the Bankers Trust Building at 280 Park Avenue, Kelly, together with Edison Price, developed a new luminaire for continuous ceiling lights and individual fixtures. Comparable to the effect of individual darklight fixtures, special louvers directed light exclusively downward, with no light visible from the side. While the rooms appeared particularly well lit, the luminaires themselves looked dark from most viewpoints except immediately underneath.

Clearly, for Kelly, the establishment of a successful visual language for the corporate American office interior was no reason to stop experimenting and improving on the established paradigms. Kelly might have also sensed that, although the luminous ceiling had significantly contributed to the creation of a visually unified and monumental architectural expression for corporate America at midcentury, its increasing ubiquity would soon come to represent the depersonalizing forces of the modern corporate environment. Kelly had recognized early on that light was, indeed, the tool to shape "reality—the real appearance of all materials"—which meant he was responsible for controlling its "visual characterization, which produces exactly what we are meant to see."[42]

Fig. 24. Eliot Noyes, Xerox showroom, New York, 1963

Fig. 25. Eliot Noyes, scale mockup of the Xerox showroom, ca. 1963

Fig. 26. The central check clearing office at Chase Manhattan Bank, New York, designed by Skidmore, Owings, and Merrill, 1961

For the Seagram Building, Kelly, Mies, and Johnson strove to create a "tower of light"; for those on Park Avenue the controlled image of a glowing tower was beautifully realized. However, for office workers spending their days in the Seagram Building's interior office spaces, cut off from exterior views and natural light, the controlled visual environment meant something quite different. Kelly and Noyes similarly used the luminous ceiling at IBM as a principal agent in creating a striking visual characterization. Entirely sealed off from the fluctuations of daylight, IBM's white room provided a constant and spatially indeterminate volume in which the company's mainframes stood solid and reassuring, stoically expressing the corporate character Noyes clearly identified with IBM—man's "control over his environment."[43] Indeed, it is precisely the control of the visual environment that informs and unifies the diverse aims and applications of architectural lighting design for the modern corporation and office landscape throughout the mid-twentieth century, and few had a more lasting impact on this new luminous environment than Richard Kelly.

Notes

This essay is based in part on two previously published articles: Margaret Maile Petty, "Illuminating the Glass Box: Architectural Lighting Design and the Performance of Modern Architecture in Postwar America," *Journal of the Society of Architectural Historians* 66, no. 2 (June 2007): 194–219, and Margaret Maile Petty, "Perpetual Noon: Fluorescent Lighting and the Modern Office," *Scapes* 7 (Fall 2008): 9–15.

1. Arnold Nicholson, "Mr. Kelly's Magic Lights," *Saturday Evening Post* (July 5, 1958): 65. Phyllis Lambert's essay in this volume speaks about the Glass House design and Kelly's involvement in more detail. See also Richard Kelly, "New Light on Living," unpublished lecture (dated July 25, 1955), Richard Kelly Papers, Manuscripts and Archives, Yale University Library; Richard Kelly, "Focus on Light," *Flair* (February 1950): 67–68; Nicholson, "Mr. Kelly's Magic Lights," 28–29, 61, 64–65; and Alison Bisgood, "A House Decorated with Light," *Vogue* (January 1, 1957): 135–137.
2. Kelly, "New Light on Living."
3. Ibid.
4. Kelly, "Focus on Light," 67. Kenneth Frampton argues for the centrality of the landscape to Johnson's concept of the Glass House in "The Glass House Revisited," *Catalogue, Institute for Architecture and Urban Studies*, no. 9 (1978): 38–59.
5. Ludwig Mies van der Rohe, "The Adam Building," draft of a letter on the 1928 project for the Adam department store, manuscript in Museum of Modern Art, later German projects, Folder 1. The design was introduced in *Das Kunstblatt* 14, no. 3 (1930): 111–113; reproduced in Fritz Neumeyer, *The Artless Word: Mies van der Rohe on the Building Art*, trans. Mark Jarzombek (Cambridge: MIT Press, 1991), 305.
6. See Dietrich Neumann, "The Barcelona Pavilion," in *Barcelona and Modernity: Picasso Gaudi Miro Dali*, exhibition catalog (Cleveland Museum of Art, 2006), 390–399.
7. Phyllis Lambert, *Mies in America* (New York: Abrams, 2001), 356–357, 510nn.46–49.
8. Ibid., 375–376.
9. Ludwig Mies van der Rohe, telegram to Richard Kelly, February 22, 1950, Richard Kelly Papers, Lake Shore Drive Apartment Folder.
10. Ibid.
11. Ibid.
12. Philip Cialdella, unpublished notes for *Richard Kelly, Selected Works*, exhibition of the Illuminating

Engineering Society of North America (IESNA), New York, 1993.

13. "New Progress in Light," *Architectural Forum* 106 (February 1957): 155.

14. "Uniform intensity of brightness over the lobby walls with fixtures minimized was the design goal to achieve simple monumentality effortlessly and elegantly. It required the courage to spend enough wattage to achieve the minimum intensity that could be expressive. It is probably the highest wattage per foot yet used in a lobby." See "Seagram Building: Definition of Structure," *Progressive Architecture* (September 1958): 139–143.

15. "Seagram Building, New York City," *International Lighting Review* 12 (1961): 68–69.

16. Ibid.

17. Ibid.

18. See Margaret Maile Petty, "Illuminating the Glass Box: Architectural Lighting Design and the Performance of Modern Architecture in Post-war America," *Journal of the Society of Architectural Historians* 66, no. 2 (June 2007): 194–219.

19. The building's curtain wall contained some sections of plate glass as large as ten by twenty-two feet—the largest sections of glass ever used in a curtain wall to that date. Dietrich Neumann, *Architecture of the Night* (Munich: Prestel, 2002), 184.

20. Fischbach and Moore also were the electrical contractors for the Seagram Building's construction.

21. Mumford and Huxtable as quoted in Neumann, *Architecture of the Night*, 184.

22. "Lighting Is Architecture: Assertion of Purpose," *Progressive Architecture* (September 1958): 145–149, and Neumann, *Architecture of the Night*, 191.

23. See Lambert's comments on the luminous ceiling, *Mies in America*, 514n.127.

24. Cialdella, *Richard Kelly, Selected Works*.

25. Jürgen Joedicke, *Office Buildings* (New York: Frederick A. Praeger, 1962), 140–141, 158–159.

26. T. H. C. [Thomas H. Creighton], "Seagram House Re-Reassessed" *Progressive Architecture* (June 1959): 140–145. Many thanks to Dietrich Neumann for calling my attention to this counterpoint to the widespread praise of the Seagram Tower.

27. Ibid., 144.

28. Nicholson, "Mr. Kelly's Magic Lights," 61.

29. "Lighting Is Architecture: Definition of Structure," *Progressive Architecture* (September 1958): 139–143.

30. Thomas Ennis, "Lighting, Once Mere Utility, Has Become an Important Element of Design," *New York Times*, October 26, 1958.

31. Their professional relationship began as early as 1945, when Noyes, then director of the Department of Industrial Design at the Museum of Modern Art, asked Kelly to serve on a jury selecting new lighting fixtures as a part of the museum's "Good Design" program. Eliot Noyes, letter to Richard Kelly, November 23, 1945, not indexed, Richard Kelly Papers.

32. The partnership between Noyes and IBM began after Noyes met Thomas Watson Jr. at the Pentagon during World War II and lasted until Noyes's death in 1977. A general source tracing Noyes's history with IBM is Gordon Bruce, *Eliot Noyes: A Pioneer of Design and Architecture in the Age of American Modernism* (New York: Phaidon, 2006), 137–186. Critical readings of Noyes's collaborations with IBM include Reinhold Martin, *The Organizational Complex: Architecture, Media, and Corporate Space* (Cambridge: MIT Press, 2003), 156–181; and John Harwood, "The White Room: Eliot Noyes and the Logic of the Information Age Interior," *Grey Room*, no. 12 (Summer 2003), 5–31.

33. Harwood, "White Room," 10.

34. Describing the Madison Avenue showroom as he first encountered it, Noyes wrote, "The large main company showroom in New York was a sepulchral place, with oak-panelled walls and columns, a deeply coffered painted ceiling, a complex pattern of many types of marble on the floor, oriental rugs . . . and various models of back IBM accounting machines sitting uneasily on the oriental rugs." Bruce, *Eliot Noyes*, 146.

35. Scott Kelly, "Eliot Noyes and Associates: Curator of Corporate Character," *Industrial Design* 13, no. 6 (June 1966): 38–43.

36. Kelly, "Lighting as an Integral Part of Architecture," *College Art Journal* 12, no. 1 (Autumn 1952): 24–30.

37. Ibid., 24.

38. Ibid., 25. Harwood notes this effect as well, arguing, "Noyes's redecoration was not only an interior design, but an exhibition staged in a shop window as well." Harwood, "White Room," 11.

39. On this see also Martin, *Organizational Complex*, 174, and Harwood, "White Room," 15.

40. See Thomas J. Watson Jr. and Peter Petre, *Father, Son and Co.* (New York: Bantam, 1994), 260.

41. I am grateful to Dietrich Neumann for calling my attention to the relevance of the Chase Manhattan Bank and Bankers Trust Building to the principal narrative of this essay.

42. Kelly, "Focus on Light," 66–69.

43. Noyes suggested, "it's easy to say that IBM is simply a maker of business machines. But if you get to the very heart of the matter, what IBM really does is to help man extend his control over his environment." As quoted in Scott Kelly, "Eliot Noyes and Associates," 43.

Light Changes

Philip Johnson, Richard Kelly, and *Stimmung* at Seagram

Phyllis Lambert

By his own account, Philip Johnson's eyes filled with tears when Mies van der Rohe offered him a partnership as co-architect of the Seagram Building: "Shall we make it Van der Rohe and Johnson?"[1] But ironically, although he had been an acolyte of Mies, Johnson was just beginning to break away, to develop his own approach to architecture.

Light

Philip Johnson's first constructed move away from Mies occurred during the remodeling of a bedroom in his Brick House, conceived as a foil to his Glass House in New Canaan, Connecticut. In 1966 Henry-Russell Hitchcock remarked on this shift, and thirty years later Johnson himself confirmed it, calling the insertion of a vaulted ceiling in the brick building "my first break from the International Style."[2]

In 1953, four years after the Brick House (also known as the Guest House) was finished, the architect remodeled two of its three rooms to form one long, narrow space, where he hung a series of canopied plaster vaults from the ceiling, carrying them to the ground on thin "pilasters" (figs. 1–2).

"The insertion of the vaults came out of discussions with Dick Kelly, my lighting man," Johnson recalled. "Lighting from around a concealed roof gives a wonderful light in the room. Having got that idea straight, then I thought at once of John Soane's breakfast room at his house in London. . . . This is the first time I used that vault. . . . It's a copy of Sir John Soane. It's the first time I used anything as definitely historical as that." Johnson later admitted that the solution had more to do with Robert Adam's remodeling of the long narrow space of the Library at Syon House.[3]

Much has been made of Johnson's use of historical sources, beginning with his now famous *Architectural Review* article of 1950, in which he cited the sources for the design, composition, and siting of the houses at New Canaan. In addition to claiming Mies as his generative model, Johnson referred to Mies's contemporaries Theo Van Doesburg, Le Corbusier, and Kazimir Malevich on the relationship of forms, and to Mies's "mentor" Karl Friedrich Schinkel for the "pure neo-classical Romantic—more specifically Schinkelesque"—way of siting buildings. He attributed to Claude Nicholas Ledoux the idea of separating the functions of the Glass House and the Brick House into two absolute cubic forms, pointed to the influence of the nineteenth-century historian Auguste Choisy's analysis of movement at the Acropolis at Athens, and quixotically, always wanting to surprise, linked his own interest in bucolic settings and eighteenth-century British models to the obscure estate of Count Pückler in Silesia.[4]

Johnson had begun to learn about architecture based on a curriculum laid out for him by Alfred Barr at the end of the 1920s, when he made a close, firsthand study of both historical and contemporary architecture in Europe. However, on his own in 1930, Johnson focused on Mies, and then in 1930 and 1931 with his recent acquaintance, Henry-Russell Hitchcock, he visited and studied work by Schinkel.

Hitchcock was influential in orienting Johnson toward the aesthetic and perceptual aspects of architecture, and even encouraged him to pursue a doctorate (a short-lived project) on Schinkel's most brilliant and eclectic follower, Ludwig Persius. The work of both Persius and Schinkel surely legitimized Johnson's own departure from Miesian modernism.

But referring to models did not constitute a "break" with Mies. Mies himself discussed historical examples: the structure of medieval barns and Gothic cathedrals; Schinkel's Altes Museum in Berlin (from which he said "you could learn everything in architecture"); and the "careful construction, absolutely honest" work of Hendrik Petrus Berlage, of which he recalled, "After I returned from Holland [in 1910] I fought with myself to get away from the Schinkel-classicism."[5] It was the difference of intention that would constitute the break. Mies's models were tectonic; Johnson's were sensually evocative. The drama of the mise-en-scène at New Canaan struck me on first visiting Johnson's domain in the

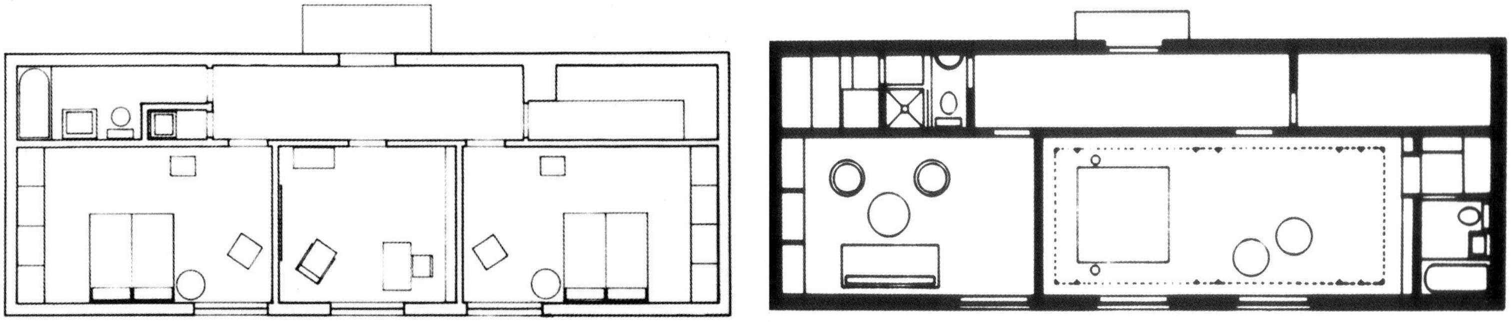

Fig. 1. Philip Johnson, Brick House, New Canaan, Connecticut. *Left*, the original plan, from 1949; *right*, the remodeled plan, 1953.

summer of 1954. The brick and glass houses and their setting had a palpable presence and were highly sensual. An ecstatic aura pervaded the guest room. One was not aware of entering a tall, narrow, windowless, tomblike space but rather was captivated by the glow of light washing the sandlike expanse of pink, silver, and gold Fortuny cloth covering the enclosing walls. Turning the knob of a substantial dimmer box that Richard Kelly had placed at the head of the bed—an early use of this new technology developed for the theater—one had the sense of nightfall in the desert, under the vaulted canopy (a sheltering firmament) as the light gradually faded.

I realize now that another model was lodged deep in Philip's psyche. Even though Johnson seems never to have referred to any but British sources for this room, he must have known another room with the same sense of enclosure, curtained walls, and magical lighting: the bedchamber that Schinkel designed between 1809 and 1810 for Queen Luise at Schloss Charlottenburg in Berlin, which was open to the public from 1918 through at least 1937 (fig. 3).[6] Barry Bergdoll's description of this remarkable chamber intensifies the comparison with the bedroom of Johnson's Brick House:

> By the simple means of white muslin stretched over rose-papered walls, light was reflected and filtered through the material to create the glowing effect of [the] sunrise, breaking down the boundaries between nature and architecture, and testing in concrete terms . . . the capacity of visual art to evoke specific moods, emotions, and states of mind.[7]

The same light-magic experienced inside the Brick House was conjured up in the glass pavilion every evening, as the induced light would slowly rise and fade among the surrounding trees (fig. 4). Johnson called this landscape his continually changing wallpaper. Added to this luminous experience were effects manifested within the glass walls. Against the dark brick floor and the large brick cylinder connecting floor and ceiling, uplights reflecting off the ceiling cast a glow over Poussin's *Landscape with the Body of Phocion Carried Out of Athens* in its picture stand (figs. 5–6). And by 1954, from a floor lamp that Johnson and Kelly had designed together (placed next to the Mies-designed daybed and table) emanated a soft pool of light.[8] The glow of the fireplace added atmosphere in cold weather.

The striking image of the steel-framed structure poised on a plateau at the edge of a precipice, the view framed by the structure of the Glass House, and the trees and valley beyond are reminiscent of Schinkel's evocative early paintings, such as *Landscape with Gothic Arcades* of 1812, which Johnson, who found Schinkel "almost as good a painter as Caspar David Friedrich," must have known.[9] Likewise, Poussin's *Phocion*, installed at the spiritual center of the house, resonates with the peopled landscape

Fig. 2. Vaults in the remodeled bedroom of Johnson's Brick House, 1953. Photograph: Bill Maris © Esto.

Fig. 3. Karl Friedrich Schinkel, bedroom designed for Queen Luise, Charlottenburg, Berlin, 1809–1810

top to bottom

Fig. 4. Philip Johnson, Glass House, New Canaan, Connecticut, 1949, night view

Fig. 5. Interior of the Glass House at night. Photograph © Ezra Stoller/Esto.

Fig. 6. Nicolas Poussin's painting *Landscape with the Body of Phocion Carried Out of Athens*, ca. 1648, inside the Glass House

and architectural elements of Schinkel's *Antique City on a Mountain* (1805): both situate a story and embed a particular view in the topography of the earth.[10] Poussin's landscape, evoking Schinkel's view, can be seen as the ideal for the site of the Glass House, which Johnson strove over the years to distance from the actual topography of the Connecticut woods. It reveals the extent to which Schinkel was on the architect's mind (fig. 7). Clearly, his break from Mies was fed by the Schinkel connection they shared but understood very differently. This break was instrumentalized through lighting design, not only because Mies's architectonic approach was out of reach for him, but also because it lay outside his own concerns, which were only beginning to surface. These concerns were nurtured by his haunting memory of the Hofgärtnerei in Potsdam in 1930: "the creation of emotional space by such casual and eclectic means."[11] Thanks to Kelly's control of artificial illumination, Johnson could bring together the pictorialism and atmospheric romanticism that he found in Schinkel *within* the tectonics Mies so admired in Schinkel, the "wonderful constructions, excellent proportions and good detailing."[12]

The introduction in North America after World War II of buildings enclosed by glass walls created new lighting problems for architects and lighting designers: solid enclosing walls that acted as reflecting surfaces were replaced by large sheets of glass that appeared black at night. This troubled Philip when he first moved into his Glass House: "There was no light—other than the sun. You can imagine the problem of reflections [at night]. If you had one bulb you saw six." Kelly, the architectural lighting consultant for the Seagram Building, developed the solution. Johnson said Kelly "founded the art of residential lighting the day he designed lighting for the glass house."[13]

He might have said that Kelly developed *a new art of lighting for a new architectural language*. Kelly's technique for lighting the Glass House, which might be taken for granted today, must have seemed revolutionary to the readers of journals in the mid-1940s. In the first sentence of one of his earliest articles from that time, he said that "good lighting is a vital part of good living," and he proposed to eliminate glare that tires the eye "by diffusing bright sources, by shielding the sources of light, [and] by arranging for a proper relation between bright objects and their surroundings." He demonstrated how these effects could create drama, even in a living room (albeit Lilly Daché's living room), where "noticeably free of glare and sharp contrasts, the general lighting is indirect—from sources subtly concealed," where certain objects like plants "are sharply silhouetted by baby spotlights, [and where] sculptures are made to reflect light . . . lighting can create drama."[14] By 1950, in an obscure periodical called *Flair*, Kelly was more polemical, claiming, under the headline "new techniques inspire exciting use in decor," lighting design to be an art. "It is not nature, but the artificial control of selected natural elements."

Fig. 7. (*Above*) Interior of Johnson's Glass House during the day; (*left*) Karl Friedrich Schinkel, *Landscape With Gothic Arcades* (Stiftung Preussischer Schlösser und Gärten Berlin-Brandenburg)

"Light and seeing are inseparable conceptions," Kelly continued. "We in fact make what we see by making things visible, and we make them appear and disappear to suit nuances of our desires." Among the effects illustrated were his use of a combination of indirect light and glittering highlight to enhance fine fabrics worn by the clients of the Stork Club in New York; color lighting to achieve distance; and dimmers to control the intensity of light and thus the sense of scale.[15] The essence of the article is a two-page spread on Johnson's Glass House titled "Romantic Lighting for a Glass House." It consists of a large and a small version of the same panoramic view photographed from the interior looking toward the exterior at dusk (fig. 8). These are also probably the earliest photographs of the house: candelabra and movable tapers provide incidental lighting in the sitting area, and a painting by Joan Miró (which would shortly be replaced by the Poussin) rests on an easel. The larger of the two images carries captions that use theatrical terms such as "bracketed," "spots," "floodlights," and "backdrop" to describe the lighting effects: lights bracketed to the eaves illuminate the lawn around the house, giving the illusion, from within, that the floor is suspended above the ground.

A mixture of spots and floodlights placed at the foot of trees, in the near and far background, light the landscape and give further perspective to the tree backdrop. At night, spotlights located on the roof of the house pick out the surrounding trees to form a luminous backdrop. Light is shot up at the ceiling inside from simple light cans in the four corners, to be diffused over the room. This provides the principal lighting of the interior.[16]

The smaller image captures the same view at night, but without any outside illumination the glass wall is black, so that "the candles and fireplace, reflected repeatedly in the glass walls, seem to have escaped out of doors to float in the air among the trees" (fig. 9).[17]

The key design invention is buried in the body of the article. After a general discussion of new technical developments in local lighting designed to meet exacting requirements for comfort in seeing under changing conditions, Kelly wrote: "To give such concentrated lighting a reasonable relation with our natural backgrounds, we require some general lighting. This need is exaggerated in the Johnson glass house by lighting the immediate surrounding landscape, in contrast to firelight and moveable tapers indoors."[18] In other words, lighting the landscape counterbalances the illumination of the interior. The continuity and flow between interior and exterior implied by this concept was a basic premise of the new architecture theorized in the 1920s.

The lighting scheme Kelly and Johnson created for the Glass House evoked Schinkel's aesthetic vision of a stage "essentially atmospheric in

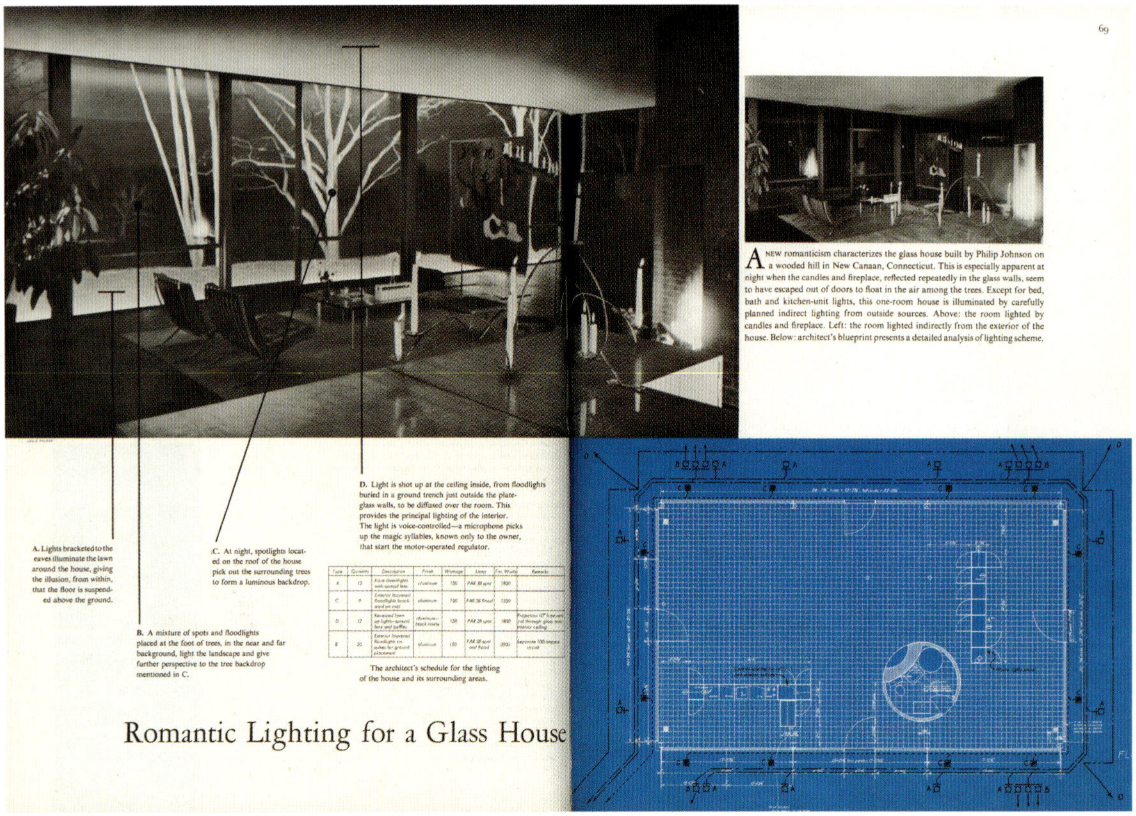

Fig. 8. Interior views of the Glass House at night, as seen in "Romantic Lighting for a Glass House," *Flair* 1 (February 1950): 68, 69

Fig. 9. Detail from the interior photo in "Romantic Lighting for a Glass House"

nature, employing lighting and painterly *Stimmung* [mood] as the main devices for the creation of theatrical effects."[19] The Glass House at night must have been somewhat garish initially: Mies would laugh and say that it made the house look like a hot-dog stand. He had proposed neon lighting to dramatize a drive-in restaurant for a commercial strip in Indianapolis and was still hoping to build it in 1950 when probably he first saw the Glass House. But Kelly and Johnson were not lighting the exterior. They had discovered how to make evident the reciprocity between exterior and interior through the use of lighting. This was something neither Johnson nor Kelly could have achieved alone—a picturesque, Schinkelesque effect that could have been achieved only within the sublime frame of Miesian architecture. Subsequently, lighting at the Glass House was continually refined, while Mies hired Kelly to help him solve the lighting for the luminous core at the Lake Shore Drive Apartments in Chicago in 1950. Kelly and Johnson worked together on numerous projects before Johnson took charge of Seagram in 1955 and contracted Kelly to consult on the architectural lighting for the building.

The sense of drama Johnson found in Schinkel's work must have drawn him to Kelly. How they met is yet to be ascertained.[20] Kelly had experimented with lighting during his high school days, and after completing courses at Columbia University in 1932, he experienced the new architecture as a lighting designer and consultant, which led him to enroll in architecture school. At Yale from 1942 to 1944, Kelly in all likelihood was exposed to the work of the peerless lighting designer Stanley McCandless, one of the earliest instructors in stage lighting and the author of the highly successful treatise *A Method of Lighting the Stage*, first published in 1932. McCandless's close attention to the instruments of lighting—fixtures and their technical characteristics—converged with the interests of Kelly, who began to consult with the founder of Gotham Lighting in the late 1930s. After obtaining his degree in architecture from Yale in the mid-1940s, Kelly served as director for the newly formed lamp department of Knoll Associates. He followed McCandless's basic concepts of light as a design method: stage lighting, which "in its brightness and darkness, its color and pattern . . . creates an atmosphere that is inherently dramatic"; and the notion that the conquest and control of the medium of light "in a sense provides a new horizon for artistic expression." Lighting, McCandless would remind his readers (and doubtless also his students), "is not really visible until it strikes some surface so that it can be reflected to the eye."[21] Kelly emphasized this point by quoting Le Corbusier: "L'architecture est le jeu savant, correct, et magnifique des formes sous la lumière" [Architecture is the masterly, correct, and magnificent play of forms under light].[22] Possibly deriving from McCandless the notions of "motivating light" (light that sets temporality and mood), Kelly was concerned with the effect on the occupants of space, and therefore would emphasize the psychological effects of his work: "To plan visual beauty by controlling light, it is important to know the psychological effect various light phenomena have on us."[23]

Kelly was a polemicist and as early as 1946 aimed to educate and convert through his writings in popular magazines. In 1952, first in *House and Garden* and then more formally and self-consciously in the

College Art Journal, he presented his principles as a "vocabulary" that expressed his theoretical position on lighting. In the *College Art Journal* article he first introduced the principles through the metaphor of painting a watercolor:

> A feeling for light and lighting starts with visual imagination, just as a painter's talent does. Think of the creation of a watercolor rendering—First, major highlights are imagined—then, graded washes of different luminosity are added and—then, the detail of minor lightplay makes the idea clear and entertains the eye.
>
> In front of the mind's eye are three elements in the perceptions of visual design—three elemental kinds of light effect which can be related to the art of painting for easier visualization: 1) Focal glow or highlight. 2) Ambient luminescence or graded washes. 3) Play of brilliants or sharp detail.[24]

With these three elements—"focal glow," "ambient luminescence," and "play of brilliants"—Kelly established the terminology and the principles that would form the foundation of his work. It is useful to consider how he applied the three elements of his thesis in practical terms for the *House and Garden* article: "1) Floor lamp and hanging lamp provide pools of light for armchair and sofa reading. This is called focal glow. 2) Ceiling spotlights spread soft, general light over fireplace wall and rug, which in turn reflect light toward [the] ceiling. This is ambient luminescence. 3) Candlelight adds [the] facets of light and play of brilliants."[25]

As an architectural lighting designer and illumination engineer, Kelly was in essence applying techniques of stage design. His three principles of lighting became a point of reference in his own field. They were absorbed into Johnson's design language, even as Johnson made the terminology more graphic, replacing the tongue-twister "ambient luminescence" with "washing the walls with light."[26] He was enamored of this new environment of controllable ambient light and focal glow and used it not only at the New Canaan Brick House but also in the modest apartment he designed for me in a New York brownstone in the mid-1950s.[27]

Gesamtkunstwerk

From the outset, Johnson was interested in the Seagram Building as *Gesamtkunstwerk*, a synthesis of elements that results in a work of "total design." Alfred Barr, director of the Museum of Modern Art (MoMA) in New York, had oriented him in this direction in 1932 when he suggested putting on an industrial design exhibition. The next year, while Johnson was the director of the museum's Department of Architecture and Design, Barr asserted that his program "would be of equal importance to anything [that] we do in painting or sculpture," and, indeed, with the exhibition Machine Art that opened in 1934, the museum gained a reputation for establishing standards in design.[28] Johnson, who knew that Mies's primary concern was the articulation of structure, form, and material, quickly grasped the fact that Seagram presented an unusual opportunity to improve on many of the standard industrial design elements used in office buildings: doors, elevator cabs, hardware, lighting and plumbing fixtures, and room partitions, as well as lettering and signage. Johnson reserved this role for himself, but his contribution to Seagram would prove to be even more far-reaching than he could have foreseen, eventually expanding to include the design of entire office floors, lighting strategies for the whole building together with Kelly, the display of artwork, the fountains on the plaza, and the design of the great rooms that merged with the public space at the plaza level. The architect and the lighting designer used powerful theatrical effects to interiorize the dramatic exterior substance of Mies's building.

Six months after Seagram opened in January 1958, the July issue of *Architectural Forum* carried a first glimpse of the completed building (fig. 10). "Seagram's Custom Look: 13 New Ideas for Better Skyscraper Design" was an unsigned, nuts-and-bolts piece written for a trade magazine. Surprisingly, the article focused on Johnson's intentions. The *Forum* critic called the building "a half-million square foot laboratory in which new and special office designs are being tested in actual use," crediting the architects with refusing "to accept a standard material or standard method if they could see ways of improving it."[29] The numerous pragmatically captioned illustrations stressed those elements destined to become part of commercial product lines, "a whole catalogue of innovations that may soon affect office building design throughout the U.S." The author captured Johnson's intentions and inadvertently pointed up the state of the building art in the late 1950s. Two of the thirteen "new ideas" were rooted in Mies's fundamental architectural conception and language: the bronze and glass curtain wall and Seagram's air-conditioning system, which "made floor-to-ceiling glass walls practical for the first time." However, one could easily imagine that the *Forum* critic's amanuensis was Philip Johnson, because eight of the other "new ideas" were his: controlled Venetian blinds, "specially designed to stop in only three positions," producing "façade patterns that always look neat"; "floor-to-ceiling doors" that "added nothing to the cost," and were made to "look like integral parts of [the] paneling," giving the "interiors greater unity"; movable floor-to-ceiling partitions, stock items redesigned and "greatly simplified in detail" for Seagram; floor-to-ceiling elevator doors revealing the custom-designed panels of an interwoven stainless steel and bronze mesh lining the elevator cabs; signage in a serifed Egyptian Bold font designed by Elaine Lustig for use throughout the building; custom faucets and other washroom fittings; and door handles and signal hardware fabricated in brushed aluminum and stainless steel at a "very, very minimal" cost over top-quality hardware, according to the manufacturer.

The floor-to-ceiling travertine slabs for an executive washroom allowed the *Forum* critic to discuss the ceiling grid and custom designed fixtures.

Fig. 10. "New ideas" number 11 to 13 from the Seagram Building, in *Architectural Forum* 109 (July 1958). Photographs: George Cserna, Alexandre Georges, Ezra Stoller © Esto.

However, there was no mention of the fact that this was clearly *not* a stock item but instead derived from a sumptuous Johnsonian concept for a travertine room. In fact, it introduced a new Philip Johnson, one who had begun to lavish rich and sensuous materials on bathrooms. Already in the late 1940s he had used leather "tiles" to line the walls of the circular bathroom of his own Glass House, forming a warm, tactile skin that exuded a musk-like scent. Ten years later another critic described the men's and women's washrooms Johnson designed for the Four Seasons restaurant as "palaces," "the former in Bardiglio Fiorioto marble and Macassar ebony, the latter in Rose Portas, rosewood, and gold Fortuny [cloth] with theatrical vanities surrounded by [low-wattage] bulbs . . . [with] marble shelves containing ashtrays adjoining each stool."[30]

The last page of the *Architectural Forum* article was devoted to three new ideas in lighting. A grouping of small images pointed to certain specific lighting effects employed in the Seagram Company offices as well as in other spaces in the building: display lights that disappear into the ceiling when not being used, and "invisible" or "concealed light sources" that "spill a wash of light over conference-room walls, and make a pool of light on [a] conference table." One passage commented on the role of lighting designers: "Lighting Consultant Richard Kelly, in collaboration with Lighting Designer Edison Price, used concealed light sources to illuminate [the] marble-faced elevator stack in [the] lobby, and to light paintings and tapestries in [the] Seagram offices. Result: one of the best-illuminated buildings ever constructed." To illustrate this last of "13 New Ideas for Better Skyscraper Design," a half page was devoted to what must at the time have been an astounding image of the Seagram Building. The *Forum* critic concluded with an evocative description that took in the urban context: "Each night, the luminous ceiling band is lit up on every floor, [and] provides a dramatic spectacle on Manhattan's sky line."[31] Lewis Mumford, whose "Lessons of the Master" appeared in his "Sky Line" column in the *New Yorker* on September 13, 1958, summed up his critical assessment of the effect of the Seagram Building shaft, the plaza, and the lighting: "It needs no ornamental fixtures other than those it has in order to increase this human quality [serenity]; all it needs—and it already has these, both by day and by night—is people capable of enjoying the primal aesthetic pleasures: ordered space, air, the spray of fountains on one's face, and sunlight or the regal mixture of black and gold that greets one from the lighted building at night."[32]

Mumford gave his version of the different hands involved in the design: "In accounting for the qualities that distinguish this edifice, one is safe in assuming that they derive, directly or indirectly, from the Master himself. To acknowledge this is not to diminish the contribution made by his associate, Philip Johnson, an avowed if by now an independent disciple."[33] Within ten days of the publication of Mumford's piece, I wrote to him: "You might be interested in knowing who did what. . . .

Fig. 11. Ludwig Mies van der Rohe and Philip Johnson, Seagram Building, New York, 1954–1957, entrance to the Four Seasons restaurant. Photograph: Ezra Stoller © Esto.

Philip played a very minor role until Mies suggested that the building would be nice lit up at night. Then came the ridiculous business about Mies's license and Mies went back to Chicago. At that point Philip's office took over."[34] Mies had felt he was being insulted and driven from New York when his application for professional membership in the state chapter of the American Institute of Architects was refused on the grounds that he had not provided evidence of an acceptable high school diploma. He left the state and returned to Chicago at the end of 1955, so from then until early February 1957, Johnson was legally the sole principal architect of the Seagram Building. For Philip, who had only recently left MoMA to open his own office, Mies's physical absence gave him a newfound authority that enhanced his growing sense of assuredness as an architect. Although he sought Mies's approval on all major design decisions, Johnson was now in charge of the office, and he remained so even after Mies's license application was accepted by July 1956. From then on Mies "visited" the office rather than headed it. Left in charge, early in 1956 Johnson began work on the lighting with Kelly for two autonomous interior spaces in the Seagram Building: executive offices for the Seagram Company and the restaurant Mies asked him to design—or, as Johnson put it, "gave up" to him.[35]

The Four Seasons was installed in the ground floor of the low east wing, within the free-span volumes Mies had created at each end. With the exception of the lighting, the "good design" elements Johnson contributed to Seagram (those lauded by the *Forum* article) constitute a body of two-dimensional elements applied to the surface planes of the building. They affect perception of the building rather than its essence. However, the restaurant Johnson designed, still unseen in 1958, would come to have an importance that exceeded what anyone could have imagined.

With the Four Seasons, Johnson achieved a Gesamtkunstwerk in which theatrical interior effects are locked into reciprocity with Mies's structural language. Furthermore, the offices for the Seagram Company and the lighting design for the building, although treated matter-of-factly in the pages of *Architectural Forum* (and by me in the letter to Mumford mentioned above) were highly distinctive. It is ironic that Johnson made his most significant contributions to the Seagram Building just as he was moving away from Mies and beginning to find his own voice.

The genius of his collaboration with Kelly in lighting the glass building was in creating at Seagram, as they had at the Glass House, continuity and reciprocity between interior and exterior spaces. These effects were epitomized in the Four Seasons restaurant, which opened in 1959. Kelly's thesis about lighting required an architectural aesthetic to soar, perhaps even to develop. Johnson's strong Miesian discipline and language, combined with his own romantic and intellectual sensibilities, supplied such an aesthetic along a six-year trajectory that led from the tentative moves made in the Glass House in 1949 to the sophisticated levels achieved at Seagram. Behind the bronze and topaz glass skin of the east wing, set back behind the building shaft and visible from the street, the shimmer of light and people in the great rooms of the restaurant imbue the place with the intriguing promise of something about to happen. The form is Mies's, but the drama belongs to Philip Johnson and Richard Kelly.

The entrance to the Four Seasons from Park Avenue draws the public across the pink granite plaza, through the glass entry cage, and past the honey-colored travertine core walls (fig. 11). The welcoming presence of these walls is maintained day and night by a wash of light regulated by astronomical and numerical clocks, devised by Kelly, which together constantly adjust the balance of brightness according to the intensity of the sun—whether midday, twilight, or the black of night. A *Progressive Architecture* critic noted that "it required courage to spend enough wattage to achieve the minimum intensity that could be expressive."[36] Kelly's darklight troffers create uniform brightness, evenly washing the twenty-four-foot-high travertine walls—an achievement not realized before. Lewis Mumford wrote eloquently about the entrance to the building: "The noble scale of the entrance is not just an outside pretense but an inside reality. . . . Even the black bands of the cove lighting in the lobby ceiling, which is of multi-toned gray mosaic, serve to point up, by their sharp contrast, the firm, undeviating integrity—and masculinity—of this design. Such purity and dignity are completely lacking in most contemporary metropolitan architecture, with its endeavor to humanize what is inhuman and to refine what remains so patently vulgar. One must almost go back to Palladio's San Giorgio Maggiore, in Venice, for anything like the same quality of mind and expression."[37]

Kelly had brought light-washed walls, his principle of "ambient luminescence," to a highly controlled level of expression. At the Fifty-second Street entrance to the Four Seasons the walls are similarly light washed, and darklights in the ceiling create an ambient luminescence on the travertine floor. This tomblike space with travertine floors and walls is no longer Mies but Johnson. We are reminded of Queen Luise's bedroom as well as the mausoleum Schinkel designed for her at Schloss Charlottenburg, and the bedroom at Johnson's Brick House in New Canaan. The memory of the guest bedroom's fabric walls was at the outset evoked by the pink and silver Fortuny cloth lining the walls of the ladies' powder room that opens off the travertine entrance to the Four Seasons. The swags of Queen Luise's drapery also reverberate in the most spectacular aspect of the two great Four Seasons dining rooms: the veil of the "Venetian" curtains made of fine-gauge aluminum chains falling in a catenary curve at the window walls. I was impressed by the genius of the idea when Philip and I visited the studio of Marie Nichols, the textile designer who developed these curtains with Kelly. Yet only when they were hung did we understand the extraordinary effect of the motion induced by the heated or cooled air rising from the convectors at the

Fig. 12. Richard Lippold, Four Seasons sculpture, 1958. Bronze and piano wire, two parts, 264 x 264 inches and 36 x 72 inches, Four Seasons Bar and Grill Room, Seagram Building, New York.

Fig. 13. Lippold's Four Seasons sculpture. Photograph: Ezra Stoller © Esto.

window wall, causing the lightweight yellow, pink, and green-gold aluminum chains to move in a slow, wavelike motion. As in Queen Luise's bedroom, "light [is] reflected and filtered through the material."[38] At times during the day the curtains are almost transparent, but in the evening they gain varying degrees of opacity and reflectivity as the maître d'hôtel changes the mood in the room, by orchestrating the intensity of "ambient light," the "focal glow" of pools of soft light on the tables, and a "play of brilliants" among sculpture and plants—thus illustrating Kelly's three principles for the creation of a seductive environment with light.[39]

Richard Lippold's sculpture in the Four Seasons Bar and Grill Room was Johnson's answer to the request of the restaurateur to create a more intimate space in the vast, high-ceilinged room (figs. 12–13). Lippold's sculpture is made of multiple quarter-inch-square bronze rods suspended from pairs of fine wires. Lippold also added a pendant to this work high on the mezzanine wall of the Bar Room. The multiple elements of these artworks, which sparkle when light is focused on them, allowed Kelly to apply his third principle of lighting: the play of brilliants. This "aesthetic ocular stimulus" plays in a private dining room just off the mezzanine. A sparkling ceiling composed of miniature incandescent lamps mounted in metal panels hovers over the room. Is this Kelly's idea or Johnson's? A gossamer sparkle curtain designed by Kelly was described by him in the *New Yorker* in April 1959 as being strung with countless electrical bulbs so infinitesimal as to be practically invisible by daylight.[40] However, the boldness of the starry field recalls the 1874 aquatint by Schinkel for his most famous stage set, for the "Palace of the Queen of the Night," which he designed for the first act of Mozart's *Magic Flute*. This image is one that anyone thinking of Schinkel's extraordinary range, and especially Philip Johnson, would know (fig. 14).

As suggested by the restaurant's name, plants form an integral part of the Four Seasons interior design. The concept of landscape architect Karl Linn was to have "permanent specimen planting, strong entities, and decorative 'exhibition' flower displays" at each season.[41] In contrast to the Glass House, where the building structure frames the landscape, at the Four Seasons the play of the natural forms of leaves and branches heightens the expanse of the disciplined architecture as diners ascend the stairs. Around the bronze housing at the base of each plant, Kelly placed uplights that cast leafy shadows and project patterns of light onto the ceiling, while the leaves themselves sparkle and shimmer. This effect is especially dramatic in the Pool Room, where at the four corners of the square pool large tropical plants both dominate the space and create an intimate environment. Downlights from the ceiling illuminate the upper leaves of the ornamental fig trees, *Ficus decora*, filtering subtle shadows onto the surface of the tables, while uplights cast dramatic shadows on the ceiling. The sparkle of the trees and the pool thus becomes the counterpart of the Lippold sculpture in the bar. Because of the geometry of the half-cubic rooms and the clarity and purity of the decorative treatment of the two solid and two transparent glass walls, despite the strategic location of the plants, the Four Seasons is not an indoor garden.

A fine balance exists between the architectural frame and the refined surfaces—the rippling chain curtains, the parchment paneling in one room, and the bookmatched French walnut paneling in the other, all bathed in light—and the intricate scale of the "pointillist" light-dappled plants (fig. 15).

These rooms were orchestrated with a theatrical sensibility where lighting played a crucial role. The subtle effects Kelly used to light the trees and pool in the dining rooms of the Four Seasons connect the interior of the restaurant with the illuminated trees and fountains on the plaza and

Fig. 14. (*Left*) Private dining room in the Four Seasons, 1960. Photograph: Ezra Stoller © Esto. (*Right*) Karl Friedrich Schinkel, set design for "Hall of Stars in the Palace of the Queen of the Night," Act 1 of Mozart's *Magic Flute*, aquatint, 1874. Photograph: Collection Centre Canadien d'Architecture/Canadian Center for Architecture, Montreal.

the glow of the Seagram Building day and night. Philip Johnson did not have to struggle with tectonics: he had only to invoke an interior environment within the space of Mies's structure. With the unleashing of his refined sensibility for light and materials, as well as his sense of history, Johnson came into his own. He brought to Mies's appreciation of Schinkel's "wonderful constructions, excellent proportions, and good detailing" Schinkel's *other* genius, for evoking *Stimmung*, or the atmosphere of a given place.

Fig. 15. The Pool Room in the Four Seasons, 1960

Notes

This chapter is based on the essay "Stimmung at Seagram: Philip Johnson Counters Mies van der Rohe," *Grey Room* 20 (2005): 18–59, which was the edited version of a talk given at the Collins Kaufman Forum at Columbia University in February 2004 at the invitation of Barry Bergdoll. It is a highly personal account based on my own experience serving as the client who represented the owner of the Seagram Company, Samuel Bronfman (and also as his daughter), during the design and construction of the Seagram Building, as well as since 1954 as director of planning for the company. In addition to my own memories I have used historical documents—my files and papers, letters and texts written at the time, documents in the Seagram archives and in the Richard Kelly Papers at Yale, an extensive bibliographical database of articles on the building, as well as the writings of Mies, Johnson, and others. The process has led to a number of insights that have in turn opened up fresh lines of investigation that might well not have been undertaken otherwise.

1. Philip Johnson, in conversation with the author, October 1954.
2. Henry-Russell Hitchcock, "Introduction," in Philip Johnson, *Philip Johnson: Architecture, 1949–1965* (New York: Holt, Rinehart and Winston, 1966), 10; Hilary Lewis and John O'Connor, *Philip Johnson: The Architect in His Own Words* (New York: Rizzoli, 1994), 37.
3. Lewis and O'Connor, *Philip Johnson*, 37.
4. Philip Johnson, "House at New Canaan, Connecticut," *Architectural Review* 108, no. 645 (September 1950): 154, 153.
5. Ludwig Mies van der Rohe, interview by Graeme Shankland, *The Listener* 62, no. 1594 (October 15, 1959): 622; "Mies in Berlin," transcript of 1966 interview with Mies for the RIAS, the American Radio University, Berlin, in Library of Congress, Manuscript Division, MvdR Papers, Container 62, 8.
6. I am grateful to Denise Bratton, who brought the parallel with Queen Luise's bedroom to my attention. I also wish to extend my gratitude to Wallis Miller, who generously helped to identify the dates when the bedroom of Queen Luise was renovated and open to the public. The 1921 and 1927 Baedeker guides *Berlin und Umgebung* list Schloss Charlottenburg and refer to rooms including the bedroom of Queen Luise, which is also mentioned in a 1937 Guide to the Museum as having been renovated in the 1930s. Dr. Burkhardt Goeres, Direktion, Schlösser und Sammlungen, e-mail to

Renata Guttman (CCA Library for author), September 23, 2004.

7. Barry Bergdoll, *Karl Friedrich Schinkel: An Architect for Prussia* (New York: Rizzoli, 1994), 31.
8. Designed in 1954 with Richard Kelly and Edison Price, this became known as the "Glass House floor lamp."
9. Philip Johnson, "Schinkel and Mies," in *Writings/Philip Johnson*, foreword by Vincent Scully, introduction by Peter Eisenman, commentary by Robert A. M. Stern (New York: Oxford University Press, 1979), 165.
10. See Kurt W. Forster, "'Only Things That Stir the Imagination': Schinkel as a Scenographer," in *Karl Friedrich Schinkel, 1781–1841: The Drama of Architecture*, ed. John Zukowsky (Chicago: Art Institute of Chicago; Tübingen: Wasmuth, 1994), 18–35.
11. Johnson, "Schinkel and Mies," 177. Johnson originally presented "Schinkel and Mies" as a speech at Congress Hall, Berlin, March 13, 1961.
12. Peter Blake, "A Conversation with Mies," in *Four Great Makers of Modern Architecture: Gropius, Le Corbusier, Mies van der Rohe, Wright; A Verbatim Record of a Symposium Held at the School of Architecture from March to May 1961* (New York: Columbia University, 1963), 94.
13. Philip Johnson, "Philip Johnson Remembers Richard Kelly," *Lighting Design and Application* 9 (June 1979): 49.
14. Richard Kelly, "The Better to See . . . ," *House and Garden* 90, no. 6 (December 1946): 152.
15. Richard Kelly, "Focus on Light—New Techniques Inspire Exciting Use in Decor," *Flair* 1 (February 1950): 66, 67.
16. Ibid., 68.
17. Ibid., 69.
18. Ibid., 67.
19. Forster, "'Only Things That Stir the Imagination,'" 24.
20. Thanks to Margaret Maile Petty, we know that both Kelly and Johnson served on the "affordable lighting" jury in November 1945, which had been set up by Eliot Noyes, then director of the Department of Industrial Design at MoMA, to stimulate better design in objects for everyday use. Margaret Maile, e-mail to author, October 18, 2003.
21. Stanley McCandless, *A Method of Lighting the Stage* (New York: Theatre Arts, 1932), 9, 16. Later editions followed in 1939 and 1947, and an emended and revised edition appeared in 1958.
22. Richard Kelly, "Lighting as an Integral Part of Architecture," *College Art Journal* 12, no. 1 (Fall 1952): 26. The quotation is transcribed incorrectly as "L'Architecture est le Jeux, savant, correct, et magnifique des formes *sur* la lumiere" (emphasis added).
23. McCandless, *Method of Lighting the Stage*, 50; Richard Kelly, "Good Lighting Is Part of Good Living," *House and Garden* 101, no. 3 (March 1952): 192.
24. Kelly, "Lighting as an Integral Part of Architecture," 24.
25. Kelly, "Good Lighting Is Part of Good Living," 138.
26. Olga Gueft, "Four Seasons Restaurant, by Philip Johnson," *Interiors* 119, no. 5 (December 1959): 168.
27. "The Light Changes," *Vogue* (January 1, 1957): 137–139. *Vogue* wrote: "In this New York pied-a-terre designed by Philip Johnson and lighted by Richard Kelly, the effect is all lightness and light—a warm surrounding luminescence that bathes everything (and everybody) in the room, seeming to come from no particular source. There are no 'islands,' no 'pools' of light surrounded by darkness . . . rather, there is a total ambiance that can be brightened or dimmed at the owner's will."
28. Quoted in Sybil Gordon Kantor, *Alfred H. Barr, Jr., and the Intellectual Origins of the Museum of Modern Art* (Cambridge: MIT Press, 2002), 303.
29. For this and subsequent quotes drawn from this unsigned article, see "Seagram's Custom Look: 13 New Ideas for Better Skyscraper Design," *Architectural Forum* 109, no. 1 (July 1958): 72–75.
30. B. H. Friedman, "The Most Expensive Restaurant Ever Built," *Evergreen Review* 3, no. 10 (November–December 1959): 112.
31. "Seagram's Custom Look," 75.
32. Lewis Mumford, "Lessons of the Master," *New Yorker* (September 13, 1958): 147.
33. Mumford, "Lessons of the Master," 142.
34. Phyllis Lambert, letter to Lewis Mumford, September 23, 1958, in Annenberg Rare Book and Manuscript Library, University of Pennsylvania, Philadelphia.
35. Philip Johnson, letter to Gene R. Summers, January 17, 1957, Ludwig Mies van der Rohe Papers, Library of Congress, Washington, D.C.
36. "Lighting Is Architecture: Definition of Structure," *Progressive Architecture* 39, no. 9 (September 1958): 140.
37. Mumford, "Lessons of the Master," 145.
38. Bergdoll, *Karl Friedrich Schinkel*, 31.
39. Kelly, "Lighting as an Integral Part of Architecture," 24.
40. Richard Kelly, quoted in [S.H.], "On and Off the Avenue: About the House," *New Yorker* (April 4, 1959): 132.
41. Karl Linn, "The Four Seasons: Collaboration for Elegance," *Progressive Architecture* 40, no. 12 (December 1959): 142.

Evolving Technology, Devolving Lighting

D. Michelle Addington

Light-emitting diodes. Electro-luminescents. Fiber optics. Smart glazing. Liquid crystals. The products available to the lighting industry have evolved rapidly during the last decade, as semiconductor-based technologies have revolutionized the emission and transmission of light. These new products have introduced unprecedented levels of versatility and control to the lighting industry. Light can be produced with any imaginable spectral profile over several orders of magnitude of intensity and directed at every angle with any beam shape. Wavelengths can be specified at the nanometer level, and switched on and off with molecular precision. The supporting electrical systems no longer require the consignment of large segments of a building's infrastructure, and the discrete size and low heat dissipation of light sources now allow their placement in any location. In short, light can be delivered wherever, whenever, and however one desires.

Architects, however, have shown little inclination toward exploiting the remarkable characteristics of these advanced technologies. As light sources have become ever more heterogeneous, architectural lighting has become even more homogeneous. Uniformly distributed white light floods interiors, regardless of whether the interior is that of a museum or a warehouse. Indiscriminate daylight spills through full height glazing, necessitating whiter surfaces and additional electrical lighting to overcome the inevitable glare. For all of the heightened attention generated by these new technologies, much of the resulting discussion has been confined to their role in energy use and not to their potential to enhance the human perceptual experience. Given that lighting is the single largest user of energy in buildings, and even more problematic, the single largest user of electricity across all sectors, one can certainly understand why the energy efficiency of light sources has garnered so much attention. The search for an energy efficient source drives much of the advanced research for many of the major lighting manufacturers, and the Department of Energy has further committed $450 million to LED (light-emitting diode) research in the confident belief that a revolutionary improvement in efficiency will render them as suitable replacements for today's technologies.[1] The potential for LEDs to bring a direct, discrete, and personal specificity to lighting design has been backgrounded as manufacturers have instead focused on developing them as replacements in conventional lighting systems.

In 1952, in an essay titled "Lighting as an Integral Part of Architecture," Richard Kelly described over thirty new lighting technologies that had emerged during the first twenty years of his practice.[2] From cold cathode lamps to precision lenses to dimmer controls, the technologies he listed touched on all aspects of lighting system design: the sources for generating light, the resources for distributing light, and the mechanisms for controlling light. Many of the products and technologies would be considered dated, and even undesirable, in current practice, but to Kelly they were the progenitors of an unprecedented versatility in "modern" lighting design. He expressed delight in the seemingly most mundane ("wonderful new candles, more light per ounce, less drip") and found potential in some of the most reviled ("mercury vapor lamps of high efficiency and spectrum, helpful and flattering to green plant life").[3] Nevertheless, none of the individual items that Kelly singled out afforded any significant development in system design, which is notable given that the time span he cites straddled a sea change in the technologies and methods available for lighting buildings. The New York World's Fair in 1939–1940 not only coincided with but was also largely responsible for the transition of lighting from a purely functional building service into a systematic component of architectural design. Before the fair, technologies were often custom produced and installations were nonstandardized. Although there certainly had been attempts to standardize lighting design, such as the "Lumen Method," developed in 1916 as a generalizable approach to the distribution of luminaires, or lighting fixtures, such methods were not widely adopted until after the introduction of fluorescent lighting at the fair.[4]

Although fluorescent technology had been patented in 1926 by a group of engineers in Germany, penetration into the U.S. market was slow to follow. According to the historian Cecil Elliott, General Electric and Westinghouse, the two manufacturers that dominated the U.S. electric lamp industry, had "accepted incandescent lighting as completely satisfactory for general purposes of illumination and viewed gaseous discharge and fluorescent lamps as suitable only for specialized functions."[5] Determined to showcase the newest and most advanced technologies, organizers of the World's Fair pressured American manufacturers to step up their development of fluorescent lighting by threatening to use European lamps. Sylvania joined with General Electric and Westinghouse in fast-tracking production and delivery of the lamps for the fair, and within just three years after their introduction to the American public, more than 34 million fluorescent lamps had been sold nationwide.[6]

Fluorescent technology was not a straightforward substitute for incandescent lighting, nor was it a routine upgrade for the discharge lamps more typically used in industrial settings. Incandescent systems required only the most basic of electrical infrastructure, and their small unit size coupled with controllable luminosity allowed for the discretionary placement of light. Mercury vapor and sodium vapor lamps required a dedicated electrical infrastructure but they could deliver light in a specific direction with very high intensity. Fluorescent lamps had few of the advantages of the existing technologies and most of their disadvantages. They required a complex electrical infrastructure that not only restricted their placement to ceilings or adjacent to cavity walls, but also necessitated additional structural support due to the weight of the magnetic ballasts that accompanied each lamp. Their discontinuous spectral profile could not begin to approach the quality of color rendering afforded by incandescents, and their lower light output coupled with a spreading photometric profile prevented them from delivering the high luminous intensity of the discharge lamps.[7] Unable to be discretely located, and also unable to produce directional light, many more fluorescent lamps were required regardless of whether they were replacing incandescent or discharge systems. How was it possible for fluorescent systems to penetrate the market for lighting design so quickly and so broadly? Certainly the forces that drove consumers to switch virtually overnight to a lighting system that was costly, cumbersome, and inflexible came from numerous fronts, not the least of which was savvy marketing from manufacturers targeting designers and architects.

In 1942, General Electric published a manual to aid its salesmen in marketing fluorescent lighting.[8] One of its chapters was devoted to arguments that could be used to counter potential customers' objections to making the switch from their current systems. Discharge lamp systems were described as creating "roller-coaster" lighting, which the manual claimed was dangerous, particularly in industrial settings (fig. 1). Only the continuous, even light provided from a ceiling system filled with fluorescent lamps was capable of delivering the high, constant light levels that were supposedly better for the eye, and safer for the body. Of course, this same ceiling lighting system was also proposed for commercial and institutional spaces, which previously used incandescents. Here the argument was more subtle. As the quantity of light delivered by the fluorescent system was much greater than conventional room lighting, the resulting contrast levels between dark surfaces and the bright light of the fluorescents was so high that it diminished visual acuity. The remedy proposed by the manual was not the reduction of lighting levels, but rather the elimination of dark surfaces (fig. 2). Regardless of whether lighting was being designed for an automotive factory or an elementary school classroom, the proposed solution was the same: homogenous light distributed evenly throughout the space.

Many of Kelly's contemporaries during the 1950s also remarked on the evolution of lighting technology over the previous decades, but they were referring to the introduction of fluorescent lighting, with its resultant planar homogeneity, and not to the small features that seemed to so entrance Kelly. Abe Feder commented that the "fluorescent lamp was hailed as the solution to all light problems," while Henry Wright claimed that the freedom in planning was the most revolutionary result: "This major shift is nowhere more dramatically evident than in the large architectural-drafting room, where it is now common to arrange blocks of drafting tables in rows of five or more in both directions."[9] Kelly's more specific references to minute technological advancements neither extrapolated into generalization nor deterministically coupled lighting technology to lighting design. In his descriptions, technologies were ren-

Fig. 1. An illustration from Charles Amick's *Fluorescent Lighting Manual*, 1942. The manual was critical of the point-source discharge lighting typically used in industry settings, claiming that the variation in light levels on a horizontal plane was dangerous.

Fig. 2. Amick's *Fluorescent Lighting Manual* on the importance of contrast. Salesmen were coached to encourage clients to use lighter-finish materials in interiors, as this would necessitate the installation of additional fluorescent lamps.

dered as precise tools to manipulate the characteristics and movement of light, nothing more. It was the role of the lighting designer to solve problems or provide design freedom using the tools at hand.

Kelly's attention to and interest in such details as "step-up transformers" and Venetian blinds might be a reflection of his early career path, during which he designed and produced lighting fixtures (known as luminaires) in addition to selling equipment from other lighting manufacturers. His light source was limited to incandescence and his fixtures were primarily intended for residential use. Nevertheless, he fully exploited every material and device for diffusing, directing, filtering, and focusing light. Baffles, louvers, and reflectors moved light; refractive and diffusive materials shaped light. While the extant sketches and drawings demonstrate a design sensibility for the object of the lamp itself, Kelly's interest was clearly more tuned toward the methods and materials for manipulating light and less toward the artifact that housed the physical components. Although a common assumption is that "light itself is the design material for Kelly, fixtures and lamps are secondary," this is belied by his exhaustive studies and drawings depicting the precise interaction between sources and materials (figs. 3–4).[10] The design of light was unquestionably his desired end, but he fully understood that materials and technologies were the necessary means.

Kelly's collaboration on projects with other designers and architects during the prewar period coupled with the inevitable material shortage brought about by the advent of World War II may well have been the impetus that sent him to Yale in 1942 to study architecture, from where he graduated in 1944. The context in which Kelly reentered the field of lighting design as an architect was much different from the one he had contributed to as a technician and product designer. Fluorescent light had eclipsed all other sources; homogenous fields of lighting had erased discretion and localization. But for Kelly, the content had changed much less than the context. The six qualities of light that he argued were necessary to control—intensity, brightness, diffusion, spectral color, motion, and direction—remained paramount, and thus what was deemed a sea change in technology to others was but a parametric fleshing out of the material means of manipulation in each quality.[11]

For all of the precision with which Kelly delineated materials, technologies, characteristics, and behaviors, he was most noted for his more conceptual description of the "three elemental kinds of light effects, namely (1) focal glow, or highlights, (2) ambient luminescence, or graded washes of light, (3) play of brilliants, or sharp detail."[12] This oft-repeated description would be recognizable to any contemporary lighting designer as but a linguistic precursor to today's three generic categories of lighting: general lighting, task lighting, and "sparkle." The fundamental categories of quotidian lighting design, however, have produced a very different lineage than do Kelly's elemental light effects. General lighting is the fundamental lighting of a space throughout which a standardized quantity of foot-candles is distributed. Task lighting is the purposeful delivery of a given intensity of light to the surface on which a task, from sewing to surgery, is performed. "Sparkle" refers to any small, high-intensity point source, such as a chandelier, beyond the direct field of view, but within the surrounding visual field. General lighting is governed by codes and standards, and the procedure for distributing luminaires is the same Lumen Method that was introduced in 1916 and later repackaged as the "Zonal Cavity Method."[13] Task lighting is supplemental lighting that generally adheres to quantitative criteria, whereas "sparkle" is a looser category, more or less justifying the installation of gratuitous luminaires. Contemporary lighting design is driven by objective measures to deliver a predetermined quantity of light regardless of the specific luminous environment or the behavior of the human eye. Essentially, the rules and methods reinforce the hegemony of an approach that was originally developed to maximize the consumption of fluorescent lighting.

The three elemental kinds of light effects posed by Kelly may seem just marginally distinguishable from the three basic categories of lighting, but there are significant differences in both conceptualization and actualization. He describes ambient luminescence as "twilight haze on a mountaintop," but defines it as "shadowless illumination [that] minimizes form and bulk."[14] Focal glow is "the campfire of all time" that manifests as "multiple foci producing a significant composition of attention." Play of brilliants is "the aurora borealis," exciting the optic nerves and heightening sensation. Poetic descriptions aside, the prosaic definitions lead not to quantifiable and repeatable results, but to the formal construction of a localized luminous environment. This environment is built on the foundation of the wash of ambient luminescence, shaped by focal glow and differentiated by the play of brilliants.

The conceptual and subjective underpinnings of Kelly's installations led many to describe him and his work as lyrical, magical, visionary. Maude Dorr, in her 1963 essay on the four most influential lighting consultants of the midcentury, singled out Kelly from his more pragmatic counterparts: "Each consultant has a different line of attack. [William] Richardson promotes color effects, Feder is concerned with . . . finding more and more efficient lamps; Kelly concentrates on spinning the elusive, subtle effects of light itself; and Edison Price has his hands immersed in the practical problems of exposed hardware."[15] In an article aptly titled "Mr. Kelly's Magic Lights," Arnold Nicholson describes Kelly as "an intense, imaginative individual who is best described as the leading advocate of the new age of light."[16] Kelly did little to dissuade such panegyric and indeed fueled it with his own prose: "to play with light is to play with magic."[17] The rhetoric, however, seems to be an incongruous cloak spread over what otherwise is a rigorous and structured process.

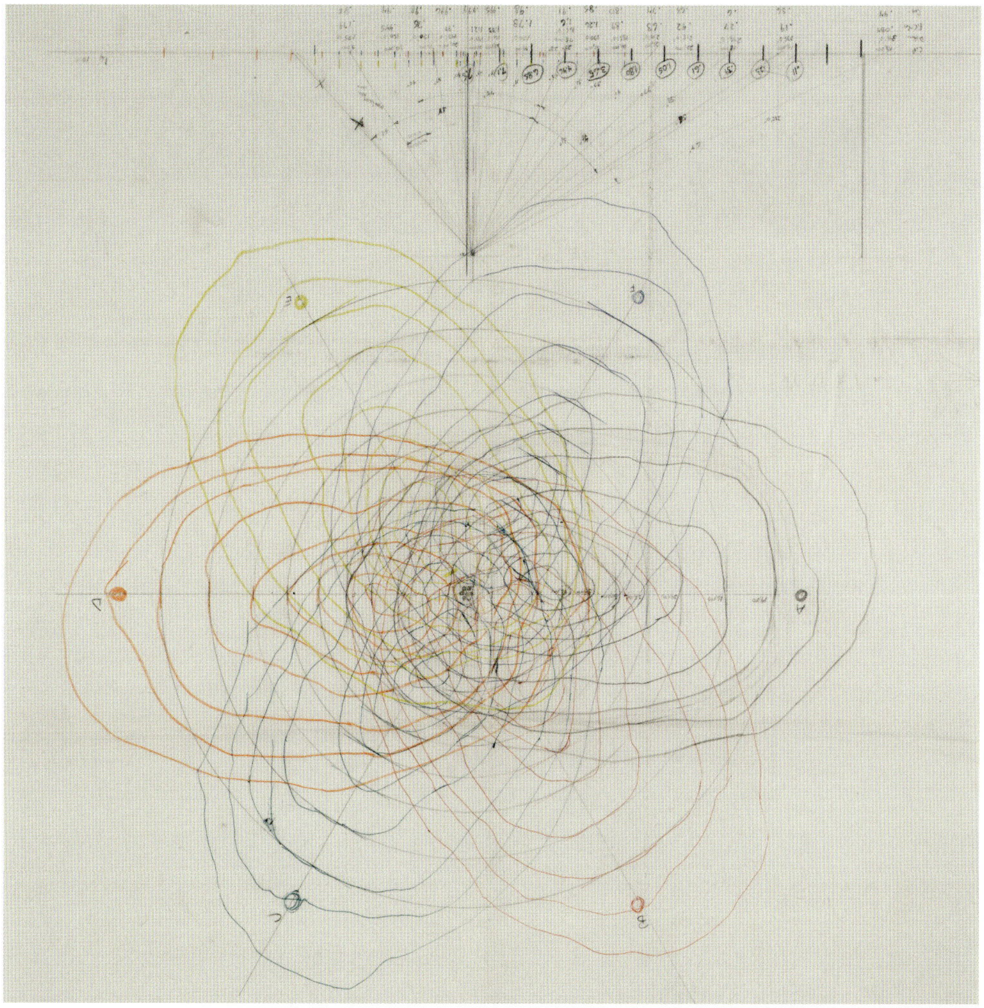

Fig. 3. Richard Kelly, sketch of lighting levels for Christ Corcovado statue, Rio de Janeiro, Brazil, 1965. Overlapping photometric curves of individual sources establish a profile of the resulting lighting plan.

Fig. 4. Richard Kelly, sketch of lighting points for Christ Corcovado statue, 1965. The arrays of marks on the statue show centerlines of each light source's photometric profile.

Returning to Kelly's delineations of new technologies and his descriptions of the qualities of light, one might recognize a staged hierarchy: more than thirty discrete technologies, systems, and materials for manipulating light, six qualities that characterize the behavior of light, and three resultant light constructions. Contemporary understanding of physics and perception would lead to the restaging of the hierarchy as four levels of increasing dependency:

1. Physical phenomena
2. Transient manipulation of phenomenological behaviors
3. Physiological interaction with transient behaviors (objective)
4. Perceptual coding of physiological response (subjective)

If Kelly's stages are mapped onto these levels, then his six qualities of light would compose the physical phenomena; the thirty-plus technologies would be means for manipulating the phenomenological behaviors; and the three elemental kinds of light represent a generalized perceptual coding of the transient behaviors. Missing from Kelly's hierarchy is level three: physiological interaction. As such, the causal links from levels two to four are bridged over with a deterministic construction. Kelly's acute observation of the human visual response rendered his empirical conclusions relatively on target even if not fully explicable or precisely describable. The inability to fully follow through with the rigor of his process may well be what resulted in his and others' overly rhetorical assessments.

The fields of neurobiology and visual psychology did not begin to form a coherent and comprehensive theory for the human visual system until the latter decades of the twentieth century. The first successful experiments to document that visual response is due to the location in the retina on which light falls took place in 1953; the discovery that retinal receptor fields are sensitive to orientation was made in 1959; the positing of the first theory linking the activities of single neurons to sensation came in 1972.[18] Contemporary lighting designers are confronted with the continually evolving and expanding field of knowledge regarding the mechanisms for perception, but Kelly did not have access to even the most basic physiological premises from which later knowledge evolved. Instead, a popular approach regarding visual perception from approximately 1910 until the late 1950s was Gestalt theory. Gestalt psychologists considered perception to be autonomous, an "as yet unspecified holistic physical process taking place in the brain."[19] It was not a question of determining the form of the link between phenomenological behaviors and perception, as they were considered to be independent theories. If Gestalt theory were mapped on the four levels of phenomena to perception, there would be a distinct severance between the phenomenological behavior of light and the visual perception of one's environment. This disconnection encouraged many architects to discuss lighting design as a direct product of the language of architectural design, and not as a process stemming from the precise manipulation and movement of light. Indeed, one might say that Gestalt theory led to an abdication of responsibility for rigorous lighting design and may well have contributed to the increasing homogeneity of interior environments even insofar as the knowledge regarding the understanding of human perception and of physical processes had dramatically expanded over the last half of the twentieth century.

Neither Kelly nor the lighting designers who were his contemporaries fell prey to Gestalt, but they also did not tread deeply into the territory of perception. In a conversation with C. M. Cutler about the role of the architect in lighting design, Abe Feder stated: "He has to master the mechanics of the given material to know what it does. I feel that from an architect's point of view, what is required isn't so much mastering a language as an awareness of the sources of light and forms."[20] Kelly certainly demonstrated the same pragmatism and rigor in working with phenomena and technology, but there does seem to be an inherent awareness that phenomena might link to perception in a causal rather than deterministic manner. The precision of his language may have begun to erode as his descriptions moved from material to "magic," but the specificity of his installations exhibit a carefully studied process of observation regarding visual perception.

In his delineation of the lighting scheme for the cafeteria in the world headquarters of IBM in New York, Kelly explained the linkage of several mechanisms that ultimately deliver light to a somewhat insignificant wall in a rather insignificant space (fig. 5).

> The walls opposite to the window-walls are made to provide indirect lighting by reflecting light that is directed upon them from a recess . . . in which are concealed continuous strips of concentrating lenses. The walls being painted light beige-grey have high reflectance and the light is of a flattering tint. The lighting from this equipment not only washes the walls with light, but illuminates the paintings on the walls. It is caused to grade out to a lower intensity both towards the top and bottom of the walls.[21]

This was an astonishingly subtle and nuanced design move, and indeed one whose perceptual results can be accurately analyzed only with current theories of neurobiology and visual psychology. The interior wall that Kelly describes above was situated in a corner room with two walls of windows. With blinds on the windows to eliminate glare, contrast levels between diffuse yet bright exterior surfaces and unilluminated interior surfaces would have rendered the space oddly dark, with the only alternative to increase the delivered foot-candles to the tables. It was basically a choice between gloominess and starkness. The graded washing of the wall, however, creates an "apparent" brightness that balances the window walls without requiring a flood of additional light (fig. 6). The principle in play is known as "lightness constancy," which is fundamentally the recognition that the visual system is capable of determining that a gray surface is still gray regardless of whether the actual illuminance is high, such as in direct sun, or quite low, such as in moonlight. Interestingly, lightness constancy was adopted by Gestaltists as evidence of the autonomy of human perception from the absolute behavior of physical phenomena. The neurobiological take on lightness constancy, however, which emerged in 1971, posits that it is instead a response to absolute conditions, particularly edge conditions.[22] The Craik-O'Brien-Cornsweet effect, first described by the eponymous scientists in the 1960s, demonstrates how edge conditions "code" the reading of relative luminance or brightness (fig. 7). The graded wash of light on the wall of the IBM cafeteria is a manifestation of the effect, creating lightness constancy between the interior surface and the window walls by manipulation of the edges.[23]

Kelly's ability to bridge from quantifiable physical phenomena to qualitative human perception is perhaps most evident in the projects that seem to be the most straightforward. From Philip Johnson's Glass

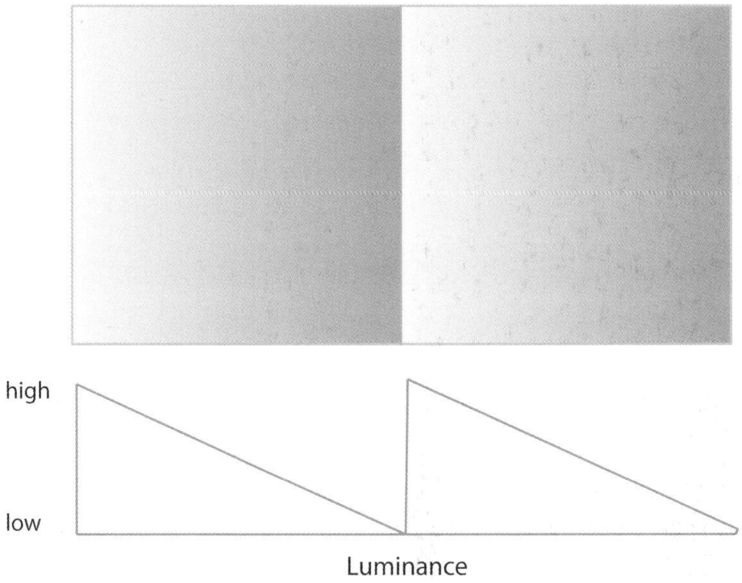

opposite page, left to right
Fig. 5. A cafeteria wall in the IBM World Headquarters, New York, where Kelly concentrated light in the center and gradually reduced levels toward both ceiling and floor

Fig. 6. At the Bankers Trust Building headquarters in New York, designed by Emery Roth and Sons, 1963, Kelly continued to use the graded wash effect but with a steeper dropoff in light levels toward the edges

this page
Fig. 7. Craik-O'Brien-Cornsweet effect. The left and right squares are identical, but the directional change of light levels at their contiguous edge dominates the interpretation.

House to Mies van der Rohe's Seagram Building, Kelly used illuminated and luminous ceilings to transition from overpowering light in the interior at night as well as from intense sun on the exterior during the day—conditions that both create glare. Arnold Nicholson recounted that Kelly believed the illumination concealed in the ceiling of the Seagram Building lobby "is probably the most intense concentration of wattage per square foot of any public building anywhere."[24] The necessity to manage contrast within the field of view demands a very high quantity of artificial light to mitigate the extremes, a realization that seems to be lost on architects and lighting designers today. Indeed, the more daylighting a building has, the more electric lighting it requires, as there is an unquestioned assumption that daylighting design demands large glazed surfaces (fig. 8).[25] What for Kelly was an intentional decision has become a default stance in lighting design.

The astonishing versatility of current technology for lighting has gone relatively untapped. New developments are pursued not for their potential in expanding the palette of lighting design, but for their insertion into the hegemonic system. The Lumen Method, in which luminaires were evenly distributed on ceilings in a grid pattern, so effectively established fluorescent lighting as the standard in the 1940s that it remains the model today. Quantitative delivery of light evenly distributed throughout a space trumps both qualitative discretion and perceptual stimulation (fig. 9). One very telling comment from Kelly regarding his choice of fixtures for the IBM cafeteria project perhaps best illustrates his reaction to homogenous lighting systems: "One of the purposes of these fixtures is to produce pools of light that grade out softly, so that the evenness of illumination in the room is relieved. . . . This gives the room the play of light needed to prevent the monotonous effect of a sea of tables."[26]

Fig. 8. Norr Group Consultants, Emirates Tower Hotel, Dubai, 2000, interior view. The high exterior light levels coupled with a large percentage of glazed surface creates a contrast level so high that interior details can't be distinguished. Additional artificial lighting will reduce contrast, improving the ability to see.

Fig. 9. John Andrews, Harvard University Graduate School of Design, Gund Hall, Frances Loeb Library, Cambridge, Massachusetts, 1972. Quantitative lighting design has produced interiors such as in this library, which has consistent high levels of lighting.

Notes

1. Light-emitting diodes are currently not as efficient at producing white light as fluorescent lighting is. Delivered light efficacies for warm white LEDs vary from twenty-five to fifty lumens per watt, whereas a comparable linear fluorescent ranges from fifty to one hundred lumens per watt. LEDs are, however, more efficient than incandescent lighting and therefore do produce less heat, rendering them a reasonable replacement in residential lighting systems, but not for commercial lighting systems, which almost exclusively use discharge lamps. See the report prepared for the Department of Energy, Office of Energy Efficiency and Renewable Energy in January 2009 titled "Multi-Year Program Plan FY'09–FY'15: Solid State Lighting Research and Development, Section 4.0 Technology Research and Development Plan."
2. Richard Kelly, "Lighting as an Integral Part of Architecture," *College Art Journal* 12, no. 1 (Autumn 1952): 24–30.
3. Ibid., 26–27. He singled out thirty-one new technologies, including eighteen technologies for artificial lighting and thirteen new devices for daylighting.
4. The "Lumen Method" emerged from the results of a 1916 experiment that determined the average uniform illuminance on an imaginary horizontal plane. See W. Harrison and E. Anderson, "Illumination Efficiencies as Determined in an Experimental Room," *Transactions of the Illuminating Engineering Society* 11 (1916): 67–91. A simulated re-creation of this experiment is documented in John An, "Evaluation of Assumptions in Building Energy Standards: A Method for Assessing the Lighting Provision" (Ph.D. diss., Harvard University, 2004).
5. Cecil D. Elliott, *Technics and Architecture: The Development of Materials and Systems for Buildings* (Cambridge: MIT Press, 1992), 264–268.
6. Ibid., 268.
7. The photometric profile describes the three-dimensional intensity falloff in light at several distances from the source. It can be considered the volumetric shape of light. The spectral profile indicates the energy level at different wavelengths—a balanced profile would have relatively similar energy levels of all visible wavelengths, whereas an unbalanced profile, typical of discharge lamps, will have a discontinuous profile with high energy spikes at particular wavelengths while possibly not containing all of the spectrum.
8. Charles L. Amick, *Fluorescent Lighting Manual* (New York: McGraw-Hill, 1942). Amick was an engineer with General Electric at their Nela Park facility in Cleveland.
9. Abe Feder, "Light as an Architectural Material," *Progressive Architecture* (September 1958): 125; Henry Wright, "Lighting Is Architecture," *Progressive Architecture* (September 1958): 115.
10. Maude Dorr, "Lighting Consultants," *Industrial Design* (June 1963): 47.
11. Kelly, "Lighting as an Integral Part," 28–30.
12. Richard Kelly, "The Versatility of Modern Lighting," *Lighting and Lamps* (March 1953): 23.
13. The fundamental calculation algorithm is unchanged from 1916; modifications have been made primarily to accommodate a wider range of luminaires and operating conditions. The term "zonal cavity" was substituted for "lumen" in 1966 to stress the importance of mounting height. The zonal cavity is the region between the luminaire and the ceiling. See An, "Evaluation of Assumptions," for an overview history of the Lumen Method and its modifications over the twentieth century.
14. Richard Kelly refers to these three light constructions in most of his interviews, lectures, and writings. See Richard Kelly, "Statement to Mrs. Edward Emerson," November 15, 1962, Richard Kelly Papers, Manuscripts and Archives, Yale University Library, for a particularly flowery version.
15. Dorr, "Lighting Consultants," 40.
16. Arnold Nicholson, "Mr. Kelly's Magic Lights," *Saturday Evening Post* (July 5, 1958): 28–29, 61–65.
17. Kelly, "Versatility of Modern Lighting," 24.
18. Ken Nakayama, "Vision Fin de Siècle," in *Perception and Cognition at Century's End: History, Philosophy, Theory*, ed. J. Hochberg (Oxford: Academic Press, 1998), 307–331.
19. Ibid., 309.
20. Henry Wright, ed., "Is Lighting Architecture?" (transcription of a discussion with Abe Feder, Richard Kelly, and C. M. Cutler), *Progressive Architecture* (September 1958): 179.
21. Kelly, "Versatility of Modern Lighting," 25.
22. E. H. Adelson, "Lightness Perception and Lightness Illusions," in *The New Cognitive Neurosciences*, ed. M. Gazzaniga, 2nd ed. (Cambridge: MIT Press, 2000), 339–351.
23. The edges addressed by the effect are actually micro-scale differentiations that are straddled by center-surround "filters" on the retina. Nevertheless, large-scale surfaces and their edges are the carriers of such micro-scale differentiation.
24. Nicholson, "Mr. Kelly's Magic Lights," 61.
25. Data collected by Vivian Loftness at Carnegie Mellon University. Cited from a lecture she delivered in Boston titled "The Environmental Performance of Buildings," November 18, 2003.
26. Kelly, "Versatility of Modern Lighting," 51–52.

Two Skylights

Matthew Tanteri

The finest examples of Richard Kelly's use of daylight can be seen in two important buildings: the Kimbell Art Museum in Fort Worth, Texas (1966–1972), and the Yale Center for British Art, in New Haven, Connecticut (1969–1974), both designed by Louis I. Kahn.[1] Similar to Kelly's custom fixture designs for manufacturer Edison Price, these buildings are the product of close cooperation between two designers, each at the peak of his career and especially sympathetic to the other's design ideas. Their collaboration on these two buildings was, in the words of Marshall Meyers, project architect for the Kimbell Museum, a "perfect communion."[2] A comparison of the two museums' skylighting solutions underscores Kelly's sensitivity to the particularities of program, site, and architecture.

Program and Site

Art museums are a distinct building type in that the elements of vision—viewer, object, and light—are foregrounded in any consideration of program. That is, how people look at art, and not simply the art itself, is crucially important to the museum's success. This aspect of the program, rather than, say, the location of the gift shop, is often shaped by the philosophy of the museum's director. At the Kimbell, founding director Richard F. Brown called for a daylighting strategy that would address a tension common to all museum lighting: how to balance the richness and variation of daylight, which can enhance the visitor's experience of art, with the sensitivity of many materials, such as fabrics, paint, and paper, that can degrade with exposure to the frequencies found in daylight. He especially wanted to emphasize the role of daylight at the Kimbell, but without endangering the works on display. The solution Kahn and Kelly finally arrived at entailed a monolithic, passive (that is, nonmotorized) lighting device: a slot cut lengthwise into the top of each ceiling vault effectively transforms each bay into an immersive lighting fixture (fig. 1).

At Yale, the lighting program was defined in a memorandum sent by the museum's director, Jules Prown, to Kahn:

> A. On a brilliant sunny day we would like to rely solely on natural light to illuminate the pictures; however, we do not want hot spots on the floors and walls.
>
> B. On bright but overcast days we would like to rely mostly on natural light for illumination, using little or no artificial light to supplement it.
>
> C. For less bright days we would use artificial light, preferably incandescent, to bring the natural illumination up to an acceptable level.
>
> D. We desire the option of eliminating all natural light from any gallery skylight.
>
> E. We do not want any beam of light to fall directly on the walls or floors.
>
> F. The light admitted to the skylight should come through clear glass or plastic, treated only to remove ultraviolet rays.
>
> G. We want to be able to sense change in the level of brightness of the sunlight available and do not object to sensing changes in the sun's position.[3]

In this case, the itemized requirements and the specific tolerances that qualify the use of daylight at the Yale Center for British Art suggested a variable approach. In response, Kelly provided a system to allow the museum greater flexibility to regulate daylight as it changed through the day and from season to season. The result would be an expanded range of visual and spatial experiences for visitors. To this day the museum employs trained personnel to manually operate an array of internally mounted shading devices to regulate direct sunlight in certain exhibition areas (fig. 2).

However the lighting program is defined, the qualities of light and consequent museum experience are affected by the site—the set of local conditions unique to a particular location. These conditions include climatic factors, such as the daily and seasonal path of the sun, weather patterns, latitude, and so on, and environmental factors, including the color of surrounding buildings, obstructions to light, viewshed, local types of plants, and more. The Center for British Art sits on the corner of one of New Haven's busiest streets, opposite Yale University's urban campus. In this area, surrounding buildings are mostly three stories in height, streets are relatively narrow, and surrounding materials are mostly hard—concrete, stone, macadam—all of which combine in a distinct urban character. These same factors limit the effectiveness of sidelighting through windows, and reinforce a strategy of top lighting. The Kimbell Art Museum, on the other hand, is a freestanding building surrounded by a well-manicured low-height landscape of plantings, pools,

Fig. 1. Louis Kahn, Kimbell Art Museum, Forth Worth, Texas, 1972, interior view with reflector installation

Fig. 2. Louis Kahn, Yale Center for British Art, New Haven, Connecticut, 1974, interior view with skylight installation

and fountains. For a museum's daylighting design to excel, its fenestration strategy must take all of these site factors into consideration.

As one example, lighting designers must construct a "design sky," an industry term for a model of the range of sky luminance distributions at a location over a period of time, which takes into account not just sunlight but reflections off clouds and the effect of the atmosphere's scattering effect on sunlight. Design skies are usually grouped under the headings of clear, partly cloudy, and overcast. New Haven has coastal New England's typical mix of conditions: overcast and partly cloudy conditions make up the majority of skies during the year. Fort Worth also has a distinctive mix of skies, with clear and partly cloudy the predominant types.

Another key aspect of daylighting design is the "solar window," which describes the hours of direct sunlight and accounts for those times any given building will be in shade. Over the course of a year, the sun's path across the sky changes within limits governed by the latitude. At 41 degrees north latitude, New Haven sits almost halfway between the equator and the north pole. This position results in a solar window midway between horizon and zenith of an imaginary dome centered on the building in question. In the summer, the sun climbs high but never gets directly overhead. In the winter, the solar path is low: surrounding buildings can obstruct direct sunlight. At a latitude of 32.5 degrees north, Fort Worth is significantly closer to the equator, giving the solar window a more vertical position in the sky. At noon, the summer sun is almost directly overhead. The solar window is modified by the design sky to arrive at an estimate of how sunny the sky will likely be. Based on a record covering the past thirty years, sunlight probability in Fort Worth is about 25 percent higher than it is in New Haven. This additional insolation inevitably affects temperature. In Fort Worth average temperatures fall into the upper range of U.S. cities, while in New Haven they are in the middle. The higher sunlight probability in Fort Worth supports a top-lighting solution where the aperture is designed solely for direct sun, while the lower probability in New Haven calls for top lighting with an aperture that accommodates a mix of sun and sky conditions.

Design Solutions

Despite the many differences in their sites, Kahn and Kelly settled on top lighting as the preferred daylighting method for the two museums. In both buildings light enters from above through a well-considered, highly articulated aperture and travels downward through inter-reflection from interior surfaces. But this is where any similarity ends, as in each of these museums daylight is utilized in a completely different way.

Given the hot, sunny climate of Forth Worth, Kahn and Kelly acknowledged the sun as an extremely powerful energy source. Allowing sunlight, in either direct or reflected form, into the interior would require balancing the benefits of daylight against the liability of heat gain and overexposure of the art collection. They also knew that a horizontal surface at this latitude would receive the greatest illumination and insolation throughout all the days of the year. With the exterior illumination level from sunlight so high, very little roof opening would be needed to achieve the recommended general illuminance level of a museum environment. At the same time, the roof would be subject to tremendous insolation and would thus require some mechanism to reduce the transfer of heat into the building envelope, through either high reflectance or thermal mass, or both. Kahn's architectural solution was simple: a series of long, cast-concrete cycloid vaults that run along a north-south axis with a narrow and continuous linear glazed slit at the top of each to let in sunlight (fig. 3). The slit is hidden by an internal winged reflector, which reflects light back up to the vault's curved ceiling. Portions of the vault are interrupted to make outdoor spaces that form the building's main entrance and several interior courtyards.

Kelly was present right from the start of the design process for the Kimbell, at the early conceptual stage even before budgets were set or structure determined. His evident success in bringing his technical knowledge and design sensitivity to bear on Kahn's thinking established a new milestone for the lighting profession by demonstrating the pivotal role a lighting designer could play in architectural design, helping to articulate a mutual understanding of program and site. For the Kimbell, Kahn made a point of crediting Kelly's involvement at "the inception of the idea of the shell, skylight and lighting fixture integration as far back as the preliminary design."[4]

In New Haven, the Yale Center for British Art would need to address the primary daylight source of overcast and partly cloudy skies, but would nonetheless also need to address the demands of direct sunlight. Although clear skies are not the prevailing type in New Haven, the probability of sunlight between June and September is well over 60 percent. Although not as simple, Kahn and Kelly's solution was equally ingenious: a series of large rectangular skylights with an exterior-mounted shading structure designed to equalize interior illuminance throughout the day and over the course of the year (fig. 4). The illuminance of the sky would necessarily vary through the day, but by carefully calculating the louver profiles, Kelly was able to guarantee a steady and even light diffused within each of the skylight wells.

The centerpiece of the Kimbell's lighting design is the winged reflector that runs along the peak of the cycloid vault and fills its interior surfaces with ambient light. Kahn had initially proposed one-way mirrored glass for the reflector, but Kelly thought plastic would be more practical.[5] The material finally used was perforated aluminum sheets, which Kelly realized would offer some degree of transparency as well as good reflectivity. Moreover, it reduced the initial cost and required far

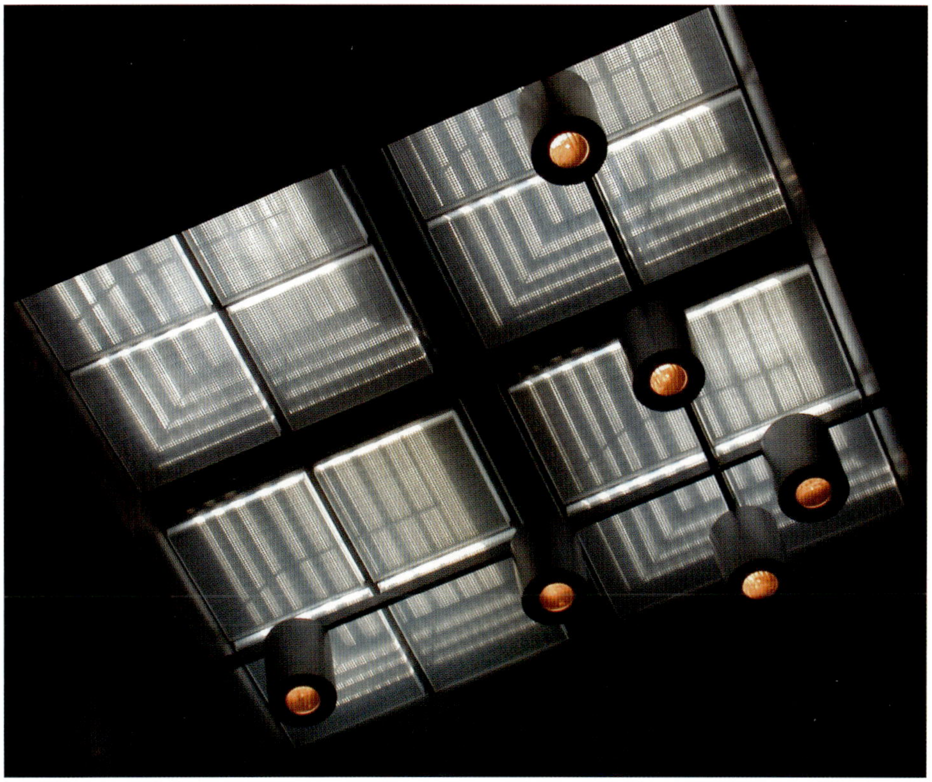

above left

Fig. 3. A reflector installation inside the Kimbell Art Museum

above

Fig. 4. A skylight installation in the Yale Center for British Art

left

Fig. 5. Reflector installation for the Kimbell Art Museum. Illustration by Cherine Saroufin.

Fig. 6. Interior of the Kimbell Art Museum with reflector installation

less maintenance than the acrylic he originally had in mind. Kelly drew the sweeping curve of the reflector, and mathematician Isaac Goodbar, then working in the office of fixture manufacturer Edison Price, verified the curve through the new technique of computer analysis. In an early design phase Kelly hid a small linear source of electric light on the underside of the reflector to illuminate the vaults at night. Always sensitive to issues of glare, Kelly calibrated the design so that neither the sun nor the electric light source could be seen from below. Ultimately, budget considerations eliminated Kelly's hidden electric light, leading him to design the track lighting that was eventually installed. The final design consists of a supporting yoke, a light track, and a frame on which is attached a curved aluminum sheet (fig. 5). Perforations allow some daylight penetration to soften the contrast between the underside of the fixture and the adjacent daylighted concrete vault. The central portion of the aluminum sheeting, rising into the skylight, was left unperforated to block direct sun. In areas where it was safe to allow occasional sunlight—the lobby, bookstore, dining room, and library—even this vertical portion of the reflector was perforated (fig. 6). For the auditorium Kelly designed a motorized shutter system so that the room could be darkened as needed.[6]

The scope of Kelly's work at the Kimbell extended further to the overall lighting program, including designing electric light to blend with daylight, advising on ways to filter damaging ultraviolet light, night lighting of the gardens, and even suggesting the plants in the courtyards to filter and further soften the daylight.

The central element of the daylighting design at Yale is a rectangular grid of skylight wells, which penetrate various levels of the four-story building. Kahn worked closely with Kelly to determine the form of the structural members that support the roof and give the skylight wells their unique character. Like the perforated aluminum of the Kimbell's skylight, the deep, slanted, and textured concrete on the inside of the wells softens the contrast between the luminous skylights and surrounding surfaces. Kelly thought that some type of shielding might allow the skylights to exploit the relatively low elevation of the sun in New Haven to protect the museum's art from ultraviolet infiltration. With the aid of computer calculations, Kelly developed what he described as "a kind of unit louver to create a sun shadow pattern on a diffusive material that then becomes the source of daylight for the paintings."[7] His louver design minimized northern light but transmitted some warm-colored southern light into the space to attain a full range of color (figs. 7–9).

Kelly's design for the skylights went through several modifications, including some investigation of motorized shutters. His second design proposal had four basic parts. Starting from the top, it consisted of a truncated pyramidal exterior louver system; a double dome of acrylic with a coating on the inner dome to filter ultraviolet light; a diffuser made from two sheets of prismatic acrylic lenses; and a hanging baffle divided into four sections to further diffuse the light. A full-scale mockup with movable louvers was constructed to test the complex design. After close study, the hanging baffle placed below the diffuser was eliminated and the diffuser went through several more stages of development involving other consultants.

The final design of the interior diffuser uses a sandwich of three light-modifying elements. They are, again from the top down: a sandblasted plastic sheet to soften the light and protect the diffuser below from dust; an egg-crate louver; and two prismatic acrylic lenses. These last two elements inverted the order of Kelly's second diffuser design. The hanging

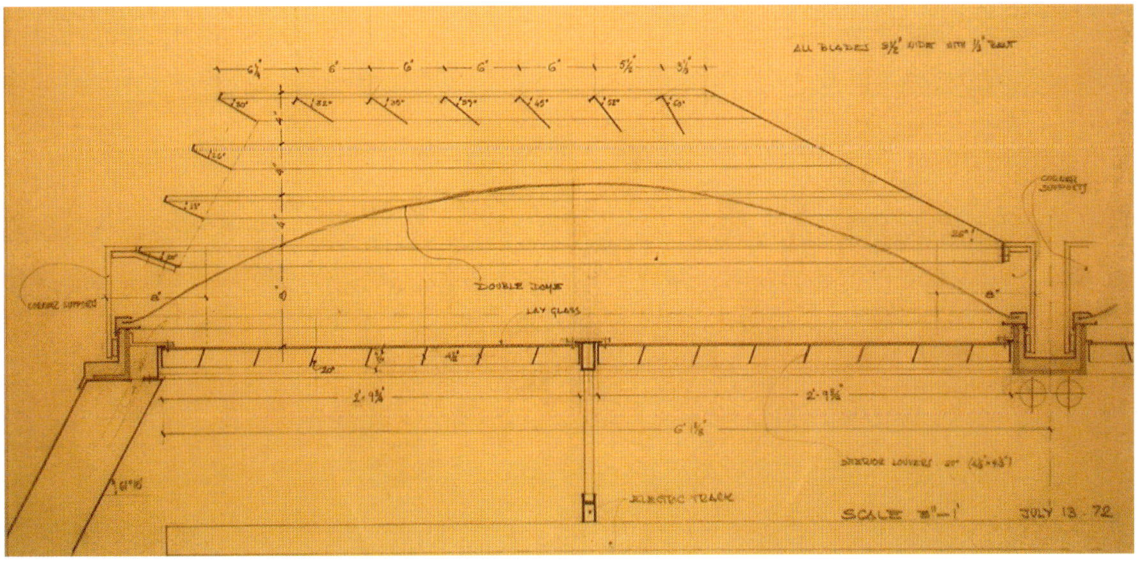

Fig. 7. The external louvers for the Yale Center for British Art, drawing by Kelly

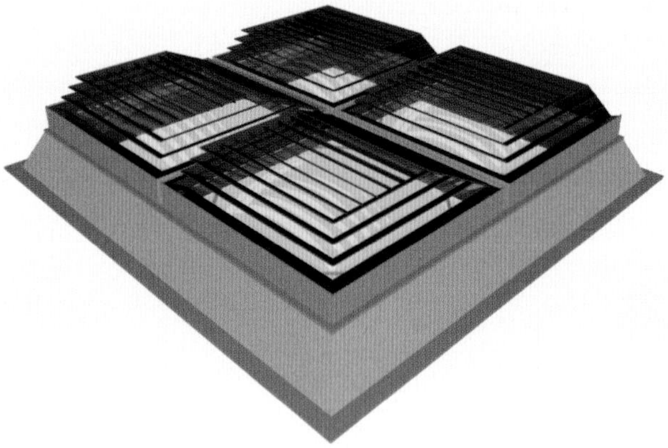

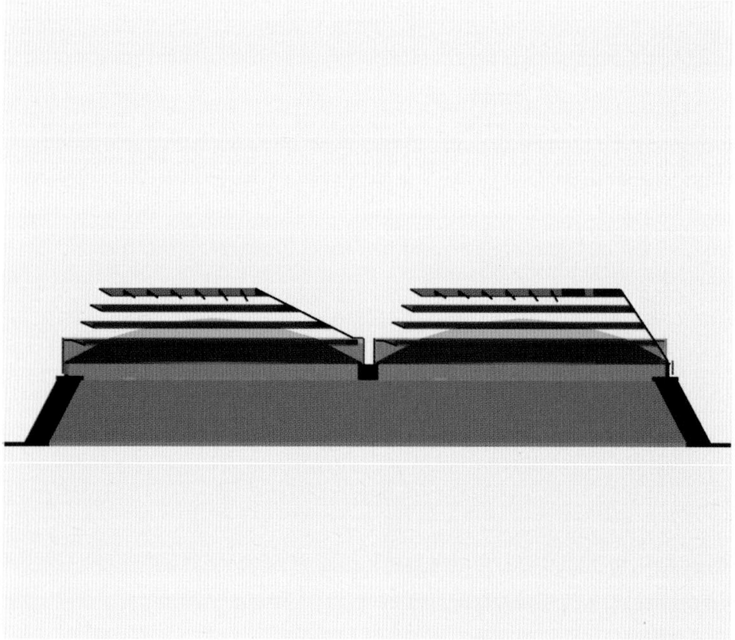

Fig. 8. The external louvers for the Yale Center for British Art, "Sun View." Illustration by Cherine Saroufin.

Fig. 9. The external louvers for the Yale Center for British Art, section. Illustration by Cherine Saroufin.

baffle that Kelly specified was replaced by a specular one-by-one-inch parabolic cube louver; the two prismatic acrylic lenses from Kelly's initial design were retained, however. Below this assembly, a lighting track supports a combination of wall washers and narrow-beam accent fixtures. Outside, above the skylights, the fixed angles of the exterior louver system moderate the changing quantity and quality of sunlight: they reduce the amount of light hitting the skylight when the sun is high in the sky and, when it is low, they catch the lower incidence of light to reflect more into the building. The result is to keep levels of daylight inside the building more or less the same throughout the day, as well as throughout the seasons. During periods of insufficient daylight, as in winter, electric light is used as a supplement.

The Kimbell Art Museum and the Yale Center for British Art represent two fundamentally different approaches to daylighting a museum with skylights. Their great difference in form and function, sensitive to details of program and site, as well as to the formal ambitions of the architecture, is a testament to Kelly's inventive spirit and Kahn's enduring conviction that, even when inside, the light of day is the foundation of spatial experience. As Kelly wrote in 1973: "The handling of forms, the meaning of a room, have to relate to daylight."[8]

Notes

1. For details about the genesis of the design of these two buildings, see Patricia Cummings Loud, *The Art Museums of Louis I. Kahn* (Durham: Duke University Press, 1989), 100–243. On the skylights in the British Art Center, see Jules David Prown, "The Architecture of the Yale Center for British Art; Published on the Occasion of the Inauguration of the Yale Center for British Art," introduction by Edmund P. Pillsbury (New Haven: Yale University, 1977), and Jules David Prown, "Paul Mellon and the Architecture of the Yale Center for British Art," in *Paul Mellon's Legacy: A Passion for British Art*, by John Baskett et al. (New Haven: Yale University Press, 2007), 13–25. According to Prown, a cheaper alternative to Kahn's and Kelly's skylight diffuser cassette designed by the general contractor, the George B. H. Macomber Company, was eventually selected for execution.

   Although the majority of Kelly's commissions were focused on artificial light, he emphasized the importance of a thorough comprehension of daylight from early on. In one of his most pertinent essays, he placed equal emphasis on nocturnal and daytime illumination; Richard Kelly, "Lighting as an Integral Part of Architecture," *College Art Journal* 12, no. 1 (Autumn 1952): 24–30. Projects such as Eliot Noyes's Ault House (1952), Philip Johnson's Davis House (1954), and the Munson-Williams-Proctor Institute in Utica (1959) show Kelly's integration of daylight and artificial light and can be seen as predecessors to his work with Kahn in Fort Worth and New Haven.
2. Marshall Meyers, telephone conversation with the author, ca. January 15, 1993.
3. Memorandum on plans of October 7 and August 26, October 11, 1971, Berg to Office of Louis I. Kahn, Yale University, Manuscripts and Archives, Kahn Collection, Correspondence Yale Mellon Office, J. Prown and H. Berg, File Box LIK 109. See also Loud, *Art Museums of Louis I. Kahn*, 206.
4. Louis Kahn, letter to Richard F. Brown, December 16, 1969, Kahn Collection, Kimbell Art Museum, Correspondence with Dr. Richard F. Brown I, 3.66–12.70, File Box LIK 37; quoted in Loud, *Art Museums of Louis I. Kahn*, 140. In his conversation with me in January 1993, Marshall Meyers confirmed Kelly's important role from early on, somewhat correcting the impression (which Meyers himself created in 1979) that Kelly came in after the design had been established (Marshall Meyers, "Masters of Light: Louis Kahn," *AIA Journal* 68, no. 11 [September 1979]: 60–62).
5. For Kahn's early ideas for a mirrored glass reflector, see Loud, *Art Museums of Louis I. Kahn*, 110.
6. According to Patricia Cummings Loud, Kelly's involvement with the design of the reflector began in November 1968 with his proposal of the plastic reflector in a letter to Marshall Meyers; Loud, *Art Museums of Louis I. Kahn*, 139. Kelly's "pocket notes" mention meetings and phone conversations with Kahn earlier in 1968, on August 22 and 28.
7. Richard Kelly, "Lighting Starts with Daylight," *Progressive Architecture* 54 (September 1973): 82–85.
8. Ibid., 84.

Catalog

Karen Bouchard, Seher Erdogan, Travis Eby, Eliza Higgins, Sandy Isenstadt,
Dietrich Neumann, Kristen Oehlrich, Margaret Maile Petty

Colonial Dining Room at J. Walter Thompson Agency, Graybar Building

Location: 420 Lexington Avenue, New York, N.Y.
Completed: ca. 1939
Architect: Unknown
Lighting installation: ca. 1939

One of Richard Kelly's earliest commissions placed him right at the heart of a central location of modernity in New York: the J. Walter Thompson Advertising Agency, led by Stanley and Helen Resor. The agency had moved into the eleventh floor of the new Graybar Building on Lexington Avenue in 1927, and Helen, a trustee at the Museum of Modern Art, had commissioned Lewis Mumford to purchase three thousand books for the office library, which were displayed (sorted by size and color) in the agency's reception area. Edward Steichen was one of the staff photographers, and the theater man and industrial designer Norman Bel Geddes (who had married Stanley Resor's niece) had created a large modern meeting and conference room at the agency in 1938—"machine-like in its efficiency" (Meikle), according to contemporary critics. Mies van der Rohe was hired in 1937 to design a country house at the Resors' estate in Wyoming (unexecuted).

The Resors' modernist leanings apparently were not at odds with the installation of a complete seventeenth-century living room from a Connecticut farmhouse as a corporate dining room in their office space. For Richard Kelly, the lighting for what became known as the Colonial Dining Room was perhaps his most literally theatrical work—in fact, theater impresario David Belasco, much admired by Kelly and known for his obsession with realistic effects, was famous for having once dismantled and rebuilt on the stage a complete room from a boarding house, down to its smallest details. As the location for the room had no access to outside walls, Kelly established perpetual sunshine in the form of hidden spotlights that would hit a scrim outside the room's windows, just as it would have done on a stage.

Kelly wrote: "The need for the reproduction of an exact and effective character through lighting is dramatized by the seventeenth-century Cape Cod house moved by J. Walter Thompson onto the eleventh floor of New York's Graybar Building for intimate advertising conferences at lunch. Here, on a depressing rainy day, artificial sunlight can warm patches of old pine flooring when a million dollars is at stake" (*Flair*).
DN

De Gracia, Victoria. *Irresistible Empire: America's Advance Through Twentieth-Century Europe*. Cambridge: Belknap Press, 2005.
Kelly, Richard. "Focus on Light." *Flair* (February 1950): 15, 66–69.
Lears, T. J. Jackson. *Fables of Abundance: A Cultural History of Advertising in America*. New York: Basic, 1994.
Meikle, Jeffrey L. *Twentieth Century Limited: Industrial Design in America, 1925–1939*. Philadelphia: Temple University Press, 1979.
"Offices of J. Walter Thompson Co., New York, by Norman Bel Geddes." *American Architect* 136 (July 20, 1929): 96–102.
Stern, Robert A. M., Gregory Gilmartin, and Thomas Mellins. *New York, 1930: Architecture and Urbanism Between the Two World Wars*. New York: Rizzoli, 1987.
Yale University Library, Manuscripts and Archives, Richard Kelly Papers.

above: Thompson Office, corporate dining room

Stork Club

Location: 3 East Fifty-third Street, New York, N.Y.
Restoration: 1940
Interior designer: LeRoy Ward
Lighting installation: 1941

The Stork Club was a nightclub in New York City from 1929 to 1965. Owned and operated by Sherman Billingsley, the club first opened at 132 West Fifty-eighth Street, but was closed down by Prohibition agents in 1931. After an interim location on Fifty-first Street, the club reopened in larger quarters at 3 East Fifty-third Street, where it remained until it closed on October 4, 1965. In 1940, architect LeRoy Ward was charged with a renovation of the club, and he hired the firm of Kelly and Thompson for the lighting of the large, high-ceilinged and windowless Cub Room. Kelly provided the indirect cove lighting at the edge of the curvilinear drop ceiling panel, which was then echoed in a series of luminous clouds floating beneath the ceiling. Made of steel, plaster, and translucent plastic, the clouds were about four feet in diameter and twelve inches deep and were lit by neon lights. As the club was used in a number of movies filmed on location, Kelly's clouds appear in the background in the club scenes of *All About Eve*, *The Wrong Man*, and *Executive Suite*, among others.

DN

Blumenthal, Ralph. *The Stork Club: America's Most Famous Nightspot and the Lost World of Café Society*. Boston: Little, Brown, 2000.

Kelly, Richard. "Focus on Light." *Flair* (February 1950): 66–69.

Yale University Library, Manuscripts and Archives, Richard Kelly Papers.

above: Stork Club, Cub Room

Bonwit Teller Store

Location: 234 Berkeley Street, Boston, Massachusetts
Completed: building, 1863; conversion into store, 1947
Architect of building: William Gibbons Preston; architects of store conversion: Leland and Larsen; designer of store interior: William Pahlmann
Lighting installation: 1947

One of the most prominent department stores in the northeast, Bonwit Teller specialized in high-end women's apparel and set the standard for a luxury shopping experience. Originally founded in New York, Bonwit Teller stores were spacious and lavishly decorated. When president Walter Hoving expanded operations to Boston, the old Museum of Natural History building in Back Bay was chosen to house the new store. Interior renovations were handled by designer William Pahlmann, who succeeded in creating a modern space inside a French Renaissance Revival building. Prevented from making any structural changes to the historic building, Pahlmann and Richard Kelly came up with a creative solution to the adaptive reuse of the museum space. As described in *Lighting and Lamps*, "the Traditional Building was married to the Modern Interior and a sturdy, beautiful Contemporary Style child was produced."

In a highly detailed article for *Interior Design and Decoration*, Kelly described the many problems inherent in lighting public spaces and identified the "comfort" level sought in department stores as a fine balance between providing sufficient intensity of lighting and preventing reflected glare. He further explained that expensive women's clothing, such as that sold at Bonwit's, should be shown in "an atmosphere indicative of the background in which they may be worn."

For the entrance to the new store, Kelly used partial floodlighting to emphasize the building's nineteenth-century architectural details and draw in customers. Indeed, the store had no shop windows and advertised itself only by a small gold plate on the facade. Inside, the main floor was brought to life "as with magic" by invisible pinpoint light fixtures concealed in a dropped ceiling. In the dress salon, appropriate ambiance was achieved by three great gold and glass chandeliers providing twenty-seven direct downlights. Twenty-four remote downlights were also employed, reflected by medallion mirrors installed in the ceiling. The central chandelier of the three held eight spotlights that were directed toward the perimeter of a plaster ceiling medallion. A low-profile luminaire of sixty bulbs and five hundred crystal pieces lit the millinery department. In addition, wall sconces held lamps softened by silk shades, and candles on a central table, protected by similar shades, helped create an ambiance of calm and sophistication. The success of the lighting installation in the Boston store, signified by both increased business and positive publicity, prompted Bonwit Teller owners to incorporate similar designs into their other shops.

SE/KB

"Bonwit Teller Leases Old Back Bay History Museum." *New York Times*, January 16, 1947.
"Bonwit Teller Shop Opened in Boston." *New York Times*, September 18, 1947.
"Decorative Lighting, Prime Factor in Store Modernization." *Lighting and Lamps* (November 1947): 45.
Johnson, Richard I. "The Rise and Fall of the Boston Society of Natural History." *Northeastern Naturalist* (2004). www.redorbit.com/news/display/?id=58933.
Kelly, Richard. "Design Journal." *Interior Design and Decoration* (June 1949): 42–47.
Loring, John. "William Pahlmann: Shaking Up Interiors with a Surprisingly Diverse Vision." *Architectural Digest* (January 2000): 14–16.
Yale University Library, Manuscripts and Archives, Richard Kelly Papers.

opposite: Bonwit Teller, millinery department

Knoedler Gallery

Location: 14 East Fifty-seventh Street, New York, N.Y.
Lighting installations: 1947 and 1955

In 1949 Richard Kelly wrote, "The lighting of sculpture falls into two schools of thought. One insists on a shadowless, open daylight kind of lighting. The other believes in directional lights with shades calculated to best emphasize the form of the individual pieces. In either case, the lighting of sculpture is a far more elaborate business than the lighting of painting." As if to illustrate this distinction, Kelly applied each approach in the two major exhibitions he was invited to illuminate and arrange at one of New York City's oldest contemporary art galleries, the Knoedler Gallery. In 1947, for an exhibition of the French sculptor Gaston Lachaise, Kelly suspended an enormous canvas disc from the ceiling and installed theater spotlights above it. The focus of the spots and their distance from the diffusing canvas determined the distribution of light underneath, leading to circles of light of different size and brightness, focusing attention on each piece of sculpture and reducing "a large room to more intimate scale" (*Flair*). Kelly was also responsible for the grouping of the sculptures, which "were all set in a kind of social grouping rather than in the usual deadly back-to-the-wall lineup."

For a 1955 exhibition of bronze figurines by Edgar Degas, Kelly wanted to emulate the diffuse light of an overcast sky by applying a somewhat dramatized form of the luminous ceiling: white silk curtains, provided by Marie Nichols, were draped in long parallel lines over tension wires. Kelly was also responsible for the placement of the wax dancers in "a charming choreography" in one gallery, and the race horses poised for action in another. Kelly explained his concept in a letter to Irving Drutman, a journalist writing for the *New York Herald Tribune*. His complex manipulation of space and light was "decidedly different from the established methods of presentation of sculpture." The sixty-eight small sculptures seemed "bigger and more important because (1) a silk gauze ceiling limits the space around them, and (2) high mounting platforms physically elevate the waxes up to and above eyelevel which gives them a slight superiority over people. . . . Not only is the composition made simpler by grouping of figures significantly, but spot lights provide these simplified centers of interest with many times more light than the mechanical accessories require to mount them. The background is dark and light-absorbing in order to eliminate the feeling of limited space."

DN

Genauer, Emily. "Degas Wax Sculptures Exhibited: Benefit Show at Knoedler." *New York Herald Tribune*, November 9, 1955.

Jewell, Edward Alden. "Gallery Displays Work by Lachaise." *New York Times*, January 21, 1947.

Kelly, Richard. "Design Journal." *Interior Design and Decoration* (June 1949): 42–47.

Kelly, Richard. "Focus on Light." *Flair* (February 1950): 15, 66–69.

Kelly, Richard. Letter to Irving Drutman, November 25, 1955. Richard Kelly Papers.

Yale University Library, Manuscripts and Archives, Richard Kelly Papers.

above left: Gaston Lachaise Exhibition, 1947, view from above the canvas disc
above right: Gaston Lachaise Exhibition, 1947, view from below the canvas disc
opposite: Edgar Degas Exhibition, 1955

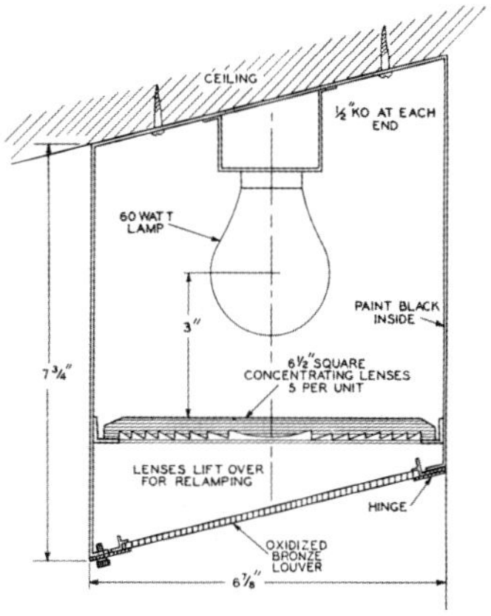

Cross Section of Window-wall Lighting.

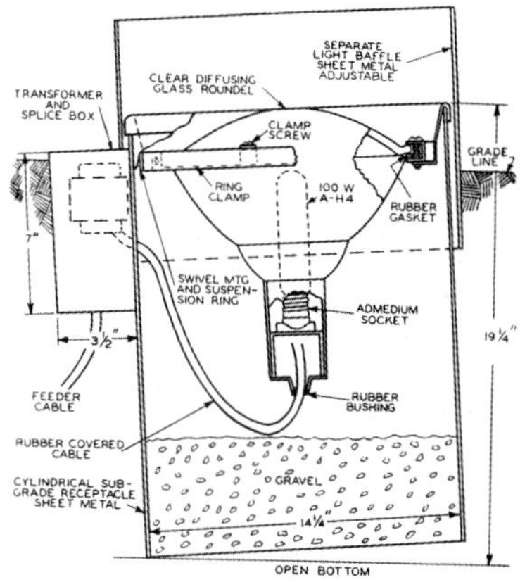

Outdoor Floodlight Installation

House Beautiful Pace-Setter House

Location: Orange, New Jersey
Completed: 1949
Architect: Emil A. Schmidlin
Lighting installation: 1949

What exactly is a Pace-Setter House? According to *House Beautiful*, "It's a house to dramatize the newest and best that's being done in the year we publish it. It's an idea house, from which you can borrow a little or a lot." Between 1948 and 1961, the magazine's annual model homes were celebrated events and each one was lavishly published. The 1949 version was designed by the Swiss-born architect Emil A. Schmidlin in Orange, New Jersey, and boasted a climate-control system and underground wiring to melt snow. Richard Kelly had been hired as the lighting designer and proceeded to apply "all the tricks of the lighting designer's art." In the living room, which, as the magazine declared, "is exciting by day, but at night . . . becomes exciting in a different way," Kelly used a carefully calibrated mix of concealed spotlights, floor lamps, and table lamps to define spaces for different functions, pick out works of art, or add a diffuse glow to the window drapery. All were controlled by new dimmer technology. In the dining room, cove lights underneath the ceiling provided the main illumination, with spotlight accents and valance lights illuminating the draperies. The garden and terrace by landscape designer Ethelbert Furlong were lit by concealed floodlights under the trees and on the roof.

The "livable modernism" that Elizabeth Gordon, the critic, taste maker, and editor of *House Beautiful*, had in mind when she launched the campaign of the Pace-Setter Houses was a deliberate counter position to the impact of orthodox European modernism in America, and in particular to the Case Study House Program initiated by the Californian *Arts and Architecture* magazine in 1945. The first six Case Study houses by California modernists like Richard Neutra were presented in 1948, the same year the Pace-Setters were launched. As noted by David Smiley, Gordon believed her readers wanted "the function of modern architecture, without the look." Thus, the 1949 Pace-Setter featured a glass-walled living room but also a traditional pitched roof. A *New York Times* article described the designer's intent: "the furniture arrangement and color schemes . . . are strictly contemporary . . . although this adherence to functionalism is by no means obvious."

For Kelly this commission offered an opportunity to showcase many of his newest ideas for practical, decorative, and atmospheric lighting effects in the home. At exactly the same time, though, he had begun working with Philip Johnson and Ludwig Mies van der Rohe on two of his most influential and important commissions, the Glass House and the Lake Shore Drive Apartments, where he would achieve a degree of clarity and minimalist simplicity far removed from his playfully decorative work at the Pace-Setter house.

KB/DN

opposite: Pace-Setter House, dressing room. Maynard L. Parker, photographer; courtesy of the Huntington Library, San Marino, California
above left: Pace-Setter House, great room
above right: Pace-Setter House, lighting diagrams

House Beautiful Pace-Setter House *continued*

"House Beautiful's Pace-Setter House for 1949." *House Beautiful* 91 (November 1949): 195–313.

Roche, Mary. "Luxurious Home to Go on Display." *New York Times*, September 30, 1949.

Smiley, David. "Making the Modified Modern." *Perspecta* 32 (2001): 39–54.

Yale University Library, Manuscripts and Archives, Richard Kelly Papers.

above: Pace-Setter House, kitchen. Maynard L. Parker, photographer; courtesy of the Huntington Library, San Marino, California.

Museum of Modern Art, Ain House

Location: New York, N.Y.
On display from May 19 to October 29, 1950
Architect: Gregory Ain with Joseph Johnson and Alfred Day

After apprenticing with Richard Neutra, California modernist Gregory Ain had created a number of increasingly popular low-cost homes in Los Angeles. He was commissioned by Philip Johnson, then director of the Architecture and Design Department at the Museum of Modern Art, to design a temporary house in the museum's garden in 1950, two years after the great success of the first such house by Marcel Breuer. The wooden house was built in cooperation with the *Woman's Home Companion* "to demonstrate that good modern architectural design is possible in a speculatively built house, which is the kind lived in by most Americans," and was estimated to cost between $15,000 and $19,500. Ain designed the one-story structure as if it were part of a larger development, carefully facing its main windows (including the thirty-two-foot-long living-room window) away from imaginary neighbors. The interior had several retractable walls to allow for flexibility.

Johnson hired Kelly to design the lighting for the house, which, Kelly claimed, would be "exceedingly cheap" and "would take care of the basic needs of any small family." Apart from using several of his movable baffle lamps, Kelly developed a thin wooden valance strip, shielding a slimline fluorescent tube, whose light would shine both upward and downward. He placed these strips along walls, underneath the ceiling, above bookshelves, and across a window (illustrated on p. 48). As in Johnson's Glass House in New Canaan from the same year, Kelly affixed downlights to the roof's perimeter to render the outside landscape visible from inside at night.

SE/DN

Baer, Barbara. "Lighting the House in the Museum Garden." *Lighting and Lamps* 57 (June 1950): 20–21, 37, 44.

Denzer, Anthony. *Gregory Ain: The Modern Home as Social Commentary*. New York: Rizzoli, 2008.

Gebhard, David, Harriette Von Breton, and Lauren Weiss Bricker. *The Architecture of Gregory Ain: The Play Between the Rational and High Art*. Santa Barbara: University of California Art Gallery, 1980.

McCoy, Esther. *The Second Generation*. Salt Lake City: Peregrine Smith, 1984.

Morrison, Harriet. "House Exhibit on at Museum of Modern Art," *Sunday News*, May 28, 1950.

"Our House with a View—To the Future." *Woman's Home Companion* (June 1950): 65–72.

"People Want Better Lighting." *House and Home* (May 1954): 166–167.

Pepis, Betty. "Ideas for Home: Unusual Floor Plan Keyed to Family Needs." *New York Times*, May 19, 1950.

Yale University Library, Manuscripts and Archives, Richard Kelly Papers.

above: Ain House, interior view

Rockefeller Guest House

Location: 242 East Fifty-second Street, New York, N.Y.
Completed: 1949–1950
Architects: Philip Johnson (in association with Landis Gores and Frederick C. Genz, Architects)
Lighting installation: 1949

The so-called Guest House had been commissioned by Mrs. John D. Rockefeller III, who used it as a private retreat and a showcase for her collection of modern art. On the narrow and deep lot of a former carriage house, Philip Johnson created a two-story structure that showed the influence of Ludwig Mies van der Rohe's courthouse projects and his recent architecture for the IIT campus in Chicago. It combined the formal language and materials of Johnson's Glass and Brick Houses in New Canaan, designed and built at the same time. A bare brick wall with a centered door faces the street and is topped by three translucent clerestory windows and a tripartite steel and glass facade on the second floor. Beyond a screened-off vestibule and built-in kitchen a deep living and dining room between white brick walls doubles as exhibition space for art by Hans Arp, Alberto Giacometti, Jacques Lipchitz, Jackson Pollock, and Mark Rothko. A plate-glass wall at the end faces an open courtyard entirely taken up by a shallow reflecting pool. Beyond it lies the bedroom, reachable only via three flat stepping stones in the pool.

Perhaps Kelly was selected for this job because he had lit several art exhibitions at the Knoedler Gallery and published recommendations for lighting art at home in *House and Garden* in 1947. He certainly followed his own advice for recessed spotlights "about 30 to 40 inches from the wall," in order to "light your pictures from the same direction of light as the artist has painted it," and he suggested that the entire wall could be lit that way, with increased intensity in the center (Kelly 1947). "The result is a projected area of light from the floor up into the corner formed by the wall and ceiling and a vertical tapering of illumination at both sides. This tapering is built up by the overlapping light from the next unit in the row of lighting units" (Kelly 1950). Kelly used recessed spotlights with highly specular Alzak reflectors (an aluminum alloy available since the 1930s). Beyond this simple task, however, he demonstrated an entire vocabulary of new lighting ideas. The guest house became as much a showcase for modern art as contemporary ideas and designs for light. In the central axis of the living and dining room Kelly placed three grids of sixteen recessed downlights, each with a suspended louvered grate underneath. The light cone emanating from the baffled recessed projector was channeled into the small squares of the louver, and glare was eliminated entirely.

Above the small terrace outside the living room and facing the pool, Kelly installed a translucent canopy that refracted and diffused daylight but also contained fluorescent lights, providing diffuse light outside the wall-high plate-glass wall and eliminating reflections from inside. This technique he might have learned from Richard Neutra when he visited him in Los Angeles two years earlier. Mrs. Rockefeller also purchased one of Kelly's and Johnson's three-legged lamps and one of Kelly's more conventional lamps.

This small commission, the first collaboration with Philip Johnson, proved fateful for Richard Kelly's career. Immediately afterward he developed the lighting for Johnson's Glass and Brick Houses in New

Canaan, and many other Johnson commissions followed. Mies van der Rohe had seen the Rockefeller Guest House in January 1950 and asked Johnson about the lighting designer. As a result, Kelly visited Mies two weeks later in Chicago and subsequently designed the lighting for the Chicago Arts Club and the Lake Shore Drive Apartments. He returned to work for Mies on the Esplanade Apartments in Chicago and the Seagram Building in New York.
DN

Jenkins, Stover, and David Mohney. *The Houses of Philip Johnson.* New York: Abbeville, 2001.

Kelly, Richard. "How to Light Your Paintings." *House and Garden* (January 1947): 112–113.

Kelly, Richard. Letter to Ludwig Mies van der Rohe, January 20, 1950.

Pepis, Betty. "A Setting for Art." *New York Times*, January 7, 1951.

"Rockefeller Guest House." Landmarks Preservation Commission, December 5, 2000; Designation List 321, LP-2079.

"Rockefeller Guest House, New York." *Architectural Forum* 9–10 (1954): 366–367.

"Rockefeller Guest House, 242 East 52nd Street: Philip Johnson, 1950." *A & U: Architecture & Urbanism* (December 1994): 242–249.

Stern, Robert A. M., Thomas Mellins, and David Fishman. *New York, 1960: Architecture and Urbanism Between the Second World War and the Bicentennial.* New York: Monacelli, 1995.

Viladas, Pilar. "Tea and Geometry: Philip Johnson Revisits the Modernist House He Designed for Blanchette Rockefeller on the Eve of Its Sale." *New York Times Magazine* (May 28, 2000), 44.

Yale University Library, Manuscripts and Archives, Richard Kelly Papers.

opposite: Rockefeller Guest House, front room. Arts of the United States Collection, University of Georgia.
above: Rockefeller Guest House, facade

Glass House

Location: 798–856 Ponus Ridge Road, New Canaan, Connecticut
Completed: 1949
Architect: Philip Johnson
Lighting installation: 1950

The view of Philip Johnson's Glass House by night represents one of the iconic images of modern architecture, and much of the credit for this belongs to Richard Kelly's lighting scheme. In its wooded setting, the glass retreat allowed Johnson to feel immersed in nature during the day, but initially, he remembered, "there was no light—other than the sun. You can imagine the problem with reflections [at night]. If you had one bulb, you saw six. When it got dark outside, there wasn't anything a lighting man could do, or so I thought. Richard founded the art of residential lighting the day he designed the lighting for the glass house" (*Lighting Design and Application*).

In the summer of 1949, Helmut Newton photographed the house by night. Three ceiling lamps are visible above the kitchen unit, and more light seems to come from a portable light source (probably the photographer's) behind the round bathroom unit. Altogether, the lighting seems inadequate. Several trees in the background, however, are already illuminated from underneath. Kelly's main concept was executed in the summer of 1950. He installed downlights around the exterior roof parapet, illuminating the steps and the lawn immediately adjacent to the house, and lit more trees from individual floodlights in the ground underneath and from spotlights on the roof. Now, similar to daytime conditions, the light from outside was stronger than the light sources inside, thus eliminating reflection and providing the illusion of a spatial continuum.

According to Kelly's article in *Flair* magazine in 1950, the ceiling of the Glass House was meant to be illuminated from the outside by upward spotlights from trenches in the lawn close to the glass walls. Supposedly, all were to be voice activated via a secret code word. It is not clear if those details were ever executed. Today, we find five Kelly-designed light cans on the floor inside, in the corners, and along the long side of the room, producing a soft halo on the ceiling. The house was "a gleaming rectangle," said a writer for the *Saturday Evening Post;* "I felt shielded and secure once I had stepped through the doorway. . . . One gets the impression of being centered, almost floating, on a sea of light."

KB/DN

Cialdella, Philip, and Clara D. Powell. "The Great Illuminator." *Lighting Design and Application* (May 1993). Reprint, www.iesny.org/Documents/RKelly-LDnAMay93Reprint.pdf.

"House in New Canaan, Connecticut; Philip Johnson: Architect." *Architectural Review* 108, no. 645 (September 1950).

Kelly, Richard. "Focus on Light." *Flair* (February 1950): 66–69.

Lambert, Phyllis. "Stimmung at Seagram: Philip Johnson Counters Mies van der Rohe." *Grey Room* 20 (Summer 2005): 38–59.

Maile Petty, Margaret. "Illuminating the Glass Box." *Journal of the Society of Architectural Historians* 66 (June 2007): 194–219.

Nicholson, Arnold. "Mr. Kelly's Magic Lights." *Saturday Evening Post* (July 5, 1958): 28–29, 61–65.

Petit, Emmanuel. *Philip Johnson: The Constancy of Change.* New Haven: Yale University Press, 2009.

"Philip Johnson Remembers Richard Kelly." *Lighting Design and Application* 9 (June 1979): 49.

Whitney, David, and Jeffrey Kipnis. *Philip Johnson: The Glass House.* New York: Pantheon, 1993.

Yale University Library, Manuscripts and Archives, Richard Kelly Papers.

opposite: Glass House, night view, ca. 1950s. Arts of the United States Collection, University of Georgia.

above: Portrait of Philip Johnson. Photographer: Arnold Newman, July 1, 1949. Arnold Newman/Getty Images.

Candlelight Restaurant

Location: Manhasset, New York
Completed: 1950
Architect: Natalie Rahv
Lighting installations: 1950

When New York restaurateur Patricia Murphy decided to establish a third Candlelight restaurant in addition to the existing locations in Brooklyn Heights and Manhattan, she commissioned the architect Natalie Rahv to remodel a former Manhasset country club into both a restaurant and a home for herself and her husband, Captain J. E. Kiernan. Located amid sprawling gardens, the restaurant boasted a seating capacity of five hundred and consisted of three large dining rooms, a cocktail lounge and bar, and a gift shop. Several years later, in 1954, Murphy opened up yet another restaurant in Yonkers, once again employing Rahv and Kelly.

For the Manhasset restaurant, the lighting scheme Kelly proposed required extensive new wiring, which greatly prolonged the installation process. Kelly illuminated the gardens by employing such techniques as floodlighting installed on the roof, upward spotlights from trenches in the ground, and downward from standards throughout the grounds. The exterior lighting eliminated the so-called black-mirror effect, making the large plate-glass walls seem to disappear for the guests inside. To light the main dining room of the Manhasset building, Kelly installed three wagon-wheel-shaped chandeliers, twelve feet in diameter, and made of brass tubing and coral-painted wood. Each chandelier held one 500- and one 75-watt lamp in its hub and an additional 75-watt lamp at the end of its fourteen spokes. Three bar-shaped chandeliers with candlelike bulb sockets graced the Coral Room, while the Garden Room was illumined by 200-watt hanging lamps in brass hoods. All rooms featured special window and plant lighting, the Coral Room having slimline lamps installed over the top of each sash window to illuminate the curtains.

SE/KB

Burke, Betsy. "Restaurant Lighting in Manhasset . . . Candlelight Restaurant." *Magazine of Light* 22 (February 1953): 9–13.
"Candlelight Restaurant: Luminous Pavilion Touched by the Orient." *Interiors* (July 1955): 76–79.
"Experts Examine the Facts of Light." *Institutions* (August 1960): 64–67.
"Mrs. Kiernan's Country Home." *Interiors* (March 1951): 88–93.
Yale University Library, Manuscripts and Archives, Richard Kelly Papers.

opposite: Candlelight Restaurant, Manhasset, night view of garden
above: Candlelight Restaurant, Manhasset, Coral Room

Desert Inn

Location: Las Vegas, Nevada
Completed: 1950; demolished 2001–2004
Architect: Jac Lessman
Lighting installation: 1950

Originally called Wilbur Clark's Desert Inn, this famous hotel and casino was the fifth resort to open along the Las Vegas Strip where it operated for almost fifty years. The interiors were designed by Jac Lessman of New York, who specialized in the planning and development of hotels, including the Roosevelt and the St. Regis in Manhattan. The Desert Inn was best known for its Sky Room located on top of a three-story tower that, for a while, made the hotel the tallest building along the Strip.

The project did not proceed on the most amicable of terms—the correspondence between Lessman and Kelly is filled with complaints and disavowals—yet the designers collaborated for over a decade. While the technical aspects of Kelly's lighting strategy for the Desert Inn went through considerable changes, mostly as a result of financial concerns, the conceptual aspects remained more or less the same. In a letter to the owner's representative, Kelly suggested expanded lighting for the front of the building and stressed the importance of color throughout the site, in order to compete with the increasingly spectacular designs of Clark's competition on the Strip. The building's "Bermuda pink" color with green trim was to be intensified, especially in contrast to the green of the illuminated landscape, by washing the back wall of the entry porch with recessed fixtures. Kelly suggested adding more olive trees to those already planted and uplighting them with mercury lamps. "Vibrant green should be tripled," he wrote. "Paint the grass the same green with a new type mercury light projector because the whole lawn goes black at night." To achieve long-range visibility, he proposed making the main building's white tile roof appear even whiter by supplementing the existing lamps with spread-lens roof lights. As part of his interior illumination scheme, Kelly devised an elliptical chandelier for the Sky Room, with sixty tiny spotlights at the ends of its radial spokes. The ceiling itself was, as the *Los Angeles Times* described it, "dotted with twinkling electric stars." The effect further enhanced the sense of spaciousness in the lounge and, in Kelly's words, "made it feel one with the surrounding desert."
SE/KB

Charleston Communications. "History of the Desert Inn." A2Z Las Vegas. www.a2zlasvegas.com/hotels/history/h-di.html.
"Jac Lessman, 85, Dies; Hotel-Resort Developer." *New York Times*, November 8, 1990.
"Luxurious Las Vegas Hotel Open Monday." *Los Angeles Times*, April 18, 1950.
Yale University Library, Manuscripts and Archives, Richard Kelly Papers.

above: Desert Inn, exterior view at night

Lake Shore Drive Apartments

Location: 860–880 Lake Shore Drive, Chicago, Illinois
Completed: 1950
Architect: Ludwig Mies van der Rohe
Lighting installation: 1950

In 1946 the Chicago real estate developer Herbert Greenwald commissioned Ludwig Mies van der Rohe to design two twenty-six-story residential towers on the Lake Michigan shoreline. The 860–880 Lake Shore Drive project provided Mies with his first opportunity to realize a glass and steel skyscraper along the lines of his unbuilt projects of the early 1920s. Arranging the two towers on an open plaza with a connecting canopy between them, Mies combined the elevator lobbies and auxiliary rooms on the ground and mezzanine floors as a single entity in the core, pulled back from the building's perimeter and exposing its crisp, square columns. This recessed core was enclosed by large transparent and translucent panes of glass, giving the structure above an appearance of weightlessness.

At night this effect would be sustained, even exaggerated, through its lighting scheme. The opaque glass–enclosed core was illuminated from within, its glow complemented by the transparency of the clear glass-walled lobby after dark. Long fluorescent lamps were installed under the ceiling immediately behind the translucent glass walls, their light spread and guided downward to cover the entire height by parabolic projector shields. On the two shorter, three-bay ends of the soffits recessed downlights created soft "pools of light" on the travertine floor, balancing interior illumination levels with the exterior. This lighting approach had a number of benefits, as Kelly described in a letter to Mies: "With your conception of the buildings, [a] linear projection of light on the ground and terrace makes apparent the open continuity of space under the buildings, makes a pleasant outlook from the lounges and also lights the ramp for underground traffic." In the success and restraint of Lake Shore Drive's lighting program we find the seeds of the extraordinary lighting solutions for the Seagram Building that Kelly, Mies, and Johnson developed together a few years later.

MMP/DN

Holroyd, Geoffrey. "American News Letter—9." *The Architect and Building News* (April 8, 1954): 400–401.
Maile Petty, Margaret. "Illuminating the Glass Box." *Journal of the Society of Architectural Historians* 66 (June 2007): 194–219.
Mills, Edward D. "860 Lake Shore Drive, Chicago, USA." *The Architect and Building News* (April 8, 1954): 402–408.
Yale University Library, Manuscripts and Archives, Richard Kelly Papers.

above: Lake Shore Drive Apartments, lobby at night

The Arts Club of Chicago

Location: 109 Ontario Street, Chicago, Illinois
Completed: 1951; demolished 1997
Architects of the building: Peter M. Leichenko and Curt A. Esser
Interior design: Ludwig Mies van der Rohe
Lighting installation: 1951; destroyed in 1997

The Arts Club was one of the younger clubs in Chicago, and since its founding in 1916 (inspired by the success of the Armory Show at the Art Institute) its mission was to bring modern art to the city. It proceeded to present the first solo exhibitions in the United States for Picasso, Braque, Calder, Rodin, Pollock, and many others. Its interiors were always designed by Chicagoans. It does not come as a surprise, then, that the club hired Ludwig Mies van der Rohe, the preeminent modernist in the city, when it moved to the second floor of a new office tower at 109 East Ontario Street in 1951. Mies got involved early enough to have an impact on the planning of the host building, and he carefully calibrated the influx of natural light by adjusting ceiling heights. The major elements of his design included a stairway, a gallery, a lecture hall, and a dining room. Emerging on the second floor, visitors found themselves transported into the crisp, minimalist environment of the gallery, which was the only semipublic space of the club.

Richard Kelly (commissioned to design the lighting after Mies had seen his work in Philip Johnson's Rockefeller Guest House in New York in January 1950) provided light "as flexible as the human eye" (Robb) for the entrance, the gallery, the restaurant, and the stage, where he, according to the *Chicago Tribune*, played his "famous tricks of light intensity manipulation." The slightly recessed entrance foyer was emphasized at night by Kelly's six downlights in its outside soffit, creating a pool of light on the sidewalk. Behind a wall-high glass membrane and flanked by curtains on either side, Mies's elegant three-flight staircase sat like an art object in the small lobby, lit dramatically from above. In the public Arts Club gallery, Mies had designed the positions of the wall-high space dividers and tall curtains to control outside light and shield the private club quarters from view during gallery hours. Kelly employed a configuration of thirty-nine wall washers, recessed spotlights for the stage, and soft downlights throughout the gallery.
SE/DN

Harrington, Kevin. "The Arts Club, 1948–1951." *Architronic* 4 (December 1995). http://corbu2.caed.kent.edu/architronic/v4n3/v4n3.06.html.

Pridmore, Jay, and George A. Larson. *Chicago Architecture and Design*, rev. ed. New York: Harry N. Abrams, 2005.

Robb, Marilyn. "The Club Reborn in Chicago." *ARTNews* 50 (September 1951): 34–35.

Schulze, Franz. *Mies van der Rohe: Interior Spaces; The Arts Club of Chicago, September 20 through November 4, 1982*. Chicago: The Arts Club, 1982.

Yale University Library, Manuscripts and Archives, Richard Kelly Papers.

above left: Chicago History Museum, entrance. Photographer: Hedrich-Blessing.
above right: Chicago History Museum, top of staircase. Photographer: Hedrich-Blessing.

Graef House

Location: Summit, New Jersey
Completed: 1951
Architect: Gordon Powers
Lighting installation: 1951

Robert Graef, a publications editor for the oil conglomerate Esso, interviewed several modern architects to design a house for him and his new bride on a modest site in suburban New Jersey, about twenty miles west of Manhattan. He selected Gordon Powers, who was then working for William Lescaze in New York but would soon move to southern California to set up his own firm. Powers organized the house as a long rectangle with a central entry to divide the bedrooms on one side from the kitchen, living, and dining areas on the other side. A garage and basement are cut into the sloping site underneath this, more public side of the house. Powers exploited the post-and-beam structure to set up a strong architectural rhythm of beams running perpendicular to the length of the house and, at the same time, draw attention out to the landscape through glazing butted into the posts.

Graef appears to already have known Kelly and in any case worked with him directly on the lighting, articulating sixteen specific conditions that he asked Kelly to address. In response, Kelly mounted rows of downlights projecting sideways from the transom fascia of floor-to-ceiling windows along both the front and back of the house, a row of surface-mounted spotlights along an interior gallery, and a row of fascia-mounted downlights along the exterior. Each row of lights runs parallel with the long dimension of the plan, offering a contrapuntal measure to the beams overhead. Although it was a relatively small house, Kelly designed a sophisticated and prolonged sequence of outdoor lighting, including downlights recessed in an overhang in front of the garage, low-wattage path lights, roof-mounted downlights, 300-watt roof-mounted "tree lights," and the downlights that shone directly onto the glass wall (illustrated on p. 54). The Residence Lighting Forum of the New York section of the Illuminating Engineering Society held its annual meeting at the Graef House in 1952 to witness the many effects Kelly had designed for it.
SI

Yale University Library, Manuscripts and Archives, Richard Kelly Papers.

above: Graef House, exterior view

Hodgson House

Location: 881 Ponus Ridge Road, New Canaan, Connecticut
Completed: 1951
Architect: Philip Johnson with Landis Gores
Lighting installation: 1951

Architects Philip Johnson and Landis Gores were classmates at the Harvard Graduate School of Design and had collaborated on such projects as the Rockefeller Guest House and the Glass House. Richard Hodgson was an engineer and a very influential television and radio executive. His residence, located directly across from the Glass House on Ponus Ridge Road, was primarily a masonry construction of special highly glazed brick. Its U-shaped plan was centered around a patio, glass-walled on three sides and open to the sky. The house was further opened to nature by the inclusion of glass walls in the living room and bedroom, opposite the patio walls, thereby allowing the viewer to look straight through the building from one side to the other. Johnson later added a bedroom wing, attached to the main house by a glass corridor.

The *New York Times* described the lighting scheme designed by Richard Kelly as "unusual and dramatic. . . . There is an elaborate arrangement of switches for picture spots, closet lamps, outdoor lighting, recessed down lighting controlled by dimmers." With a control panel placed near the couch in the living area, "the owner will be able to control the mood of light on outdoor planting, pictures, walls, and reading lamps with a flick of the three dials." Kelly again used the small Alzak shovel reflectors he had employed to illuminate the artwork in the Rockefeller Guest House the previous year. Recessed downlights in the overhang above the patio walkway and additional perimeter lights illuminated the ground and vegetation immediately outside the glass walls and thus removed the reflections on black glass walls at night. This concept was supported by the carefully selected surface materials, from black tile inside to reflective white gravel on the outside.

SE/KB

"A Connecticut House for a Television Executive." *Architectural Record* (March 1953): 156–161.

Haeberly, Mabel. "Residence in New Canaan Soon to Shed 'Winter Wraps' to Display Modern Design." *New York Times*, May 6, 1951.

Jenkins, Stover, and David Mohney. *The Houses of Philip Johnson*. New York: Abbeville, 2001.

Yale University Library, Manuscripts and Archives, Richard Kelly Papers.

above: Hodgson House, interior view to courtyard. Photograph: Ezra Stoller © Esto.

Remodeling of Singer and Sons Showroom

Location: 32–38 East Nineteenth Street, New York, N.Y.
Completed: November 1951
Interior designers: Bertha Schaefer and Richard Kelly
Lighting installation: November 1951

When Joe Singer of the M. Singer and Sons furniture company decided to remodel the company's large exhibition space, he hired Bertha Schaefer and Richard Kelly. Schaefer had been instrumental in promoting modern European art and furniture in the United States. In 1924 she had founded her Interiors gallery and in 1944 the Bertha Schaefer Gallery of Contemporary Art. She also designed many pieces of furniture herself, several to be produced by the firm of M. Singer and Sons. As an interior designer she had a strong interest in lighting, having been one of the first to employ the new fluorescent lights in residential applications in the early 1940s.

Kelly had worked with Bertha Schaefer earlier in 1951, when he lit her showroom at the National Home Furnishings Show. In a letter to Joe Singer, Kelly explained his intention "to free the furniture and the imagination from architectural enclosure and limitation." For this he would "proportion useful spaces," and establish "a visual order of significance" with the help of the relation of tonal values in the dark shell of the walls, columns, and ceilings, the soft, light, continuous floor, the rich sheltering screen panels and curtains, and finally the brilliant highlights of the exhibits. Kelly installed a rich array of downlights in tracks on the darkened ceiling and created additional effects by washing curtains, walls, and fabrics with light from above. The weeklong trade show that opened the new space showed twenty-one pieces by the three Italian architects Gio Ponti, Ico Parisi, and Carlo di Carli, and fifteen by Schaefer.

DN

"Across the Seas of Collaboration for the New Singer Collection." *Interiors* 110 (December 1951): 120–129.
Pepis, Betty. "Following Sculptural Lines." *New York Times*, November 4, 1951.
Yale University Library, Manuscripts and Archives, Richard Kelly Papers.

above: Singer and Sons Showroom, interior view

Lee Ault House

Location: 90 Lambert Road, New Canaan, Connecticut
Completed: 1952
Architect: Eliot Noyes
Lighting installation: 1952

Architect Eliot Noyes was the director of the Industrial Design Department at the Museum of Modern Art from 1940 to 1946, and afterward an industrial designer at Norman Bel Geddes's firm, where he cultivated a long-lasting and seminal relationship with IBM. Noyes was the first of the "Harvard Five" group of architects to move to New Canaan, where he designed a number of residential projects. One of his earlier works was a house commissioned by Lee Ault, the editor of *Art in America* magazine and the owner of a substantial art collection. Noyes devised an H-shaped structure whose two outer wings with bedrooms, kitchen, and the garage were connected by a glass-walled living-dining room and adjacent art gallery, both facing open courtyards. In a 1968 article in *Art in America*, Noyes recalled: "The programme for the design of the house, right from the beginning, was to offer diverse spaces and good lighting for installing this magnificent collection while also providing all the normal needs of a family, and to intermesh art with living. As an architectural problem this was about as interesting and rewarding an assignment as I ever hope for!"

A long skylight close to the gallery's display wall provided additional daylight. Richard Kelly placed "Baby Spotlights" between the skylight's vertical baffles to illuminate individual paintings at night. Along the perimeter of the glass-enclosed living room and gallery, he placed recessed circular fixtures in the protruding soffit of the roof. Another sequence of downlights, farther apart from one another, was placed in the suspended frame along the edge of the two courtyards. This staggered transition allowed the exterior living space to remain an integral part of the house at night. Kelly dispersed spot lighting throughout the landscape to delineate a selective view of the trees and garden plants at night.
SE/KB

Bruce, Gordon. *Eliot Noyes: A Pioneer of Design and Architecture in the Age of American Modernism*. London: Phaidon, 2006.
"Recent Work of Eliot Noyes: Four Houses." *Architectural Record* (November 1958): 166–180.
"Eliot Noyes." *Architectural Record* 124 (November 1958): 166–180.
Kelly, Richard. "How to Light Your Paintings." *House and Garden* (January 1947): 112–113.
"The Newest Arts in Lighting." *House and Garden* (March 1958): 86–89, 108.
Noyes, Eliot. "Wall Houses." *Art in America* 56 (January 1968): 56–65.
Yale University Library, Manuscripts and Archives, Richard Kelly Papers.

above: Ault House, facade at night
opposite: Ault House, illumination over paintings

Franklin Savings Bank

Location: Forty-second Street and Eighth Avenue, New York, N.Y.
Completed: 1901
Architects: York and Sawyer
Lighting installation: 1952

In 1952, the president of the Franklin Savings Bank realized that the growing brightness of nearby Times Square made the bank's Beaux Arts structure increasingly invisible at night, and he commissioned the McNutt Electric Company to give the building "one of the finest installations of lighting in the country." McNutt in turn hired Richard Kelly as consultant. Kelly responded to the ubiquitous floodlighting in the area, which, he claimed, flattened form and "obscured detail in its unnatural and unartful glare." Instead, he developed a new approach that he called "flare lighting," as it "uses light sources to highlight the details which make the building distinguished: . . . cornice, frieze, pilasters and their capitals, as well as the rustication of the stone work . . . with a play of light and shadow." It was, Kelly wrote, "a strong modern counterpart of the Renaissance use of flares or torches." In order to dispel the "dead" look of the tall windows (15 feet wide and 30 feet tall) at night, they received special curtains of a new material to serve as reflectors and refractors of light. This was Kelly's first major collaboration with the fabric designer Marie Nichols, with whom he later developed the metal curtains for the Four Seasons restaurant. Nichols suggested the material Dynel, which was manufactured by Union Carbide and Carbon and had typically been used for tire fabrication, but was now being promoted as a cheap synthetic substitute for wool. According to *Time* magazine: "Dynel will be to wool what nylon is to silk." The curtain was woven in a large mesh, relatively lightweight, and it picked up the light cast on it from inside and diffused it efficiently. Kelly employed the brand-new General Electric 300-watt sealed-beam Pyrex lamp and worked with the firm of Treitel Gratz (which had recently received the commission to manufacture Mies van der Rohe's metal furniture for Knoll) on the development of the light fixtures.

DN

"Enter Dynel," *Time*, December 11, 1950.
"Flare Lighting Accents Building Design." *Electric Construction and Maintenance* (October 1953): 90–92.
Stern, Robert A. M., Gregory Gilmartin, and John Massengale. *New York, 1900: Metropolitan Architecture and Urbanism, 1890–1915*. New York: Rizzoli, 1983.
Yale University Library, Manuscripts and Archives, Richard Kelly Papers.

above: Franklin Bank, exterior view at night

Hechinger House

Location: Washington, D.C.
Completed: 1952
Architects: The Architects Collaborative; Robert S. McMillan, designer
Lighting installation: 1952

In 1951, The Architects Collaborative (TAC) was commissioned to design two houses on adjacent lots in Washington, D.C., for John Hechinger, the owner of a chain of hardware stores, and his brother-in-law, Richard England. Walter Gropius, chairman of the Architecture Department at Harvard at the time, had founded TAC in 1945, but he put an associate, Robert S. McMillan, in charge of the design. The two houses were built on a sloping site facing west and were early examples of modernist homes in the Washington area. Both display different applications of the firm's design vocabulary of cubic massing, modified by voids and added volumes, balconies, and terraces. Wood siding alternates with stucco and brick, and large windows line the spacious living room. Kelly employed several of the key lighting techniques that he had been developing since 1949 for the Glass House and Hodgson House, both by Johnson, and would continue to apply at other residential commissions such as the Davis House in 1953.

In the living room, he installed recessed spotlights in the ceiling both inside and outside of its glass wall, creating dramatic scalloping effects when the curtains were drawn and illuminating the terrace outside when they were open, in order to eliminate reflection and extend the perceived space. Dimmable individual recessed ceiling fixtures were provided for task lighting throughout the house. In the bedroom Kelly designed thin strip lighting for the top inside edge of the custom-made, built-in headboard, eliminating the need for separate reading lights. John Hechinger followed Kelly's work on the project closely and engaged him in discussions about his "sensational" lighting scheme. However, Hechinger also later noted the constant humming of the dimmers (even when not in use) and Kelly's inscrutable billing practices.

SE/DN

"Congenial Individuals on One Plot." *House and Garden* (July 1952): 47–51, 93–94.

Gropius, Walter, ed. *The Architects Collaborative, 1945–1965*. New York: Architectural Book Publishing, 1966.

Harkness, John C., ed. *1945–1969: The Work of the Architects Collaborative*. Vol. 4 of *The Walter Gropius Archive: An Illustrated Catalogue of the Drawings, Prints, and Photographs in the Walter Gropius Archive at the Busch-Reisinger Museum, Harvard University*. Edited by Winfried Nerdinger. New York: Garland, 1990–1991.

Lewis, Robert J. "Gropius-Designed House Is 'Composition in Cubes.'" Washington *Evening Star*, December 15, 1951.

Lewis, Robert J. "Rectangles Dominate This Design." Washington *Evening Star*, December 29, 1951.

Moeller, Gerard Martin. *AIA Guide to the Architecture of Washington*, 4th ed. Baltimore: Johns Hopkins University Press, 2006.

Yale University Library, Manuscripts and Archives, Richard Kelly Papers.

above left: Hechinger and England Houses, exterior view. Photograph: Ezra Stoller © Esto.
above right: Hechinger House, living room. Photograph: Ezra Stoller © Esto.

Museum of Modern Art, Sculpture Garden

Location: 11 West Fifty-third Street, New York, N.Y.
Completion Date: 1952
Architect: Philip Johnson; Landscape consultant: James Fanning
Lighting installation: 1952

In 1946, after a twelve-year absence, Philip Johnson returned to his position as director of the Architecture and Design Department at the Museum of Modern Art. His directorship, along with the success of his 1950 west-wing design, allowed him to oversee and collaborate with landscape architect James Fanning on the redesign of the Abby Aldrich Rockefeller Sculpture Garden. Their formal design subtly divided the 107-by-200-foot lot into four outdoor "living rooms." Each zone was defined through the use of reflecting pools, trees, and grouped plantings. A fourteen-foot glazed brick wall was used along Fifty-fourth Street to complete the enclosure to the north of the site. This height was accomplished by lowering the garden level by two feet and establishing a conceptual "ceiling" height within the space. A review published in the *New York Times* in 1953 praised the project as a "handsomely designed garden: "a unique space has been provided, with a series of vistas . . . so that sculpture may be displayed to its best possible advantage."

This garden was Richard Kelly's second commission from the museum (after the lighting of the temporary Ain House in the museum's garden in 1950) and part of his continuing collaboration with Johnson. To highlight the foliage at night and turn the north wall into a glowing backdrop for the artworks, Kelly specified uplights with daylight filters concealed at the foot of the trees and the wall. Baffled spotlights with pale pink filters and downlight shields were mounted on the sixth-floor parapet adjacent to the site. At the two reflecting pools, Kelly installed spotlights under each bridge. These were complemented by pool lights fabricated with clear lenses and bronze housings.

EH

Beneés, Miroslava Marie. "Making a Modern Sculpture Garden: The Museum of Modern Art, New York." *GSD News* (Winter–Spring 1993): 8–9.

Elderfield, John, ed. *Philip Johnson and the Museum of Modern Art.* New York: Museum of Modern Art, 1998.

"Museum Garden Is an Outdoor Living Room for Sculpture Display." *Architectural Forum* 99 (July 1953): 136–137.

Stern, Robert A. M., Thomas Mellins, and David Fishman. *New York, 1960: Architecture and Urbanism Between the Second World War and the Bicentennial.* New York: Monacelli, 1995.

"A Transformed Sculpture Garden to Open at Modern Art Museum." *New York Times*, April 18, 1953.

Yale University Library, Manuscripts and Archives, Richard Kelly Papers.

above: Museum of Modern Art Sculpture Garden, view from above

Morosani House

Location: Litchfield, Connecticut
Completed: 1953
Architect: Edward Durell Stone
Lighting installation: 1953

Edward Durell Stone began to design the Morosani House in 1949. Consonant with a modernist vernacular of the time—International Style simplicity with the long and low horizontal lines of Wright's Prairie Style—it was perhaps the last building of Stone's early career, before he began work on the American embassy in New Delhi, India, and his subsequent designs that raised new questions of ornament and human scale for modern architecture. The house has an L-shaped plan, with four bedrooms and private baths composing the long leg, capped by a large playroom and a short, almost square leg containing a master bedroom suite, living room, kitchen and dining room, and an indoor patio with a sunken pool. The public spaces at this end are articulated by a masonry fireplace wall between the living room and patio and a wide overhead shelf, topped with foliage, separating the patio from the dining room.

Stone, who taught architecture at Yale beginning in 1946, hired Kelly in 1953 to design the lighting for the Morosani House. The clients told Kelly their grand plans for the lighting, and he did not disappoint, calling for nearly two dozen different types of fixtures, many of them custom designed, and creating one of his most elaborate residential designs. He allowed for multiple lighting schemes in all major rooms of the house, and filtered light through colored lenses, through foliage, and through water. He designed more than two hundred feet of "curtain lights," consisting of alternating pink and blue bulbs set in a metal trough with an angled composite lens to color and spread light downward onto the window walls or curtains drawn across them. In response to the house's extensive glazing, Kelly placed three dozen downlights along the exterior perimeter, and many more throughout the surrounding yard.
SI

University of Arkansas Libraries, Special Collections, Edward Durell Stone Papers.
Yale University Library, Manuscripts and Archives, Richard Kelly Papers.

above: Morosani House, living room, drawing by Kelly

Yale University Art Gallery

Location: 1111 Chapel Street, New Haven, Connecticut
Completed: 1953
Architect: Louis Kahn with Anne Tyng and Douglas Orr
Lighting installation: 1953

"Conceptually, visually and functionally, Mr. Kahn's tetrahedral [ceiling] slab, which is really THE feature of the Gallery, must be termed a major success. . . . [T]o stand in Weir Court on a calm evening and to look through the transparent walls to the layer upon layer of tetrahedrons, permeated by their inner glow, is to feel that this building has a vitality of its own: permanent and worthy of endurance." Boris Pushkarev, writing for *Perspecta* in 1956, observed a quality here that had become a significant aspect of modern glass-fronted architecture: at night, its interior spaces, and in particular the ceilings, could dominate a building's appearance from outside. The characteristic pattern of concrete triangles and tetrahedrons that Louis Kahn and Anne Tyng had developed for the open gallery spaces (initially used both for instruction and exhibition purposes) looked like a continuous space frame. Structural difficulties, however, required instead a series of forty-foot-long slanted concrete beams with non-load-bearing diagonal elements between them. Kahn's declination of the formal from the structural resulted in a surprisingly successful solution for the gallery's appearance, acoustics, and technical infrastructure. The triangular spaces between the hollow tetrahedrons were open to the ducts and pipes underneath the ceiling slab and thus became the places for the lights. The advantages of a drop ceiling in rendering the fixture invisible here coincided with that of an open ceiling allowing freedom in placing and adjusting the lights. Since their potential positions were predetermined by the grid, however, and their particular setting required careful calibration of the light flow, special fixtures had to be developed. Edison Price, Century Lighting (where Yale professor Stanley McCandless was a consultant), and Swivelier, Inc., developed proposals for the Mobile Gallery Lights. Edison Price won this part of the commission (Century Lighting did most of the rest), and developed two special fixtures, the Elipsol, which was used to illuminate nonexhibit areas with a focusing mechanism to control illumination and distribution, and the Parlite, for the individual lighting of art objects. The ceiling itself glowed calmly in the reflection from the light on walls and floors, punctured rhythmically by the bright triangles containing the light fixtures.

DN

"Building Engineering: 1. Tetrahedral Floor System: Yale's New Design Laboratory Conceals Lighting and Ductwork with a 31-Inch-Deep Floor Structure." *Architectural Forum* 97 (November 1952): 148–149.

Loud, Patricia Cummings. *The Art Museums of Louis I. Kahn*. Durham: Duke University Press, 1989.

Pushkarev, Boris. "Order and Form: Yale Art Gallery and Design Center Designed by Louis Kahn." *Perspecta: The Yale Architecture Journal*, no. 3 (December 1956): 46–59.

Wiseman, Carter. *Louis I. Kahn: Beyond Time and Style; A Life in Architecture*. New York: W. W. Norton, 2007.

Yale University Library, Manuscripts and Archives, Richard Kelly Papers.

opposite: Louis Kahn in the gallery. Photograph © Yale University Art Gallery, 2010.
above left: Yale University Art Gallery, interior view. Roberto Schezen © Esto.
above right: Yale University Art Gallery, facade at night

William A. Burden Apartment

Location: 1025 Fifth Avenue, New York, N.Y.
Completed: 1925; redesigned 1954
Architects: Warren and Wetmore
Apartment redesign: Philip Johnson
Lighting installation: 1954

In contemporary home magazines, the lighting design for this Fifth Avenue apartment owned by the president of the Museum of Modern Art received as much attention as its innovative architecture. Philip Johnson, then director of the Architecture and Design Department at MoMA, installed a shallow plaster dome with an oculus in its center underneath the unusually high ceiling of the living room, recalling the famous breakfast-room "canopy" at the home of nineteenth-century British architect Sir John Soane and his demonstration of the "poetry of architecture." While Johnson's dome floats similarly without visible means of support, the original's skylight and influx of daylight along its edges could not be adopted here. Instead, Richard Kelly had soft incandescent light (from Kliegl three-inch concentrating lens strips) flood down from the sides and illuminate the center, controllable via dimmer. As described in the March 1955 issue of *Interiors*, "the light is a directionless presence that, shining on white draperies and walls, gives the room an ethereal luminosity."

Contemporary photographs provide insufficient evidence about the actual quality of light in the living room. The suspended plaster dome prevented Kelly's preferred method for lighting artwork, namely through recessed downlights "about 30 to 40 inches from the wall." The dome's smooth plaster surface was penetrated only once, somewhat awkwardly, for a single spotlight above an oversized planter.

The dining room displayed an entirely different concept: Kelly and Johnson developed an open, suspended ceiling grid ("a Mondrian design in lighting," according to *House and Garden*) from whose thin metal bars tiny light bulbs illuminated the ceiling, and a black copper box provided pinhole spotlights for the table. They were arranged so as to cast five intersecting circles of light, exactly matching the outer dimensions of the Johnson-designed table. The result, wrote Kelly, was "brittle, sharp highlights on silver and crystal, to excite the optic nerve, whet the appetite, and stimulate conversation." The multicolored silk curtains by Marie Nichols were grazed with light from the metal structure above, its impact softened by an additional interior gauze curtain.

In a bedroom planned "for a man," Kelly again brought down the height of the room by adding a luminous ceiling, creating diffuse illumination, while adding bright lights similar to those seen in theater dressing rooms around a mirror. In the master bedroom the writing and dressing tables directly faced the windows between built-in cabinets and shelves, while at night they were brightly lit by banks of bulbs set directly into the window frames.

KB/DN

opposite: William A. Burden Apartment, living room

William A. Burden Apartment *continued*

"Good Decorating Begins with a Plan." *House and Garden* (October 1954): 132–133.
"Light: Element of Décor." *New York Times*, February 25, 1957.
"Lighting: The Designer's Fourth Dimension." *Interiors* (February 1958): 92–94.
"Lighting for Design and Mood." *Interiors* (March 1955): 94–95.
"Modern Setting." *Vogue* (June 1954): 90–91.
Pepis, Betty. "An Architectural Apartment." *New York Times*, June 27, 1954.
Yale University Library, Manuscripts and Archives, Richard Kelly Papers.

above: William A. Burden Apartment, dining room. Guerrero/House and Garden © Conde Nast Publications.

Davis House

Location: Wayzata, Minnesota
Completed: 1954
Architect: Philip Johnson
Lighting installation: 1954

Richard Davis was an avid art collector and senior curator of the Minneapolis Institute of Arts. When his house was featured in *Fortune* magazine as an example of the return to opulence in postwar building, he stated, "We had in mind a country house sufficiently flexible in plan for normal family life and frequent entertaining, and sufficiently pure and sophisticated for our large and rather personal art collection." Philip Johnson's plan consisted of two distinct brick volumes with remarkably few apertures, organized around a central interior glass-walled courtyard. This arrangement allowed for large, unbroken wall surfaces to display artwork as well as maximum exposure to daylight. The 450-square-foot patio became a main source of illumination by day and by night. The court had a coffered ceiling of plywood, which was roofed over with translucent corrugated plastic during the winter months, and with screens against insects in the summer. Daylight bulbs of ten watts were concealed inside the coffers, minimizing glare. These were supplemented by spotlights to accent plants and a fountain. Kelly suggested two nighttime illumination schemes: the "stylized" lighting of the individual plants as seen through the glass walls, or the curtains drawn across the glass and lit from the patio beyond as "luminous backdrops." Johnson had provided narrow strip skylights close to the northern and southern walls—an arrangement similar to that at Eliot Noyes's Ault House two years earlier. Kelly treated the skylights similar to the courtyard: wooden louvers would help to evenly distribute the light from above, prevent direct sunlight from reaching the artwork underneath, and hide spotlights between them from view. At night these incandescent lights provided "firelike" glow and a "cozy night-time feeling, different from daylight." Kelly would continue experiments with a joint positioning of daylighting and light fixtures throughout his career, as for example in the Munson-Williams-Proctor Arts Institute of 1959 or the Yale Center for British Art in 1974.

SE/KB

Jenkins, Stover, and David Mohney. *The Houses of Philip Johnson*. New York: Abbeville, 2001.
"A Modern Expression of the Formal House." *House and Garden* (March 1957): 72–75.
"Philip Johnson: Three Recent Works." *Interiors* (July 1954): 62–71.
"The $250,000 House." *Fortune* (October 1955): 133–142.
"What Patios Can Do for Your House: Indoor Gardens Can Be a Source of Light." *House and Home* (August 1954): 110–115.
Yale University Library, Manuscripts and Archives, Richard Kelly Papers.

above: Richard Davis House, interior view to courtyard

Philip Johnson Brick House

Location: 798 – 856 Ponus Ridge Road, New Canaan, Connecticut
Completion date: 1949; interior remodeling: 1953
Architect: Philip Johnson
Lighting installation: 1954

Long eclipsed by the Glass House as a much photographed and referenced icon of midcentury modernism, Philip Johnson's Brick House was built at the same time only a few feet away, as a carefully composed counterpart and deliberate opposite. Similar in width but not as deep as the Glass House, the Brick House consisted of a plain box of sheer brick walls, interrupted only by the entrance door and three circular porthole-like windows in the back providing daylight for the three rooms. When remodeling its interior in 1953, Johnson combined two of its rooms into one ten-by-twenty-six-foot rectilinear space for a bedroom, covering two windows with movable fabric panels, to achieve complete darkness inside. A pair of flat pendentive plaster domes was suspended from the ceiling and linked to the ground by improbably thin double columns. A nod to the suspended ceilings in Sir John Soane's early-nineteenth-century house in London, and perhaps to the plaster domes in German Rococo churches, this interior represents the first time that Johnson moved beyond a strictly defined Miesian vocabulary. In the same year, he designed a similarly suspended saucer dome in the Burden apartment in New York City. Smooth softened corners and domed ceilings became recurring elements of Johnson's designs in the following years and inspired other modernists such as Edward Durell Stone.

Between the billowing baldachins and the actual ceiling, Kelly installed incandescent lights, whose indirect glow reflected off the golden Fortuny damask fabric on the walls and movable panels. The author of an *Interiors* article, probably Olga Gueft, wrote: "The only light is a mysterious, shadowless glow from all sides that outlines the domes and floors. Rheostatically controlled, it is easily set anywhere between night and 4000 glareless watts." A *Saturday Evening Post* article on Kelly described the room's emotional effect: "We sat under the domed ceiling in these exotic surroundings, bathed in reflected light which slowly began to fade. . . . When, after a minute or two, it had dropped to a level at which it would have been difficult to read, the room seemed to have expanded to twice its size. There was no feeling of confinement at any level of light." The placement of the lights and provision of a dimmer allowed for cycles of imaginary sunsets and sunrises — echoing the glass house's role as a baldachin and belvedere. The choice of Fortuny fabric for the walls was particularly apt, since it had been developed originally for the reflection of floodlight in theater stage sets. Together, the Glass and Brick Houses translate a number of nineteenth-century ideas about space perception and illusion into contemporary architecture, and Richard Kelly's role was central to making this strategy convincing.

KB/DN

Haerberly, Mabel C. "All-Glass Home on Ponus Ridge Startles New Canaan Residents." *New York Times*, December 12, 1948.

Jenkins, Stover, and David Mohney. *The Houses of Philip Johnson*. New York: Abbeville, 2001.

Johnson, Philip. "House at New Canaan, Connecticut, Architect: Philip Johnson." *Architectural Review* 108 (September 1950): 152 – 160.

Lambert, Phyllis. "Stimmung at Seagram: Philip Johnson Counters Mies van der Rohe." *Grey Room* 20 (Summer 2005): 38–59.
Nicholson, Arnold. "Mr. Kelly's Magic Lights." *Saturday Evening Post* (July 5, 1958): 28–29, 61–65.
Pepis, Betty. "The Light Touch." *New York Times*, August 8, 1954.
"Philip Johnson: Three Recent Works." *Interiors* (July 1954): 62–71.
Whitney, David, and Jeffrey Kipnis. *Philip Johnson: The Glass House.* New York: Pantheon, 1993.
Yale University Library, Manuscripts and Archives, Richard Kelly Papers.

opposite: Philip Johnson Brick House, exterior
above: Philip Johnson Brick House, bedroom. Arts of the United States Collection, University of Georgia.

Eliot Noyes House

Location: Country Club Road, New Canaan, Connecticut
Completed: 1955
Architect: Eliot Noyes
Lighting installation: 1955

Eliot Noyes left New York City and his position as the first director of the Industrial Design Department at the Museum of Modern Art in 1946 to pursue his own practice in New Canaan, Connecticut. The Noyes House is the second and more influential of the two modern houses the architect designed for his family in New Canaan, and the only one still extant. The layout is that of a rectangular plan with living and sleeping rooms separated by a garden courtyard and connected by covered but open walkways. The east and west exterior walls are made from large movable glass panels providing unobstructed views between garden, living area, and wooded landscape, while the remaining walls are constructed of local fieldstone. Similar to Kelly's lighting strategy for reducing nighttime glare at Philip Johnson's Glass House and Gregory Ain's MoMA demonstration house, a majority of the interior lighting was eliminated, and the house was illumined mainly from the exterior. To accomplish this, the lighting plan included downlights in the outside soffits adjacent to the courtyard as well as along the open walkways. This alternative approach maintains visual connection between the interior living space and the exterior courtyard at night. Kelly's initial design proposal included dimmers, but due to budget constraints, they were cut. Instead, to maintain electrical efficiency, lamp wattage was controlled. The family residence was one of multiple collaborations between Noyes and Kelly.
EH

Bruce, Gordon. *Eliot Noyes: A Pioneer of Design and Architecture in the Age of American Modernism*. London: Phaidon, 2006.
Earls, William D. *The Harvard Five in New Canaan*. New York: W. W. Norton, 2006.
"Eliot Noyes." *Architectural Review* (May 1957): 362.
"Eliot Noyes." *Architectural Record* 124 (November 1958): 166–180.
"Here Is One of New Canaan's Most Admired New Houses." *House and Home* 10 (October 1956): 168–169.
"House: New Canaan, Connecticut." *Progressive Architecture* (December 1956): 98–105.
"Patio Splits Two-Zone House." *Architectural Record* 121 (Mid-May 1957): 125–128.
Yale University Library, Manuscripts and Archives, Richard Kelly Papers.

above: Eliot Noyes House, exterior view to courtyard. Photograph: Ezra Stoller © Esto.

711 Third Avenue

Location: New York, N.Y.
Completed: 1956
Architect: William Lescaze
Lighting installation: 1956

William Lescaze, best known for designing the landmark Philadelphia Savings Fund Society (PSFS) Building with George Howe in 1932, which is widely recognized as the first International Style skyscraper, made a modest attempt at adapting its aesthetic to the constraints of New York's mandated setbacks in 1956. At his office building at 711 Third Avenue, a heavy eleven-story tower, clad in blue glazed brick, rises without interruption from its wider six-story base and a two-story transitional section. The developer William Kaufman hoped to make a "bid for prestige in New York's competitive office market," and, advised by Lescaze, commissioned a stainless-steel sculpture by José de Rivera and a large-scale mosaic mural by Hans Hofmann for the lobby.

Lescaze brought in Richard Kelly, who dramatically floodlit the recessed "blue tower to make it the most noticeable office building in the midtown area." He used the brand-new General Electric five-hundred-watt PAR-64 flood lamp, and kept the costs down by limiting the lighting to three sides of the building and to the hours from dusk till midnight. On the street level Kelly proposed a continuous band of downlights in the first-floor soffit, "which will brightly light the sidewalks and 'float' the dark band of floors above it."

The tall elevator lobby in the heart of the building, behind a perimeter of stores, had no access to natural light, but it became the building's most striking feature. Entirely forgoing conventional light fixtures, Kelly installed strips of recessed downlights in slim troughs in the dark blue ceiling around the elevator core and along the outer edge. Hoffman's sixteen-foot-high glass mosaic mural was subtly washed with warm light from above, bringing his vibrant multicolored composition in luminous harmony with the dark brown marble walls enclosing the space. The recessed ceiling lights in dense sequence close to the wall represented an idea Kelly had already pondered in 1950 in the context of his work for Mies van der Rohe's 860–880 Lake Shore Drive. They point ahead to the application at the Seagram Building two years later. This experience with the lighting of highly polished but dark marble might have led to Kelly's advice to use travertine instead of polished dark marble in the first-floor lobby at the Seagram Building.

In response to a letter from Lescaze complaining that the lobby lighting was "spotty" and "uneven," Kelly explained his aesthetic intentions: "The unevenness of the illumination was not evident to me except as it was planned. For example: the very evident pools of light on the floor along the walls are not undesirable, and it is important in those cases to keep the light off the walls. Unevenness in a larger sense is certainly desirable for drama and interest."

MMP

"About Art and Artist." *New York Times*, February 16, 1956.
"Art in the Lobby." *Interiors* (February 1957): 85.
"Color and Art Help an Office Building." *Architectural Forum* 105 (October 1956): 154–155.
Lanmon, Lorraine Welling. *William Lescaze, Architect*. London: Associated University Presses, 1987.
Stern, Robert A. M., Thomas Mellins, and David Fishman. *New York, 1960: Architecture and Urbanism Between the Second World War and the Bicentennial*. New York: Monacelli, 1995.
Yale University Library, Manuscripts and Archives, Richard Kelly Papers.

above: 711 Third Avenue, elevator lobby with Hans Hofmann mural

General Motors Technical Center

Location: Warren, Michigan
Completed: 1956
Architect: Eero Saarinen and Associates
Lighting installation: 1956

One of the outstanding architectural projects of its era, the corporate headquarters, research, and design centers for General Motors consisted of twenty-five low-slung buildings sited in dynamic tension with one another. *Architectural Forum* immediately proclaimed it "a historic symbol of industrial progress." The Finnish-American architect and product designer Eero Saarinen used aluminum, steel, glass, and glazed brick as vocabulary in a strikingly elegant and personal version of modern architecture in which strong sculptural elements, such as suspended stairs, reflecting pools inside and out, an expressive water tower, and a sculptural screen by the artist Harry Bertoia, contributed to an aesthetic of refined and livable modernism that matched GM's marketing mission.

The degree of Kelly's involvement with the project is not entirely clear, but certain effects and techniques implemented in the GM center would be hard to imagine without his input. There are luminous ceilings throughout as well as recessed wall washers and spotlights for the illumination of artwork. The so-called Styling Auditorium, for example, a freestanding 186-foot clear-span dome sheathed in aluminum, contained a circular viewing platform where new automobiles could be examined by GM engineers and visitors. To give the illusion of a daylit sky the dome's cove lighting used a mixture of incandescent and mercury vapor lamps, consuming 225 kilowatts of power and providing 140 foot-candles of brightness throughout.

In the lobby of another building, a pool underneath the main stair was lit by underwater lamps, adding color and shimmering light to the entire space. Outdoors, Kelly used small-scale floor lamps adapted for outside exposure to create a sense of intimacy and enclosure throughout the complex. Few designers other than Kelly, who had worked with Saarinen previously, would have been able to meet simultaneously the exacting standards of automobile designers as well as the aesthetic ambition of the architect.

SE/SI

Brawne, Michael. "Looking Up: Suspended Ceilings as an Element in Interior Design." *Architectural Review* (September 1958): 160–170.
"GM's Industrial Versailles." *Architectural Forum* (May 1956): 122–130.
Maile Petty, Margaret. "Illuminating the Glass Box." *Journal of the Society of Architectural Historians* 66 (June 2007): 194–219.
Pelkonen, Eeva-Liisa, and Donald Albrecht. *Eero Saarinen: Shaping the Future.* New Haven: Yale University Press, 2006.
"A Tour of the GM Technical Center's Interiors." *Architectural Record* (May 1956): 151–158.
Yale University Library, Manuscripts and Archives, Richard Kelly Papers.

above left: General Motors Technical Center, styling division: private executive dining room of Harley Earle
above right: General Motors Technical Center, styling division: color room with all-louver luminous ceiling

The Frick Collection

Location: 1 East Seventieth Street, New York, N.Y.
Completed: 1914
Architects: Carrère and Hastings
Lighting installation: 1957

Henry Clay Frick, a Pittsburgh coke and steel magnate, had, in 1910, purchased land on the northeast corner of Fifth Avenue and Seventieth Street in Manhattan and commissioned the firm of Carrère and Hastings to build a mansion—more magnificent, he hoped, than that of his rival Andrew Carnegie. The private home with its collection of European paintings became a public gallery in 1935, and several additions were made by the architect John Russell Pope. In 1957, Richard Kelly began his redesign of the outdoor and indoor lighting for the museum, striving to maintain the domestic atmosphere of the original mansion. Kelly's intentions were to "make people aware of the museum and garden, yet not hit the passer-by in the eye."

Kelly achieved these subtle effects by using "many dozens of overlapping, weak light sources" to illuminate the facade "very dimly and softly." These included incandescent lights placed slightly below the ground level to illumine the trees surrounding the building, with similar recessed fluorescent lights focused on the hedges. The main facade of the building was highlighted with directed lighting to emphasize sculptural details and architectural elements, such as the supporting columns. The grand exterior staircase was lit from its base, emphasizing its horizontality in marked contrast to the strong verticality of the three arched windows of the facade. "The spectral light color is everywhere," Kelly wrote, "either originally or filtered, a very pale blue-light similar to moonlight. The exception to this is golden light on the silk curtains of the three arched windows, symbolizing the cultural wealth of the Collection in a beautiful setting."

KO/KB

Allison, David. "Outdoor Lighting: An Expanding New Technology." *Architectural Forum* (July 1960): 128–133.

Stern, Robert A. M., Gregory Gilmartin, and John Massengale. *New York, 1900: Metropolitan Architecture and Urbanism, 1890–1915*. New York: Rizzoli, 1983.

Stern, Robert A. M., Gregory Gilmartin, and Thomas Mellins. *New York, 1930: Architecture and Urbanism Between the Two World Wars*. New York: Rizzoli, 1987.

Yale University Library, Manuscripts and Archives, Richard Kelly Papers.

above: Frick Collection, facade at night

International Arrivals Building, Idlewild Airport

Location: New York, N.Y.
Completed: 1957
Architect: Skidmore, Owings, and Merrill; Design coordinator: Wallace Harrison
Lighting installation: 1957

The international terminal building by Skidmore, Owings, and Merrill was the first to be completed at Idlewild's new "aerial city." Arriving passengers would pick up their luggage and meet customs and immigration agents in a U-shaped terminal building, before entering the large arrivals hall, with an enormous Alexander Calder mobile suspended from its 50-foot-high and 180-foot-wide arched ceiling.

Richard Kelly, in charge of lighting the hall, carefully calibrated the contrast between the cool brightness of the luminous ceilings in the areas of customs supervision and health control, and the warmer, welcoming light of the arrivals hall. While the enormous arched ceiling was dotted with recessed downlights, the real challenge lay in the illumination of the ceiling itself from below over a considerable distance and with as little glare as possible. Kelly had never before lit a curved surface of such magnitude. In order to produce a unified wash of light across the entirety of the arch, substantial calculations were required. Minimizing the man-hours needed to run the calculations, Kelly used "new electronic calculating machines," after which further physical experimentation was completed to finally determine that the expanse could be washed with two hundred 500-watt sealed-beam lamps, one placed every six inches in concealed troughs across both ends of the arch. To assure consistency in the appearance of the light-washed ceiling throughout the varying conditions of the circadian cycle, a Luxtrol dimmer connected to an astronomical clock would gradually change the light's intensity. In addition, three other levels of brightness could respond to the number of people in the hall, as "the more people there are in a room, the more light there is needed, and vice versa" (Clute).

Kelly also addressed the view of the building from the outside, identifying the low parabolic arch as the new "Golden Door" into America. He buried sealed-beam projector lamps in small precast concrete pits to illuminate the exterior soffit of the parabola at the east and west ends of the building. Additional exterior baffle downlights directly above the entrance were, according to Kelly, designed to "express the welcome of entrance by reflected glow below eye level."

MMP/DN

Clute, Eugene. "Distinctive Lighting at New York International Airport." *Lighting* (January 1958): 23–25.
"Idlewild—New York International Airport." *Architectural Record* 130 (September 1961): 151–160.
"International Arrivals Building and Airline Wing Buildings." *Interiors* (April 1958): 109.
"New Aerial Gateway to America." *Architectural Forum* (February 1958): 78–87.
Yale University Library, Manuscripts and Archives, Richard Kelly Papers.

above left: Idlewild Airport, International Arrivals Building, downlights above entrance
above right: Idlewild Airport, International Arrivals Building, spectators' lounge above customs hall
opposite: Idlewild Airport, International Arrivals Building, arrivals hall

Penn Center Transportation Building and Greyhound Station

Location: Philadelphia, Pennsylvania
Completed: 1957
Architect: Vincent G. Kling
Lighting installation: 1957

The Transportation Center in Philadelphia was part of an ambitious urban renewal project replacing the elevated railroad tracks leading to Broad Street Station in the center of the city. The director of the City Planning Commission, Edmund Bacon, had originally asked Louis Kahn, who declined, and instead Vincent G. Kling designed the master plan in 1950 and several of its high-rise office and apartment buildings. The Transportation Center Building and Greyhound Station was erected in 1956. According to the artist Ellsworth Kelly, it was his friend Richard Kelly (no relation) who had received the lighting commission for the lobby of the Transportation Center and the adjacent Coach and Four restaurant of the Greyhound Bus Station, and who asked him to design sculptural screens as space dividers in the restaurant—"something which I can light." When Kling saw the designs for the seven brass installations, he commissioned Ellsworth Kelly to do a much larger screen for the main lobby and asked Richard Kelly to design the lighting for it. Ellsworth Kelly's first commissioned sculptures were "a summation of the chance based and cutout work" he had done in the early 1950s in France. He worked closely with Richard Kelly to develop a sculpture that would "catch the light." The sequence of 104 colored anodized aluminum panels arranged at different angles was almost twelve feet tall and sixty-five feet long. Kelly proposed a dimmable system of hot cathode fluorescent lamps, which was much discussed by the involved engineers and designers, because of its heat.

The entire sculpture and its supporting mechanism were produced by Edison Price and his assistant Isaac Goodbar in their workshop. They also supervised the anodization and color application. According to Ellsworth Kelly, the owner did not like the sculpture and never switched on the lights that Richard Kelly had designed for it, except at Christmas. When the Transportation Center was demolished, the sculpture was purchased by Jo Carole and Ronald Lauder and donated to the Museum of Modern Art. Richard Kelly also designed the lighting for the Transportation Center's public spaces, as well as the Greyhound Bus Terminal's interior courtyard landscape, as an "area of fantasy" (*New York Times*). **DN**

"Experts Examine: The Facts of Light." *Institutions Magazine* (August 1960): 64–67.
McKee, Guian A. "Blue Sky Boys, Professional Citizens, and Knights-in-Shining-Money: Philadelphia's Penn Center Project and the Constraints of Private Development." *Journal of Planning History* 6 (February 2007): 48–80.
"Penn Center Transportation Building and Concourse." *Architectural Record* 121 (May 1957): 190–196.
Storr, Robert, and Ellsworth Kelly. "Interview with Ellsworth Kelly." *MoMA Magazine* 2 (June 1999): 2–7.
"Transportation Center Penn Center." *Progressive Architecture* 38 (June 1957): 168.
Weart, William. "Philadelphia Bus Station." *New York Times*, February 24, 1957.
Yale University Library, Manuscripts and Archives, Richard Kelly Papers.

opposite left: Penn Center, Greyhound Post House, facade at night
opposite right: Penn Center Transportation Building, Ellsworth Kelly sculpture, with Richard Kelly standing beneath
above left: Penn Center, Coach and Four Restaurant, Ellsworth Kelly screen
above right: Ellsworth Kelly, Sculpture for a Large Wall, 1956–1957. Anodized aluminum, 104 panels, 136 x 78½ x 12 inches. The Museum of Modern Art, New York, gift of Jo Carole and Ronald S. Lauder, 1998. Originally commissioned by Pennsylvania Transport Center, Philadelphia. © Ellsworth Kelly; digital image © The Museum of Modern Art/licensed by SCALA/Art Resource, N.Y.

Seagram Building

Location: 375 Park Avenue, New York, N.Y.
Completed: 1957
Architects: Ludwig Mies van der Rohe and Philip Johnson
Lighting installation: 1957

A "tower of light," Mies van der Rohe's monumental glass and steel tower for the Seagram Corporation on Park Avenue, was described by the *New York Times* on its completion as "made of dream stuff: air and light as well as bronze and concrete. And it is light which makes the most spectacular contribution . . . by day for work, by night for drama."

Two principal illumination strategies were developed collaboratively by Richard Kelly, Philip Johnson, and Mies. First, on each floor above the lobby, a twenty-foot-deep luminous ceiling, designed in partnership with the manufacturer Lightolier, reached from the glass-curtain wall inward. With a unique dual lamping and circuit control system, it provided two distinct levels of illumination. During the day the ceiling's primary lamp circuit produced roughly 85 foot-candles — ostensibly to counter glare from the outside; in the evening, the secondary circuit along the perimeter used separate lamps running at one-quarter power to produce light levels near 20 foot-candles. These lights were intended to be seen from the sidewalk, and thus allowed for the illumination of the tower as a singular unit. The fifty-two-inch-square translucent panels were set in an anodized aluminum-trimmed modular grid — exactly replicating the tower's bay structure as expressed in applied bronze mullions on the facade. Furthermore, the ceiling panels were specially engineered to emit a nondirectional light pattern, with an "absence of any design or configuration in the diffusing panels," to provide the most uniform and "natural" illumination possible.

Second, the lobby and plaza illumination contributed significantly to the nighttime appearance of the building, anchoring the glowing tower with a powerfully illuminated central core and strong perimeter lighting at its base. Kelly's lighting throughout the lobby emphasized the scale, drama, and processional narrative of Seagram's entrance. He developed a recessed indirect lighting system able to wash evenly the length and breadth of the core's travertine-sheathed elevator banks with warm incandescent darklights, making the twenty-four-foot-high walls appear to glow. Apparently, Mies had first planned to use polished green marble, but Kelly had recently had mixed success with lighting polished marble at 711 Third Avenue and Mies's Esplanade Apartments, so he suggested travertine. At 860 – 880 Lake Shore Drive, Kelly had installed downlights only on the two shorter sides of the building. At the Seagram plaza much more intense lighting levels were needed. Recessed downlights are installed in the soffits around the perimeter of the building and along the front glass wall, in addition to two rows in the protruding canopy. The luminous footprint of the tower on the plaza floor helped maintain the transparency of the lobby's glass walls, readied the eye for the intense illumination of the core, and carried the suggestion of the building's interior glow onto the plaza. Kelly ensured the consistent appearance of the illuminated core and lobby by automatically regulating the light levels throughout the day with the help of timers and an astronomical clock. In 1958 *Architectural Forum* described the Seagram Building as "one of the best-illuminated buildings ever constructed."
MMP/DN

Jordy, William. "Seagram Assessed." *Architectural Review* 124 (December 1958): 374–381.
Lambert, Phyllis. "How a Building Gets Built." *Vassar Alumnae Magazine* (February 1959): 13–19.
"Lightolier Ceiling to Keep Bronze Skyscraper Aglow." *New York Times*, April 7, 1957.
Maile Petty, Margaret. "Illuminating the Glass Box." *Journal of the Society of Architectural Historians* 66 (June 2007): 194–219.
"New Progress in Light." *Architectural Forum* (February 1957): 152–155.
"Seagram Building, New York City." *International Lighting Review* 12 (1961): 68–69.
"Seagram Building Lobby." *Illuminating Engineering* (May 1959): 314.
"Seagram's Bronze Tower." *Architectural Forum* (July 1958): 66–77.
T.H.C. [Thomas H. Creighton]. "Seagram House Re-Reassessed." *Progressive Architecture* (June 1959): 140–145.
Yale University Library, Manuscripts and Archives, Richard Kelly Papers.

opposite: Seagram Building, view to lobby and elevator banks
right: Seagram Building at night. Photographer: Andreas Feininger/Time & Life Pictures/ Getty Images.

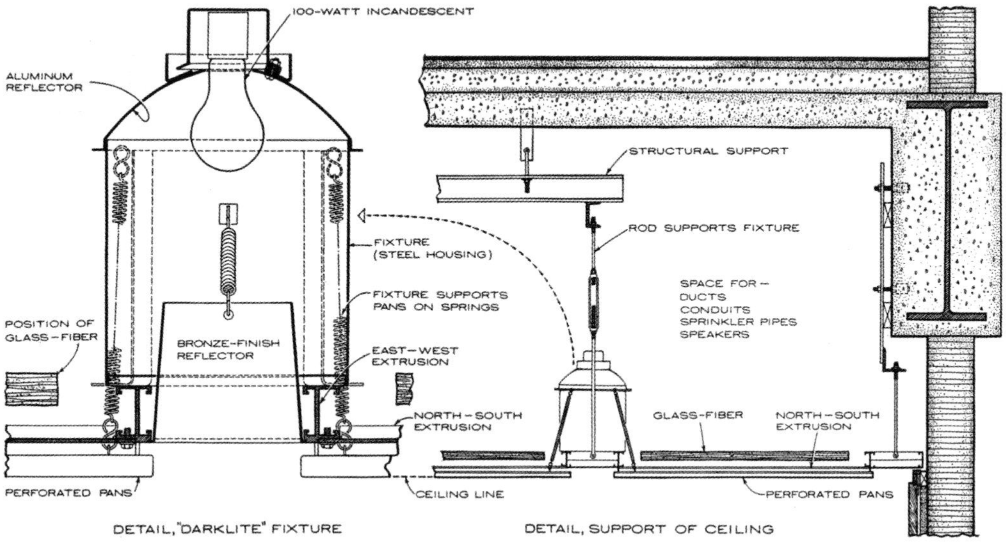

Four Seasons Restaurant, the Seagram Building

Location: 375 Park Avenue, New York, N.Y.
Completed: 1958
Architect: Philip Johnson
Lighting installation: 1958

The two rooms of the Four Seasons restaurant are perhaps Philip Johnson's most successful public spaces. Mies van der Rohe left the design of the space to Johnson, who maintained the former's sense of elegance, spaciousness, and carefully chosen materials, but also achieved a level of charm and festiveness that Mies would have found harder to conjure. The restaurant on the twenty-four-foot-high entrance level of the Seagram Building has two spacious rooms of equal size, the Pool Room in the north and the less formal Grill Room in the south. As the name indicates, the restaurant intended to celebrate the seasons in both its menu and its appearance. Among the most talked about features were the "curtains," narrowly spaced, thin metal chains in three tones of gold-anodized aluminum, whose gentle hanging curves covered the tall windows from floor to ceiling. The rising air from ventilation ducts moves the chains in subtle, rhythmic waves—apparently different in each season, depending on outside temperature. The fabric designer Marie Nichols was officially given credit for them, but their design had grown out of a series of experiments Kelly had undertaken with Nichols in search of a "metal type fabric" to "diffuse, transmit and reflect light adequately." Both had collaborated previously on the Franklin Bank in New York.

The most glorious focal point of the Grill Room is the Richard Lippold sculpture above the bar, which consists of hundreds of vertical gold-dipped brass rods of differing lengths, lit by sixteen recessed lamps in the ceiling.

Throughout the space, light fixtures are generally not visible, placed either beyond the edge of the suspended ceiling, their light grazing the metal curtains or wooden walls on the perimeter, or sending focused beams of light down onto the tables twenty feet below. The result is an astonishingly open room with enough luminous focus on each dining table to create a sense of spatial intimacy. The drama is heightened in the Pool Room, where underwater lights glow mysteriously, and bluish uplights underneath seventeen-foot-tall fig trees make their leaves shine and cast shadow patterns on the ceiling. Kelly's collaborator Edison Price developed and patented a number of new fixtures tailored to the space, in particular a range of different "darklights" with precisely focused yet glare-free beams. *Interiors* magazine perhaps best described the mood of the Four Seasons restaurant: "One singular paradox of the design is that despite the exceptional richness of its materials and workmanship, it is essentially colorless and unobtrusive. It is not a stage setting: rather it is a theatre that is not to date, nor tire the audience, but to focus on a perpetually changing mise-en-scène, an endlessly improvised drama—of the four seasons of nature, of the world's greatest metropolis, and of the pleasant rituals of serving and being served, eating, drinking and conversing."

DN

opposite: Four Seasons, Pool Room. Jeff Goldberg © Esto.
above: Four Seasons, darklight fixture diagram

Four Seasons Restaurant *continued*

Cooley, Renee, and Matthew Tanteri. *Richard Kelly Selected Works: An Exhibition of Works Presented by IESNY and the Richard Kelly Grant.* New York: Illuminating Engineering Society of New York, 2007.

Jordy, William. "The Mies-less Johnson." *Architectural Forum* (September 1959): 114–123.

"Metal Type Fabric Held Lighting Need." *New York Times*, February 23, 1954.

"More Elegance at the House of Seagram." *Architectural Record* (November 1959): 201–204.

Pepis, Betty. "Curtains of Steel Help to Improve Lighting in Room." *New York Times*, September 19, 1955.

Price, E., et al., "Lighting Fixtures." U.S. Patent no. 3,098,612, filed September 18, 1959, patented July 23, 1963.

Price, Edison. "Price Fixtures at Four Seasons." Letter to the editor, *Interiors* 10 (May 1960): 8.

Stern, Robert A. M., Thomas Mellins, and David Fishman. *New York, 1960: Architecture and Urbanism Between the Second World War and the Bicentennial.* New York: Monacelli, 1995.

"Two Masterpieces: The Guggenheim and the Four Seasons." *Interiors* 5 (December 1959): 79–87.

Yale University Library, Manuscripts and Archives, Richard Kelly Papers.

Richard Kelly Apartment

Location: 1140 Fifth Avenue, New York, N.Y.
Completed: 1921
Architect: Fred F. French Company; Interior design: David Miller
Lighting installation: 1958 and following

With no client to please or outside budget to meet, Richard Kelly was able to use his own prewar apartment on Fifth Avenue and Ninety-fifth Street as a laboratory for experimentation with his oft stated three basic elements of lighting: overall illumination, concentrated "focal glow," and a play of brilliance, or "sparkle." Not being able to recess downlights into the ceiling, Kelly used tracks that allowed him to move lamps as needed and dimmers to control their intensity. In the library, preexisting ceiling beams forced him to suspend the tracks beneath them. Additional shaded reading lamps allowing vertical movement were suspended from the ceiling. The same system was used in the combined sitting, kitchen, and dining area, where Kelly also placed "high hat" spotlights above the sink and stove. In the bathroom he installed a luminous ceiling with fluorescent tubes hidden behind plastic panels and incandescent bulbs attached to the mirror for more focused illumination.

Kelly never lost the taste for the theatrical that he first put to use while devising stage lighting as a student at Columbia University. This is most evident in his apartment's formal sitting room. As described in the *New York Herald Tribune*, "Here the windows are aglow with what appear to be dozens of miniature stars woven into the East Indian burlap draperies." Kelly had pierced the curtains with hundreds of tiny bulbs that were attached to brass strips on the inner sides. Forty-seven spotlights behind wooden screens ring the perimeter, grazing the walls and curtains with light from above. *House and Garden* noted: "Guests sipping after-dinner coffee are treated to a breathtaking spectacle. First, the room is darkened while at the curtained window wall, 'stars' glimmer, grow brilliant, are then overtaken by a wash of light that grows to sunrise radiance. . . . Later, as conversation ripens, side walls and window wall are dimmed, but table lamp behind sofa glows brightly."

KB

"Background Lighting—Instant Magic." *House and Garden* (September 1961): 120–129, 166–168.

Kellogg, Cynthia. "Some Light on Lighting." *New York Times Magazine* (May 18, 1958), 72–73.

Morrison, Harriet. "Highlighted Home of Designer on Tour." *New York Herald Tribune*, April 19, 1960.

Reif, Rita. "Dimmer Controls Put Additional Focus on Home Lights." *New York Times*, March 3, 1959.

Yale University Library, Manuscripts and Archives, Richard Kelly Papers.

above left: Kelly Apartment, entryway
above right: Kelly Apartment, library

Kneses Tifereth Israel Synagogue

Location: 575 King Street, Port Chester, New York
Completed: 1958
Architect: Philip Johnson
Lighting installation: 1958

Designed at a pivotal point in Philip Johnson's career, the Kneses Tifereth Israel Synagogue belongs to a group of buildings that, in the words of Ada Louise Huxtable, "look toward the past knowledgably, although they never copy it, and can be mistaken for nothing but of the present." The modern steel-frame structure consists of a separate oval-shaped foyer and a thirty-seven-foot-high main hall divided into a sanctuary and a social hall by eight-foot-tall removable partitions. It is in the remarkable ceiling of the main hall where Johnson acknowledges his architectural predecessors. "In order to introduce more spiritual feelings into what has been the rather cold style which we call modern," he explained in *Architectural Record*, "I have . . . introduced vaulted 'sails' of plaster which are intended to give a sense of containment to the space and also to act as light baffles for daylight and artificial lighting." As in Johnson's redesign of his Brick House bedroom and the Burden apartment in New York, but on a much grander scale, the hall's seven vaults recall the breakfast-room ceiling of John Soane's house in London.

Richard Kelly's lighting scheme plays an essential role in Johnson's design. The transition from the exterior to the foyer and from there to the main hall is designed to create a sequence from light to dark to light again. The vast interior space is illuminated during the day by rectangular seven-inch stained-glass window slits, with panels of different colors interspersed with those of clear glass. The suspended ceiling both reflects daylight and conceals the fixtures used for nighttime illumination. Six downlights are installed in each rib and, behind the sails' curving sides, dimmer-controlled spotlights are directed toward the side walls, producing an effect that makes the building "glow like a box of jewels" at night. As *Architectural Record* noted: "This may well be the most significant story of this rewarding building. To a structural system of great precision and beautiful proportions has been added a concern for light, and color, and the way people use and experience buildings: with *all* their senses and *all* their intellects."

KB

Brawne, Michael. "Looking Up: Suspended Ceilings as an Element in Interior Design." *Architectural Review* (September 1958): 160–170.

Dixon, John Morris. "Philip Johnson's Port Chester Synagogue Looks Good at 50, But Faces Functional Risks." *Docomoco US New York/Tri-State Newsletter* (Summer 2005): 3, 12.

Huxtable, Ada Louise. "He Adds Elegance to Modern Architecture." *New York Times Magazine* (May 24, 1964), 18.

Jacobus, John M., Jr. *Philip Johnson*. New York: Braziller, 1962.

"K.T.I. Synagogue, Port Chester, N.Y." *Architectural Record* (June 1955): 186–188.

"K.T.I. Synagogue, Port Chester, N.Y." *Architectural Record* (December 1959): 124–129.

Yale University Library, Manuscripts and Archives, Richard Kelly Papers.

opposite: Kneses Tifereth Israel Synagogue, interior view. Arts of the United States Collection, University of Georgia.

above: Kneses Tifereth Israel Synagogue, exterior view

Munson-Williams-Proctor Arts Institute

Location: 310 Genesee Street, Utica, New York
Completed: 1959
Architect: Philip Johnson
Lighting installation: 1959

The Munson-Williams-Proctor Arts Institute is a regional fine arts center, originally founded in 1919 and named after three generations of one Utica family. Designed by Philip Johnson, the museum followed structural principles established several years earlier by Mies van der Rohe at Crown Hall, on the campus of the Illinois Institute of Technology in Chicago: a pure solid, elevated several feet above ground level, is straddled by deep girders resting on exterior piers to create an open and unimpeded interior, where two floors of galleries surround a large skylit courtyard. Aboveground the box is entirely opaque, while belowground Johnson introduced a dry moat to allow for floor-to-ceiling glass on three sides.

In keeping with Johnson's design, Kelly called for deep vertical baffles to soften the daylight in the central court, such as the ones he had used at the Davis House, also designed by Johnson for an art collection, and for overhead artificial lighting in the galleries. As Kelly made clear in an article for *Museum News*, he aimed to eliminate the "chaotic brightness shifts and color changes" inherent in daylight, as well as preserve uninterrupted wall surfaces for exhibition purposes. Kelly, in consultation with his longtime collaborator Edison Price, developed a remarkably flexible lighting system of fixed recessed fixtures and surface-mounted supplemental lighting for the galleries that together allowed a broad range of effects and could accommodate different types of art exhibitions.
SE/SI

Jordy, William. "The Mies-less Johnson." *Architectural Forum* (September 1959): 114–123.
Kelly, Richard. "Museum Lighting." *Museum News* (May 1959): 16–19.
"Museum of Art, Munson Williams Proctor Institute, Utica, New York." *Architectural Design* 31 (August 1961): 342.
"A New Museum for the Munson-Williams-Proctor Institute." *Arts and Architecture* 75 (February 1958): 29.
"The Perfect, Professional Museum." *Architectural Forum* 113 (December 1960): 90–95.
Yale University Library, Manuscripts and Archives, Richard Kelly Papers.

above left: Munson-Williams-Proctor Institute, gallery view. Photograph: Ezra Stoller © Esto.
above right: Munson-Williams-Proctor Institute, central court. Photograph: Ezra Stoller © Esto.

New York University Institute of Fine Arts, Duke House

Location: 1 East Seventy-eighth Street, New York, N.Y.
Completed: 1912; renovated, 1958–1959
Architect: Horace Trumbauer
Architects for renovation: Robert Venturi, Paul Cope, and Mather Lippincott
Lighting installation: 1959

Nanaline Duke, the widow of tobacco magnate James B. Duke, and their daughter Doris donated the family's thirty-two-room mansion on Fifth Avenue to New York University in 1958 for use by its Institute of Fine Arts. Like many of Horace Trumbauer's designs, the house was based on a French neoclassical precedent: the eighteenth-century Hôtel Labottière in Bordeaux. Robert Venturi, in association with Paul Cope and Mather Lippincott, was given the renovation project as one of his very first commissions after leaving the office of Louis Kahn. The architects were faced with the task of converting the mansion into a practical educational building housing classrooms and a library without destroying its original character.

Venturi consciously chose to protect the building's original interiors. To avoid harming the wooden panels and decorative work, the shelving, projection equipment, and lighting were all installed so as to require few contact points with the walls. On the second floor, seven bed and sitting rooms were remodeled into a library, with each room housing a different field or period of art. As Venturi stated in *Complexity and Contradiction*, their approach was "to touch the inside as little as possible and to create harmony between the old and the new through contrasting juxtapositions: to separate the joint between the old and new layers, to create change by adding to rather than modifying the existing interior elements, to consider the new elements furniture rather than architecture and to use furniture and equipment which is commonplace and standard but enhanced by its uncommon setting." Following these criteria, they installed plain steel shelving to hold the library's book collection. Kelly, who had been brought in to create a modern lighting scheme adapted to the mansion's new uses, designed metal brackets that attached directly to the uprights of these shelves and held the lighting fixtures that illumined the books. Most of the mansion's original fixtures were retained but were supplemented with such features as recessed flush lighting in the library ceiling, to facilitate note taking. In the study rooms, individual lamps designed by Kelly were hung above the tables. These were attached to movable rings set into tracks on the ceiling, allowing individuals to adjust the height and position as needed, and removing the clutter of cords and floor outlets. Kelly had used just such a design in his own New York City apartment.

KB

Brownlee, David B., David G. DeLong, and Kathryn B. Hiesinger. *Out of the Ordinary: Robert Venturi, Denise Scott Brown and Associates*. Philadelphia: Philadelphia Museum of Art, 2001.

Dolkart, Andrew S. *Touring the Upper East Side, Walks in Five Historic Districts*. New York: Landmarks Conservancy, 1996.

Dunster, David, ed. *Venturi and Rauch: The Public Buildings*. London: Academy Editions, 1978.

"Rhythmic Play Between Tradition and Modern Converts Fifth Avenue Mansion to Scholastic Institution." *Interiors* (March 1960): 120–125.

Venturi, Robert. *Complexity and Contradiction in Architecture*. New York: Museum of Modern Art, 1966.

Yale University Library, Manuscripts and Archives, Richard Kelly Papers.

above left: New York University Institute of Fine Arts, Duke House, library lamps
above right: Duke House, hallway

Quincy House, Harvard University

Location: 58 Plympton Street, Cambridge, Massachusetts
Completed: 1959
Architects: Shepley, Bulfinch, Richardson, and Abbott
Lighting installation: 1959

Quincy House was added to the Harvard campus in the postwar years, the "Eighth House" (as it was originally called) to fit President A. Lawrence Lowell's vision of a "gentlemen around the breakfast table" system of housing, which he inaugurated in the 1930s. Each of these houses contained not only a dormitory but also a library, dining hall, apartments for faculty, commons rooms, and other spaces. The firm of Shepley, Bulfinch, Richardson, and Abbott was required to incorporate Mather Hall, a Georgian Revival building already on campus, into its design. To this traditional structure, the architects added an eight-story modernist high-rise to contain student housing, along with a two-story commons wing and a separate library. Presumably referring to Mather Hall, the architects wrote: "A conscious effort was made to counterbalance the rich detailing of carved pediments, incised cornices, and other Georgian paraphernalia by special lighting effects. Students being in residence mostly during winter months of short daylight, it was thought that a carefully worked-out pattern of lighting . . . would fulfill this purpose best" (*Progressive Architecture*).

Kelly spoke of the design in a brochure for Luxtrol light controls: "Because Quincy House is a residence, we wanted to make the lounge spaces and dining room as gracious and non-institutional-looking as possible. Although it is the home of hundreds of young men, Quincy House must have the atmosphere of the individual homes from which they came." The intensity of lighting was controllable, so that a single room such as the dining hall could be lit for quite different purposes, including meetings, concerts, and lectures. More people in a room required stronger lighting, "because people soak up light," while for smaller groups, a homelike effect was created with dimmers. Special downlights were installed on the main staircase to highlight the features of a relief sculpture by Constantino Nivola, while recessed fixtures created pools of light on the lobby floor. The same fixtures were employed on the exterior, forming circular patterns of light along the walkways. On the facade, the illumined windows stood out against the dark wall, creating a geometric pattern of horizontal and vertical rectangles. Contrasts in the architectural design were complemented by contrasts in the lighting: "We achieved [the] effect with light and shadow, background light and focal pools of light. . . . Quincy House provides an example of how adjustable lighting is used to make large areas comfortable and appealing."
KB

"Case History No. 5: Dining Hall." Luxtrol Light Controls publicity brochure, ca. 1959.
"The Eighth House." *Progressive Architecture* (September 1960): 134–141.
"Eighth House Will Perpetuate the Open Mind in the Ivory Tower." *Interiors* (February 1958): 80–81.
"Quincy House." *Architectural Record* (February 1959): 160–161.
Yale University Library, Manuscripts and Archives, Richard Kelly Papers.

above left: Harvard University, Quincy House, facade at night
above right: Harvard University, Quincy House, general purpose room

La Fonda del Sol Restaurant

Location: Time-Life Building, 1271 Avenue of the Americas, New York, N.Y.
Completed: 1960
Architect (interior design): Alexander Girard
Lighting installation: 1960

One of the most memorable restaurant designs in early 1960s New York was at La Fonda del Sol. Located inside the new Time-Life Building, the restaurant was designed by Alexander Girard, who was widely recognized for his contributions to American textile design. Commissioned by Jerome Brody of Restaurant Associates, Inc., who also managed Philip Johnson's Four Seasons, the restaurant imitated a Mexican village and featured a "sun" theme based on motifs derived from various Latin American countries.

Kelly's lighting scheme for the restaurant complemented Girard's theme, creating the illusion of an outdoor dining space. The dropped ceiling, meant to simulate grilles used for shade in hot climates, was a screen made of diamond-shaped wood and aluminum pieces. Pinhole lights above the screen simulated the sky and created an effect like that of "10,000 twinkling stars." An adobe house set under a "blacked out" ceiling surrounded the bar area. Kelly concealed darklights designed by Edison Price around the perimeter, thereby making it seem to glow against the "shadowy horizon." Built into the walls of the adobe house and the main dining room were glass-enclosed, air-conditioned niches housing hundreds of folk art objects selected from Girard's personal collection. These were specially lit by cool fluorescent lights of a very low brightness that would protect the valuable art objects yet ensure that they were still brilliantly showcased. A cocktail lounge outside the adobe house imitated a sidewalk café at sunset. Lit during the day by filtered sunlight streaming through vertical window blinds, the scene was illumined at night by fluorescent lights from above. According to the *New York Herald Tribune*, the most beautiful part of the restaurant was actually the ladies' room, and one of its most extraordinary aspects was the lighting. Kelly installed candle-size light bulbs in rows on the ceiling. Reflected in a mirror and repeated in a trompe l'oeil mural, the seemingly endless rows of light created a stunning effect. La Fonda del Sol was described by the *New York Herald Tribune* as "a feast for the eye, independent of the food. Above all the decor refreshes tired psyches, banishes belligerent reactions, and sets digestive juices harmoniously aflow."

SE/KB

Claiborne, Craig. "Latin American Zest on Midtown Menu." *New York Times*, December 9, 1960.
Claiborne, Craig. "3 City Restaurants Boast Dramatic New Interiors." *New York Times*, September 22, 1960.
"The Inn of the Sun." *New York Herald Tribune*, September 29, 1960.
Piña, Leslie A., and Stanley Abercrombie. *Alexander Girard Designs for Herman Miller*, 2nd ed. Atglen, Pa.: Schiffer, 2002
Yale University Library, Manuscripts and Archives, Richard Kelly Papers.

above: La Fonda del Sol Restaurant, interior view

Chase Manhattan Bank

Location: One Chase Manhattan Plaza, New York, N.Y.
Completed: 1961
Architect: Skidmore, Owings, and Merrill (Gordon Bunshaft)
Lighting installation: 1961

David Rockefeller, president of Chase Manhattan Bank, commissioned Skidmore, Owings, and Merrill to design the bank's new downtown headquarters in 1955. Under the supervision of Gordon Bunshaft, SOM developed a striking sixty-story aluminum and glass tower rising from a plaza set into the tight surrounding urban fabric. *Progressive Architecture* described the completed building, confidently standing apart from its older masonry neighbors, as a "shaft of light introduced into a dungeon." Coming on the heels of the Seagram Building, it adopted many and improved on some of its features. A remarkable 70 percent of its 2 1/2-acre site was given to open space, including a circular sunken courtyard with Isamu Noguchi sculptures and a reflecting pool. Unlike the Seagram, the much taller 813-foot tower rose uninterrupted as a perfect geometric body, accessible on all four sides. The light color of the aluminum cladding, the openness of the lobby with its banking hall, and the display of a superb contemporary art collection conveyed a sense of banking as a civic-minded, accessible, and transparent operation. The longitudinal footprint allowed a more functional distribution of offices along the perimeter, forty feet deep on the southern side, thirty feet deep on the north.

Richard Kelly was involved in every aspect of the lighting design. Seagram's image of a glowing tower of light, thanks to luminous ceilings around the perimeter, was not pursued here. The ceilings in most offices are equipped with more economical individual Lightolier units, or with a series of recessed downlights in the less bright executive areas. A continuous luminous ceiling is used in the computer department, where 80,000 square feet of Smithcraft Integrated Lighting was installed. It featured open white coffers with fluorescent lights inside.

As in the Seagram Building, the lobby's elevator cores are lit from recessed darklights in the ceiling, but since the walls are significantly higher (thirty feet versus twenty-four), the light hits the walls about six feet lower, resulting in a scalloping upper edge of lights. Milky-white diffusing glass turns the revolving doors into luminous cylinders. Instead of the concentrated perimeter lighting at the Seagram Building, the soffits outside feature a regular grid of downlights with a less intense illumination on the ground.

Because of the sloping terrain and the need to provide vehicular basement access, the surrounding plaza is raised above the adjoining streets. Kelly designed banks of floodlights on neighboring buildings to keep the plaza safe, and to complement the soft pool of light on the ground. **SI/DN**

"The Chase, Portrait of a Giant." *Architectural Forum* 115 (July 1961): 66–95.
Stern, Robert A. M., Thomas Mellins, and David Fishman. *New York, 1960: Architecture and Urbanism Between the Second World War and the Bicentennial*. New York: Monacelli, 1995.
"Tower with a Front Yard." *Architectural Forum* 106 (April 1957): 110–115.
"Towering HQ for N.Y.'s Chase Manhattan Bank to Leave 70 Percent of Site Open." *Progressive Architecture* (May 1956): 86–87.
Yale University Library, Manuscripts and Archives, Richard Kelly Papers.

above left: Chase Manhattan Bank, waiting room for executive offices
above right: Chase Manhattan Bank, central check clearing office
opposite: Chase Manhattan Bank, exterior view

Dumbarton Oaks Gallery

Location: 1703 Thirty-second Street, Washington, D.C.
Completed: 1962
Architect: Philip Johnson
Lighting installation: 1962

Philip Johnson was commissioned in 1959 to design a garden pavilion for the Robert Woods Bliss Collection of Pre-Columbian Art at Dumbarton Oaks, a noted research institution located in the Georgetown district of Washington, D.C. Johnson proposed an interplay between the art and its garden setting with a grid of eight intersecting twenty-five-foot circular galleries—"spools of space," as *Architectural Forum* put it—each enclosed in curved glass and supported by eight columns, and all framing interstitial potted trees and overlooking an open central court and fountain.

Johnson, by now Kelly's most important patron, called upon him to design lighting effective for a museum but in sympathy with the pavilion's rigorous formal simplicity. To that end, Kelly accentuated the shallow domes atop each gallery with hidden cove lighting to wash the vault above and downlights recessed into the ceiling at the impost to brighten the floor below; he accented the column of water that rose from the central fountain with four underwater uplights; and, outside, he called for fascia-mounted downlights to illuminate and differentiate the glass-walled corridor that led to the nine-square pavilion.
SE/SI

Alexis, Karin. "A Tribute to Washington Classicism from Philip Johnson." *Washington Business Journal*, February 22, 2008. http://washington.bizjournals.com/washington/stories/2008/02/25/focus16.html.

Dumbarton Oaks Research Library and Collection Museum Pre-Columbian Collection. "Philip Johnson Pavilion." Washington, D.C.: Dumbarton Oaks Research Library and Collection. www.doaks.org/museum/pco_collection/philip_johnson_pavilion.

Petit, Emmanuel. *Philip Johnson: The Constancy of Change*. New Haven: Yale University Press, 2009.

"Recent Work of Philip Johnson." *Architectural Record* 132 (July 1962): 113–128.

Yale University Library, Manuscripts and Archives, Richard Kelly Papers.

above: Dumbarton Oaks Gallery, interior view. Photograph: Ezra Stoller © Esto.

Lincoln Center, Philharmonic Hall (Avery Fisher Hall)

Location: New York, N.Y.
Completed: 1962
Architect: Max Abramovitz of Harrison and Abramovitz
Lighting installation: 1962

The Philharmonic Hall at Lincoln Center was the first among a suite of buildings for Manhattan's new performing arts complex. Richard Kelly worked closely with Max Abramovitz on the lighting design as well as the selection of materials and color. Kelly even supervised the fabric selection for the auditorium seating. To camouflage the acoustical props and devices introduced by the hall's acoustician, Leo L. Beranek, Kelly and Abramovitz decided to paint the walls in a strong, unifying royal blue. The retractable acoustical "clouds," suspended from a metal grid under the ceiling, however, were covered in gold leaf and each adorned by a small sparkling light bulb.

At night, the auditorium walls were lightwashed on the outside to become visible beyond the enclosing glass walls. On each floor recessed lights in the ceiling and low-wattage bulbs provided a warm ambient glow. Ada Louise Huxtable found the building "handsome by day" and remarkably beautiful by night: "from the outside, the drama of light, movement and color, seen through the glass walls, enclosed by the great tapered frame, makes the structure a spectacular success in action" (*New York, 1960*).

Soon after its completion, Kelly commented in *Industrial Design* that "the lighting issue was submerged in the roar over the acoustics." Indeed, the sound was immediately criticized by the audience and by musicians who claimed they were unable to hear each other on the stage. After a few years of unsuccessful attempts at improving the acoustics, Philip Johnson and John Burgee were asked to completely redesign the interior. Their new space opened as Avery Fisher Hall in 1976.

KO/DN

Dorr, Maude. "Lighting Consultants." *Industrial Design* (June 1963): 40–47.

"Lincoln Center, New York." *Architectural Record* 132 (September 1962): 133–148, 196–204.

"Lincoln Center Starts Building Philharmonic Hall." *Architectural Forum* 110 (June 1959): 7.

Newhouse, Victoria. *Wallace K. Harrison*. New York: Rizzoli, 1989.

"Philharmonic Hall, Lincoln Center, New York City, N.Y." *Architectural Forum* 110 (June 1959): 12.

Stern, Robert A. M., Thomas Mellins, and David Fishman. *New York, 1960: Architecture and Urbanism Between the Second World War and the Bicentennial*, 2nd ed. New York: Monacelli, 1997.

Yale University Library, Manuscripts and Archives, Richard Kelly Papers.

Young, Edgar B. *Lincoln Center: The Building of an Institution*. New York: New York University Press, 1980.

above left: Lincoln Center, Philharmonic Hall, auditorium
above right: Lincoln Center, Philharmonic Hall, exterior at night

Bankers Trust Building

Location: 280 Park Avenue, New York, N.Y.
Completed: 1963
Architects: Henry Dreyfuss and Emery Roth and Sons
Lighting Installation: 1963

Emery Roth's Bankers Trust Building, located about ten blocks south of the Seagram Building on Park Avenue, showed how the latter's generosity of space had failed to become a repeatable paradigm. The plot of land was smaller, and railroad tracks underneath it led to constraints in the spatial layout. The main banking hall had to be moved up to the mezzanine level, its luminous ceiling visible from the street.

Some of Kelly's vocabulary is clearly in evidence, such as a dense row of downlights around the perimeter of the building, where, simultaneously, hidden lamps aim upward at the underside of the soffits. The protruding penthouse roof above the fourteenth floor reflects the beam of uplights on the terrace. Luminous screens are visible on two floors for mechanical systems in the setback tower above. Lobbies on the first floor and on the executive levels feature the wall washers known from the Seagram Building.

But, for Kelly, who "introduced an unusual blending of brightness patterns throughout traffic and work areas," this project was also a place for considerable innovation. With Edison Price he developed a new fixture for the luminous ceiling, which directed light almost exclusively downward, through specially designed parabolic louvers, so that the luminaires seemed as if they were "not lighted when seen from a normal viewing angle." Instead, floors and walls seemed to be emanating light. The directional filter helped to concentrate the light from the thirty-watt fluorescent lamps above it, and increased the average light level at the workplace by 24 percent. Price had applied for a patent for these louvers in 1959, and it was granted on January 16, 1962.

In a complete reversal of the Seagram Building's "tower of light" approach, here the first floors looked as if they were not lit at all. Consequently, Kelly returned to the idea of floodlighting the facade from the outside. Several PAR 64 500-watt narrow-beam projectors in baffled boxes along the planters on the edges of the sidewalk shine upward and graze the facade's pattern of precast masonry and glass.
DN

Fisher, W. S. "New and Different." *Light* 32, no. 1 (1963): 10–15.
Stern, Robert A. M., Thomas Mellins, and David Fishman. *New York, 1960: Architecture and Urbanism Between the Second World War and the Bicentennial.* New York: Monacelli, 1995.
"Who Turned Out the Lights?" *Retailer's Review* 8 (May–June 1963): 5–9.
Wilson, Jeannette Light. "What's New in Illumination." *Building Products* (May 1964): 12–16.
Yale University Library, Manuscripts and Archives, Richard Kelly Papers.

above left: Bankers Trust, executive lounge
above right: Bankers Trust, first floor lobby
opposite: Bankers Trust, exterior view at night

Dulles International Airport

Location: Chantilly, Virginia
Completed: 1963; expanded 1966
Architect: Eero Saarinen
Lighting installation: 1963–1966

Eero Saarinen was hired to design the terminal and the control tower at Dulles Airport by the engineering firm Ammann and Whitney, which had received the government commission for a second airport in the Washington, D.C., area—the first civilian airport designed specifically for jets. Saarinen's terminal building provided two floors, the upper one consisting of one continuous space, 600 feet long and 150 feet wide, under a hanging roof of reinforced concrete, suspended from two rows of sixteen concrete pylons, 40 feet apart.

Edgar Kaufmann Jr. was more observant than any other critic in describing Saarinen's sculptural building and its appearance at night: "The terminus is lit by a few downlights from the roof (a necklace of these lies outside each window bay), echoed loosely in the reflected image of uplights from the balustrade. A more direct brilliance comes down from the lighted ceilings of the ticket and concession structures and the door canopies, properly serving areas of focused activity. Up from the roofs of the ticket and concession structures, a wash of light is spread over the center of the hanging roof, which thus is lit at each edge and in the center, leaving in semi-shadow the areas where curved glass walls meet curved roof plane—a sensible, gentle act." Indeed, the lighting of the hall's great space, the area in front of it, and the mighty roof, thrusting upward while punctured by the pylons one expects to support it, proved to be a complex and delicate task. Richard Kelly solved it with great elegance. From the flat roofs of the central check-in and commercial structures, floodlights illuminate the swoop of the ceiling, fading toward the top. On the outside, however, beyond the curved glass facade, the continuing concrete skin is lit from a series of uplights in the balustrade on the ground.

The first floor houses the baggage-claim area for arriving passengers as well as offices. Here, we find a continuous luminous ceiling, similar to the one provided in Idlewild's arrival area. Documents in the archive show that Kelly was also involved in the lighting of some of the outside areas near the tarmac and the parking lot.

DN

"A New Airport for Jets." *Architectural Record* (March 1960): 175–182.
"Our Two Largest Airports." *Progressive Architecture* (August 1963): 86–101.
Pelkonen, Eeva-Liisa, and Donald Albrecht. *Eero Saarinen: Shaping the Future*. New Haven: Yale University Press, 2006.
"Washington to Get a Swooping Saarinen Air Terminal." *Progressive Architecture* (March 1960): 57–59.
Yale University Library, Manuscripts and Archives, Richard Kelly Papers.

above: Dulles International Airport, exterior view at night. Photograph: Ezra Stoller © Esto.

Humble Oil and Refining Company (ExxonMobil Building)

Location: 800 Bell Avenue, Houston, Texas
Completed: 1964
Architect: Welton Becket and Associates
Lighting installation: 1964

The Humble Oil Building, currently known as the ExxonMobil Building, was the tallest building in Texas when it was built. It was designed by the Los Angeles architect Welton Becket, who headed one of the largest architecture firms in the world at the time. The building's design featured innovative architectural solutions, such as an air-conditioning system integrated into the ground-level parking area and, on every floor, seven-foot cantilevers on every floor that blocked out the summer sun.

Richard Kelly was hired as a consultant primarily for the exterior and the street-level lighting of the building, and his comprehensive reports described in detail the ways in which various lighting effects could be employed for the facade, roof, and entrances. In a plan that recalled lighting designer Bassett Jones's unexecuted scheme of 1924 for the Chicago Tribune Tower, Kelly wished to install, in his own words, "a crown formed by a repeating pattern of warm colored light sources (recalling firelight) occurring completely around the parapet at the 45th floor." These light sources, studied closely for their atmospheric effects in charcoal and pen drawings by Kelly, were in some designs "steam plumes," with three 1,500-watt floodlights positioned in eighteen pipes of twelve-foot length, and in others, treelike forms, described as "chandeliers," eighteen inches in diameter and holding glass or plastic globes as luminaires extending radially from the "trunk." Perhaps most astonishingly, Kelly suggested that the ring of fire could be formed by actual gas flames mounted every few feet above the parapet. In order to emphasize the building's verticality, Kelly recommended the placement of cool colored lights to illuminate the marble columns of the north and south facades. In addition, horizontal bands of cool light would encircle the three mechanical equipment floors, while a warmer band of light would surround the forty-second-floor soffit. Kelly stated that these bands would tie together the otherwise randomly lighted effect of the building's windows at night. Although the clients were very impressed by Kelly's dramatic scheme for the roof, they were ultimately swayed by financial concerns and limited his contribution to the facade and entryways. A year after the building's completion, the owners decorated the plaza for the Christmas holiday season with treelike lighting fixtures that closely emulated Kelly's early sketches and created a field of flickering lights.
SE/KB

"Design Against Sun and Glare." *Architectural Record* 134 (October 1963): 173–178.
Hunt, William Dudley. *Total Design: Architecture of Welton Becket.* New York: McGraw-Hill, 1971.
Jones, Bassett. "Structures in Light." *Light* (April 1924): 6.
Yale University Library, Manuscripts and Archives, Richard Kelly Papers.

above left: Humble Oil and Refining Company, exterior view at night
above right: Humble Oil and Refining Company, Kelly's sketch for the forty-fifth floor

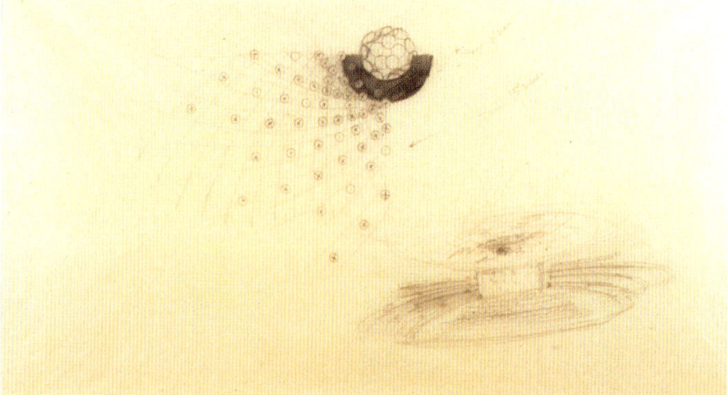

Lincoln Center, New York State Theater

Location: New York, N.Y.
Completed: 1964
Architect: Philip Johnson
Lighting installation: 1964

Lincoln Center was conceived in the mid-1950s under the banner of urban renewal as a cultural beacon and urban complex in the tradition of the commercially successful Rockefeller Center. Designed by architect Philip Johnson, the New York State Theater was the second of three large theaters to flank the plaza at the center of Wallace K. Harrison's master plan. Richard Kelly designed the lighting for all the buildings of the complex except for the interior of the Metropolitan Opera House.

Kelly illuminated Johnson's multistory lobby entrance with canister downlights that reflected brilliantly off the marble mosaic floor. Similar but smaller fixtures illuminated waiting areas immediately outside the theater beneath the terrace and balcony where patrons could mingle during intermissions around the cocktail bar. Inside the theater, one of Kelly's key concepts, the play of brilliants, came to the fore, as an appropriate backdrop for an exciting theatrical experience. Spotlights in the ceiling were concealed by a geometric starburst of curvilinear anodized bronze and aluminum bars inset with six-inch-diameter metallic star fixtures made from thermoformed Plexiglas. At the center of the auditorium sparkled a brilliant chandelier composed of spherical cullets, a design based on the structure of titanium diamond crystals (Cooley and Tanteri). The star motif was repeated on each of the three rows of balconies, where Kelly placed decorative spherical globe lights. Each of these fixtures was backed by a reflector creating patterns of diamondlike scintillation. On the exterior toward the plaza, Kelly lit each column with one stem-mounted dodecahedron downlight, complemented by angled downlights on the interior column face.

TE/EH

Cooley, Renee, and Matthew Tanteri. *Richard Kelly Selected Works: An Exhibition of Works Presented by IESNY and the Richard Kelly Grant.* New York: Illuminating Engineering Society of New York, 2007.

Kelly, Richard. "Lighting's Role in Architecture." *Architectural Forum* 102 (February 1955): 152, 169, 172.

Martin, Ralph. *Lincoln Center for the Performing Arts.* Englewood Cliffs, N.J.: Prentice-Hall, 1971.

"Plexiglas in Lighting." Case Study 7, commercial brochure in Richard Kelly Papers.

Schulze, Franz. *Philip Johnson: Life and Work.* New York: Knopf, 1994.

Stern, Robert A. M., Thomas Mellins, and David Fishman. *New York, 1960: Architecture and Urbanism Between the Second World War and the Bicentennial.* New York: Monacelli, 1995.

Varnelis, Kazys, ed. *The Philip Johnson Tapes: Interviews by Robert A. M. Stern.* New York: Monacelli, 2008.

Yale University Library, Manuscripts and Archives, Richard Kelly Papers.

above left: Lincoln Center, New York State Theater, exterior view at night
above right: Lincoln Center, New York State Theater, Kelly's sketch for the chandelier
opposite: Lincoln Center, New York State Theater, auditorium, view to chandelier above. Photograph: Ezra Stoller © Esto.

Urban Lighting Projects: Corcovado Statue of Christ, Flamengo Park, Sugar Loaf Mountain

Location: Rio de Janeiro, Brazil
Completed: 1964
Architects: Heitor da Silva Costa, designer, and Paul Landowski, sculptor (Statue of Christ); Roberto Burle Marx, landscape designer (Flamengo Park)
Lighting installation: 1964

In 1964 Kelly was invited by Carlos Lacerda, governor of the State of Guanabara in Brazil, for a visit to discuss a number of lighting projects for the state's capital, Rio de Janeiro. Kelly spent about a week in Rio in December 1964. Brazil had seen tumultuous times in recent months. On March 31, 1964, a military coup with covert American support had ended the government of President João Goulart, and a military dictatorship had taken over. For several months it still seemed as if new elections would be held fairly soon, and Lacerda intended to run for president. His highly visible improvement projects for Rio in 1964 were intended to increase his profile as a public-minded and visionary politician. Kelly met with Governor Lacerda on December 7 and developed ideas for the projects they had discussed over the following days, which he laid out in a series of letters to the governor and the chairwoman of the city's development committee, Maria Lota de Macedo Soares.

The most pressing commission was the new and improved illumination of the Christ statue on Corcovado Mountain, sitting atop a 710-meter (2,329 feet) granite peak, and standing 39.6 meters (130 feet) tall. The local engineer Heitor da Silva Costa had designed the statue in 1921, based on a sculpture by the French artist Paul Landowski. Now, for the first time, the statue was going to be completely and competently lit. Pope Paul II had already been asked to inaugurate the new lighting remotely from Rome on New Year's Eve. Kelly worked very quickly to develop a temporary installation, with clustered floodlights in seven locations surrounding the statue, successfully illuminated for the first time on December 31, 1964; Brazilian technicians later converted Kelly's makeshift arrangement into a permanent installation.

The second large project that Kelly was asked to consider was the lighting of Flamengo Park, which had recently been created on a stretch of land by Rio's downtown waterfront that had been claimed for the 1922 centennial exhibition and used only sporadically since then. Now, a new Museum of Modern Art had been built there by Affonso Eduardo Reidy, and Brazil's most prominent landscape designer, Roberto Burle Marx, had designed the park. Philip Johnson had recommended Kelly as "the only man in the world who could advise you properly on the illumination of your beautiful park. It is the kind of work, only on a larger scale, that he has done so successfully for me." John Marstaller, who worked in Kelly's office at the time, remembers it as a "giant sprawling land area with forest-like groves, paved strolling areas, athletic facilities, but also two freeways through the park. All was to be lighted at night for warm weather nighttime usage. Kelly developed the first high-mast lighting installation, allowing relatively few very tall light poles housing groups of individual directable floodlights. Kelly worked with Burle Marx personally in Rio, but brought back plans and layouts to be drawn up in the office, as well as illumination levels to be calculated by his in-office illumination engineer." Kelly wrote to Macedo Soares: "This

could be the most beautiful, human, urban place not only in South America but in the world." He suggested tall poles with invisible luminaries lighting up wide areas of green, complemented by smaller, shadowy areas with the "scintillation of beautiful, small, lower lights." Kelly had some new "metallic vapor" lamp in mind, which makes "green plants look fresh and people's faces glamorous."

Kelly then outlined briefly his philosophy: "What people see with their eyes registers in the subconscious mind and heart, through natural subliminal actions, as truth. Creation of such a night-image as I spoke of above would do more to make the jewel of the harbor of Rio live in man's memory as a trade-mark of the whole Brazilian nation than information centers and tons of printed paper and newspaper stories. Such an image lives for everyone's lifetime."

The third large project that Kelly was asked to consider for Rio's new nocturnal landscape was the illumination of Sugar Loaf Mountain, whose characteristic steep form dominated the city's horizon. Kelly wrote to Governor Lacerda on December 9, 1964: "I think that your project of illuminating the Sugar Loaf is very workable and easily done." Kelly decided on four locations for the equipment, to "make the true shape and height of the Sugar Loaf apparent to everyone in all parts of Rio, and also to ships arriving in the harbor. The four locations are: one on the north-east of the Ponta do Leme; a second half-way out above Praia Vermelha; the third behind the eastern height of Orca; and the fourth on the point southeast of the Fort of S. Joao. None of the beams of strong light coming from these locations would disturb anyone, anywhere."

"I feel it would be a mistake to try to floodlight the entire mountain equally, but rather I would like to create a glowing top, crowned with new scintillation for the small park," he continued. "I would let the glow at the top diminish gradually down the sides and increase again only at the base of the rock. This arrangement seems to me to be suggestively descriptive and strong in subtlety to bring out the real character of the Sugar Loaf in all its solidity and majesty. . . . As you yourself said when I saw you Monday, the nighttime image of the harbor of Rio can be one of the Brazilian nation's greatest symbols."

During Kelly's visit, Governor Lacerda asked him to study a new low-cost housing project, which had been financed by the Kennedy administration's Alliance for Progress program of the 1960s. Originally named Villa Progresso, its name was changed to Villa Kennedy after the president's assassination. Kelly suggested a similar approach as in Flamengo Park: to modify and partially shield the existing tall street lamps, and complement them with the sparkle of small shaded light sources. This concept was not executed. The housing complex soon deteriorated into a slum.

DN

Kelly, Richard. Letter to Governor Carlos Lacerda, December 9, 1964, Yale University Library, Manuscripts and Archives, Richard Kelly Papers.
Kelly, Richard. Letter to Miss Maria Lota de Macedo Soares.
Marstaller, John. E-mail to Dietrich Neumann, October 26, 2009.

opposite left: Christ the Redeemer statue at night. Photograph: William J. Hebert/Stone/Getty Images.
opposite right: Flamengo Park at night. Photograph: Pulsar Imagens/Ricardo Azoury/LatinContent/Getty Images.
above: Sugarloaf Mountain at night. Photograph: Walter Firmo/SambaPhoto/Getty Images.

PEACHTREE CENTER

Peachtree Center

Location: Atlanta, Georgia
Completed: 1966
Architect: John Portman
Lighting installation: 1966

"Uniform, glare-free night lighting . . . is drawing architects and builders to the 30-story Peachtree Center office building in downtown Atlanta. . . . [It] has emerged as a beacon on the Atlanta skyline [and] attracts the eyes of evening strollers, motorists on distant expressways and air travelers," wrote the *Washington Post.* The reinforced-concrete office tower was the first building of a planned eight-acre complex to be developed in the following decade. Public attention for the pioneer was crucial for the ongoing success of this development, which justified the substantial costs of $150,000 for the installation of Richard Kelly's lighting scheme plus annual electricity and maintenance costs of another $12,000. Architect and developer John Portman commented that "the uniformity of lighting achieved here is a great technical advance. . . . Exterior lighting is much neglected by architects and builders, yet this type of lighting is the only way to preserve a structure's integrity and values after the sun goes down." In fact, this was a "landmark of urban development whose significance would not be lost under the stars."

In one of his few floodlight illuminations of an office tower, Richard Kelly developed a system of 264 diagonally directed narrow-beam floodlights that sent 270,000 watts from projectors at the base, creating a uniform lace pattern across the facade, which apparently was as bright at the top as at the bottom. According to Kelly, this was "exceedingly rare and . . . actually unique for a building of this size."

Just one year later, attention was focused on Portman's next building in this complex, the Regency Hyatt Hotel with a twenty-four-story atrium, considered by some critics "the most overwhelming architectural experience of the century." The lighting design, however, went to one of Kelly's competitors, Seymour Evans Associates.

DN

"Atlanta, the Hopeful City." *Fortune* 74 (August 1966): 155–156, 160, 162.
"Back to Babylon." *Interiors* 126 (July 1967): 68–77.
"Lighting Highlights New Atlanta Building." *Washington Post*, August 13, 1966.
"Regency Hyatt House: A Permanent Happening in Atlanta." *Interior Design* 38 (September 1967): 136–149.
Yale University Library, Manuscripts and Archives, Richard Kelly Papers.

opposite: Peachtree Center, exterior view at night. Photograph: John Portman & Associates.
above: Peachtree Center, exterior view from below. Photograph: John Portman & Associates.

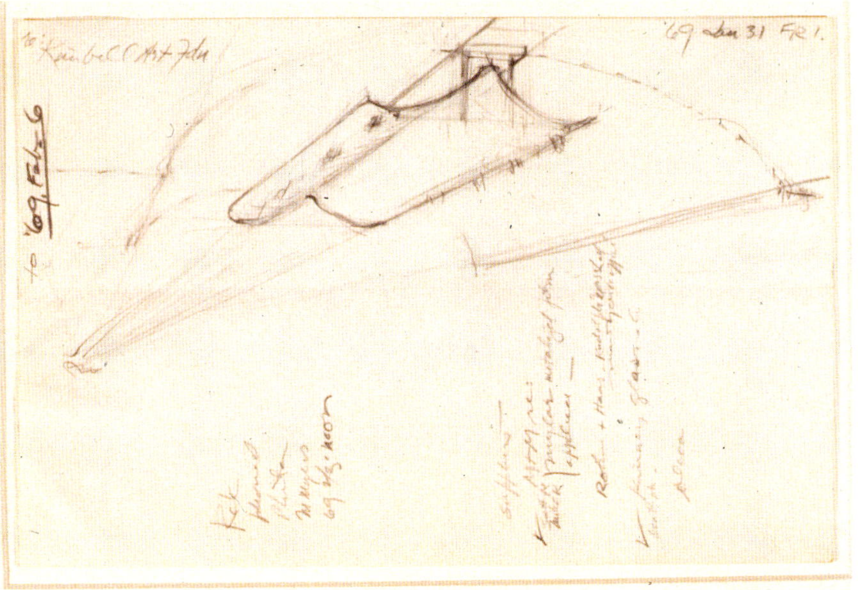

Kimbell Art Museum

Location: 3333 Camp Bowie Boulevard, Fort Worth, Texas
Completed: 1972
Architect: Louis Kahn
Lighting installation: 1972

In his lighting design for the Kimbell Art Museum, Richard Kelly answered Louis Kahn's call for an effective means of illuminating a museum interior by natural daylight without compromising the safety of the artwork on display. One of Kahn's final designs, the Kimbell was conceived with light in mind. In a 1967 lecture, he spoke of the effect he hoped to achieve: "I am designing an art museum in Texas. Here I felt that the light in the rooms structured in concrete will have the luminosity of silver. . . . This light will give a touch of silver to the room without touching the objects directly, yet give the comforting feeling of knowing the time of day" (quoted in Brawne). As Kelly remarked in *Progressive Architecture*, the Kimbell "is a great big museum built from scratch. Lou [Kahn] very excitedly thought of a structure of long barrel vaults, which opens up space and allows for change; there are no columns or wall to limit space. The vaults span 100 feet, and because 20 feet has been established as a good dimension for a room in which to view paintings, they are 20 feet wide, with 10 feet between them. Since everybody wanted the feel of daylight in the museum . . . the vaults are slotted to let in daylight. Right away there's a problem—contrast—as the slots would always be in the line of sight in barrel vault construction."

Kelly, in collaboration with Kahn and Edison Price, devised an ingenious solution to the problem of illuminating the barrel vaults. To diffuse the bright Texas light from the exterior to the interior of the gallery spaces, a long perforated metal reflector was placed under the slot at the top of the barrel vaults. The winged reflector was opaque at the point where it rose into the skylight in order to block direct sun and perforated on its undersides to allow some light to filter through and diminish the contrast between it and the concrete vault. This piece of "transparent metal" allows the color and variation of sky tone to be indirectly seen inside the gallery spaces. Daylight permeates the space at a fraction of its natural brightness, and reflectors hold incandescent lights for times when natural illumination is not practical.

Kelly, as quoted by Der Scutt, summarized his achievement: "All variety of daylight is manipulated in the Museum toward creating a delightful interior space for seeing great art. On sunny days the galleries form the excitement and color of the day. On cloudy days, the light is reflected into the interior with cool softness. Even fleecy or fierce clouds are visible inside."
KO/KB

Brawne, Michael. *Kimbell Art Museum, Louis I. Kahn*. London: Phaidon, 1992.

Cooley, Renee, and Matthew Tanteri. *Richard Kelly Selected Works: An Exhibition of Works Presented by IESNY and the Richard Kelly Grant*. New York: Illuminating Engineering Society of New York, 2007. www.iesny.org/Documents/RK_works_May07.pdf.

Kahn, Louis. *The Construction of the Kimbell Art Museum*. Turin, Italy: Skira Editore, 1999.

Kelly, Richard. "Lighting Starts with Daylight." *Progressive Architecture* 54 (September 1973): 82–85.

Loud, Patricia Cummings. *The Art Museums of Louis I. Kahn*. Durham: Duke University Press, 1989.

Scutt, Der. "Richard Kelly, 1910–1977: A Personal Memento." *Lighting Design and Application* (October 1979): 56–58.

Yale University Library, Manuscripts and Archives, Richard Kelly Papers.

opposite: Kimbell Art Museum, interior view with reflectors. Photograph: Ezra Stoller © Esto.
above: Kimbell Art Museum, Kelly's sketch of light reflector

Yale Center for British Art

Location: 1080 Chapel Street, New Haven, Connecticut
Completed: 1974
Architect: Louis Kahn
Lighting installation: 1974

The Yale Center for British Art was architect Louis Kahn's second commission for Yale University, coming almost twenty years after his Yale University Art Gallery of 1951–1953. The Center for British Art was designed specifically for the British art collection of Paul Mellon, a Yale graduate who funded the building, and included a museum, library, and auditorium, as well as ground floor retail shops. From the project's conception, museum director Jules Prown stressed the importance of light, requesting as much natural illumination as possible. When Louis Kahn died unexpectedly in 1974, the project was overseen by the firm of Pellecchia and Meyers, architects who had worked closely with Kahn in the past.

Kahn selected Richard Kelly as the building's lighting consultant in 1970 after their collaboration on the Kimbell Art Museum in Fort Worth. In both museums, the maximization of natural light was stressed as a major programmatic element. From the beginning, both designers were intent on using daylight as the primary light source for viewing the artwork. To do so they had to design a solution that would shield the paintings from exposure to direct sunlight. After numerous experiments by both Kelly and Kahn, a complex double-domed skylight that would diffuse natural light and minimize UV rays was adopted. The dome consisted of two layers of Plexiglas, the interior one of which was UV protected. Between the two layers a structural "T" member supported customized louvers directing light through a translucent cellular panel to the space below. The diffused skylight system was deployed over the entire roof and allowed for specified light control as required. Electric light was added below each module on tracks for use only when necessary, most commonly during the winter months.

EH

Abercrombie, Stanley. "Yale Center for British Art." *Contract Interiors* 136 (July 1977): 52–59.
Dean, Andrea Oppenheimer. "A Legacy of Light." *AIA Journal* 67 (mid-May 1978): 80–89.
Gast, Klaus-Peter. *Louis I. Kahn: Complete Works*. Munich: Deutsche Verlags-Anstalt, 2001.
Jordy, William H. "Kahn at Yale." *Architectural Review* 162 (July 1977): 37–44.
"Kahn's Last Work Opens at Yale." *Progressive Architecture* 58 (May 1977): 21.
Kelly, Richard. "Lighting Starts with Daylight." *Progressive Architecture* 54 (September 1973): 82–85.
Loud, Patricia Cummings. *The Art Museums of Louis I. Kahn*. Durham: Duke University Press, 1989.
"Opus Posthumous." *Progressive Architecture* 59 (May 1978): 76–81.
Prown, Jules David. "The Architecture of the Yale Center for British Art; Published on the Occasion of the Inauguration of the Yale Center for British Art." New Haven: Yale University, 1977.
Prown, Jules David. "Paul Mellon and the Architecture of the Yale Center for British Art." In *Paul Mellon's Legacy: A Passion for British Art*, by John Baskett et al., 13–25. New Haven: Yale University Press, 2007.
Scully, Vincent. "Yale Center for British Art." *Architectural Record* 161 (June 1977): 95–104.
Spiker, David, and Kirk Train. "The Yale Center for British Art." *Perspecta* 16 (1980): 50–61.
"Yale Center for British Art and British Studies, New Haven, Conn." *Architectural Record* (August 1974): 84.
Yale University Library, Manuscripts and Archives, Richard Kelly Papers.

above left: Yale Center for British Art, view across light court. Jeff Goldberg © Esto.
above right: Yale Center for British Art, Kelly's sketch for the skylight
opposite: Yale Center for British Art, skylight. Photograph: Roberto Schezen © Esto.

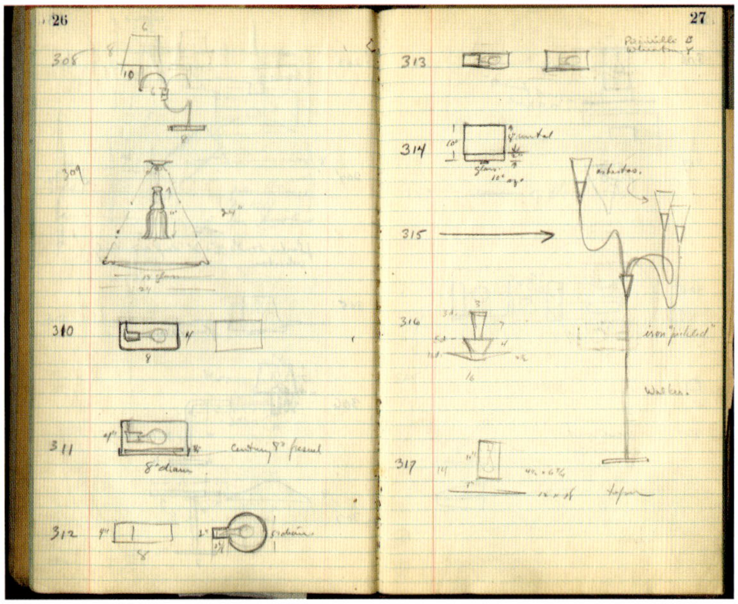

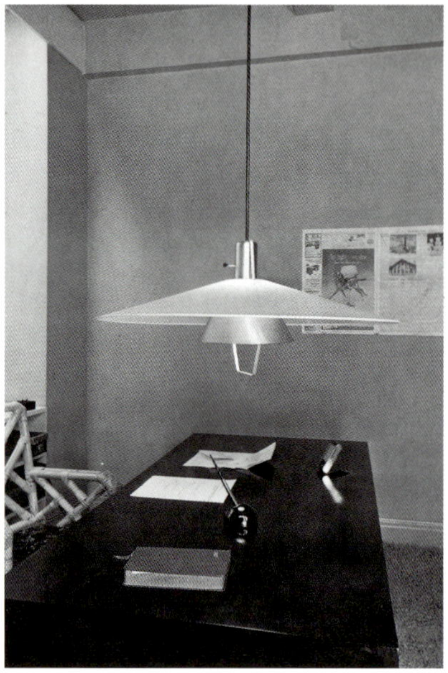

Lamp Designs

Completed: 1940–1959
Designer: Richard Kelly

While still a freshman at Columbia, Richard Kelly began his professional career designing lamps and fixtures and continued throughout his many years as a lighting designer. His papers contain several color sketches for lamps carrying the stamp of his firm Kelly and Thompson, which existed between 1938 and 1942, and an undated sheet with numerous thumbnail sketches of lamp designs with three-digit identifying numbers. With his simple and elegant designs of metal and glass, Kelly clearly aligned himself with other modernist lamp designers at the time, such as Kurt Versen, Walter von Nessen, and Poul Henningsen.

His first commercially available lamp, an aluminum and steel table lamp with a paper shade from 1940, made it into the Museum of Modern Art's exhibition of 1941–1942, organized by Eliot Noyes, titled *Useful Objects of American Design Under $10*. Thanks to its small glass dome on top, the lamp was able to cast a "focal glow" downward and provide some visible sparkle at the top. A saucer-topped design was employed for the Floating Baffle Lamp Number 711, which, according to Kelly's list of available lamps, could be reeled up and down from the ceiling to below eye level to meet the demands of the user and prevent glare.

In 1952 Kelly and Philip Johnson designed a bronze and aluminum floor lamp for the Glass House that was manufactured in small numbers by Edison Price. This early version was forty-one inches high, and consisted of a bronze light canister suspended between three vertical bronze struts, which sent its light up toward a polished circular reflector screen, from where it was distributed again downward. To avoid glare as much as possible, the light canister had interior baffles that prevented diagonal reflections from the interior of the can. The three legs proved unstable, and later versions of the lamp were produced with four. Besides the Glass House in New Canaan, this lamp shows up in a number of Kelly and Johnson's collaborative designs, such as the Burden Apartment and the Davis House, both from 1954.

The Home Fashions League, a group of women designers, gave Kelly one of its Trailblazer Awards in 1955. The winners were acknowledged for creating "a genuine departure in the design and styling of contemporary home furnishing" (*New York Times*). Kelly's Number 722 lamp was described as conventional in appearance but notable for its interior lighting arrangement, which consisted of a circle of six down bulbs for diffused light and two up bulbs for light to be reflected off a ceiling. Together, the bulbs provided enough lighting for a large room. Kelly had the lamp photographed as a double exposure, highlighting the eight-bulb arrangement as viewed through the shade.

For the 1953–1954 renovation of the Barbizon Plaza Hotel in New York, Kelly produced his perhaps best-known lamp design (and also the only one he patented): a wireless chandelier, which became an icon for the Barbizon and a milestone in fixture design. Kelly imagined the chandelier as "a galaxy of stars," and felt it epitomized "sparkle," one of the three fundamental types of light that he had described in several of his essays. Inspired by this vision, Kelly collaborated with the fabricator and engineer Edison Price. In what was promoted as the world's first wireless light fixture, low-voltage electrical current ran straight down a long nickel rod to a central hub, then out in all directions along twenty-

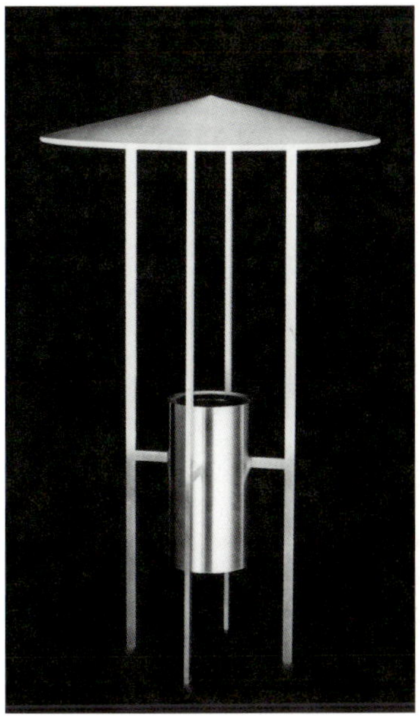

four narrow nickel rods, which branched again into four more nickel rods, each of which sprouted a small six-volt bulb, 192 in all. Inspired by Buckminster Fuller's contemporary "tensegrity" structures, the individual rods were held in place by thin wires. Twelve feet in diameter and slowly rotating in place, the entire metal chandelier weighed 140 pounds and was internally stable and self-supporting. It was also easily raised and lowered for replacing the bulbs when necessary. Kelly adapted the design to a smaller version dubbed the Star Cluster Fixture, intended for home use, but it never went into production.

Another much talked about chandelier was the one for the New York State Theater in Lincoln Center. Ten feet in diameter, the globular chandelier was completely covered with fifteen- and twenty-one-inch multi-sided "light diamonds," based on the structure of titanium diamond crystals. New designs by Kelly were also used in his 1959 installation for the Duke House at New York University, where he installed hanging lamps, adjustable by height and position, and each containing a ring of light behind an opaque shade. His Number 720 glass-bottom-cylinder table lamp was used on the library tables. Most of Kelly's later lighting designs eliminated visible fixtures in favor of hidden lights that were recessed in the ceiling or the soffit of a cantilevered roof. Sometimes, as in Johnson's Glass House, a simple black cylinder with baffles inside to prevent glare would be used to send light straight up to be reflected off the ceiling.

SI/DN/KB

"Alteration: Barbizon Plaza." *Progressive Architecture* 35 (May 1954): 118–119.

Cialdella, Philip, and Clara D. Powell. "The Great Illuminator." *Lighting Design and Application* (May 1993). Reprint, www.iesny.org/Documents/RKelly-LDnAMay93Reprint.pdf.

Cooley, Renee, and Matthew Tanteri. *Richard Kelly Selected Works: An Exhibition of Works Presented by IESNY and the Richard Kelly Grant*. New York: Illuminating Engineering Society of New York, 2007.

Eidelberg, Martin P., ed. *Design, 1935–1965: What Modern Was: Selections from the Liliane and David M. Stewart Collection*. New York: Musée des Arts Décoratifs de Montréal, 1991.

Flinchum, Russell. *American Design*. New York: Museum of Modern Art, 2008.

Kelly, Richard. "Lighting as an Integral Part of Architecture." *College Art Journal* 12 (Autumn 1952): 24–30.

Pepis, Betty. "Furniture Shown in Varied Designs." *New York Times*, July 13, 1954.

Pepis, Betty. "Prizes Presented on 11 Home Items." *New York Times*, March 24, 1955.

Pepis, Betty. "Trailblazing at Home." *New York Times*, March 13, 1955.

Yale University Library, Manuscripts and Archives, Richard Kelly Papers.

opposite left to right: Richard Kelly, miscellaneous lamp designs, pencil on paper, undated

Richard Kelly, table lamp, ca. 1940. Aluminum, steel, oak base, paper shade, and reflector bulb, 17¾ x 14 inches, manufactured by Kelly and Thompson, United States. Gift of the designer, 378.1942, © The Museum of Modern Art/licensed by SCALA/Art Resource, N.Y.

Richard Kelly, Floating Baffle Lamp Number 711, ca. 1950s, manufactured by Middletown Manufacturing Company

above left to right: Richard Kelly and Philip Johnson, floor lamp, 1952. Brass and painted metal, 42 x 25 inches, manufactured by Edison Price.

Richard Kelly and Philip Johnson, floor lamp, 1952, drawing

Richard Kelly, Number 722 Floor Lamp, 1955, height 62 inches, manufactured by Middletown Manufacturing Company

Barbizon Plaza Hotel Chandelier, 1954

New York State Theater Chandelier, 1964

Chronology of Works

The following is based on Richard Kelly's "Life Notes," which he wrote on September 4, 1974, assembling a list of his most important projects and accomplishments. We have deliberately left the information as Kelly provided it (only clarifying the chronological sequence and correcting some spelling errors), even if the degree of his involvement in the different projects seems to have varied considerably.

1935

Miss Marian Willard House, Locust Valley, Long Island, N.Y., with Jose L. Sert, architect

General Electric Exhibition House, eleventh floor roof, 3 Rockefeller Plaza, New York, with Hornbostel, Richardson, and Woodner

1936

E. I. DuPont and Company (stock broker), Wilmington, Del., with Fordyce and Hamby, architects

1937

A. M. White House, Long Island, N.Y., with Richard Kimball and Ellery Husted, architects

1938

Newbold Morris House, Southampton, Long Island, N.Y., Kimball and Husted, architects

Wheaton College, Norton, Mass., Caleb Hornbostel and Richard Bennett, architects

Tiffany and Company, New York (new building, main floor), with James Gordon Carr, architect

1939

New York World's Fair, Masterpieces of Art (building and installation), with Harrison and Fouillhoux and Abramovitz, architects

New York World's Fair, American Express Exhibit

New York World's Fair, American Home Building (Living Kitchen), with Fordyce and Hamby, architects

1940

Stork Club Room, New York, with Sherman Billingsley, owner

1942

Nelson Rockefeller House, Seal Harbor, Maine, with Wallace Harrison, architect

1945

Edgar J. Kaufmann Jr. Apartment, New York, E. J. Kaufmann Jr., architectural designer

1946

Lilly Daché Apartment, New York, Calbert Coggeshall, designer

1947

Edgar Kaufmann Sr. house, Palm Springs, Calif., with Richard Neutra, architect

Philadelphia City Planning Exhibit "Better Philadelphia," with Oscar Stonorov, architect

Warren Tremaine House, Santa Barbara, Calif., with Richard Neutra, architect

Joseph Magnin and Company (women's apparel store), Sacramento, Calif., with Victor Gruen, architect

Container Corporation of America, Chicago, Ill., with Maria Bergson, designer, among others

1948

Bonwit Teller (store remodeling), New York, with William Pahlman, designer

1948–1949

Philip Johnson's house (The Glass House), New Canaan, Conn., with Philip Johnson, architect

1949

Bonwit Teller (store in remodeled museum), Boston, with William Pahlman, designer

Matthew Fox Penthouse, New York, with Kahn and Jacobs, architects

1950

Henry Ford II (office suite), New York, with Skidmore, Owings, and Merrill, architects

860 Lake Shore Drive (apartment house), Chicago, with Ludwig Mies van der Rohe, architect

Wilbur Clarke House, Las Vegas, Nev., Jac Lessman, designer

The Desert Inn, Las Vegas, Nev., Jac Lessman, architectural designer

Rockefeller Guest House, New York, Philip Johnson, architect

Virgin Isles Hotel, St. Thomas, V.I., Harold Sterner, architect

1951

Henry Ford II (house, new wing), Southampton, Long Island, with Philip Johnson, architect

Museum of Modern Art, new West Building, New York, with Philip Johnson, architect

900 Lake Shore Drive (apartment house), Chicago, with Ludwig Mies van der Rohe, architect

Chicago Arts Club, Chicago, with Ludwig Mies van der Rohe, architect

Willard Gallery, 26 East Fifty-sixth Street, New York, with Jose L. Sert, architect

Jean de Menil House, Houston, Tex., with Philip Johnson, architect
St. James University (restaurant, classrooms, museums, campus), Houston, Tex., with Philip Johnson, architect (Kelly was probably referring to St. Thomas University)
Hanover Inn Coffee Shop, New Hampshire, Richard Kelly, architectural designer
Richard Hodgson House, New Canaan, Conn.

1952
Brandeis University, dining hall and recreation building, with Eero Saarinen, architect
Brandeis University, dormitories, with Eero Saarinen, architect
Drake University, dormitories, with Eero Saarinen, architect
Promenade Apartments (apartment house), with Ludwig Mies van der Rohe, architect
"Good Design" (permanent exhibition, Merchandise Mart), Paul Rudolph, architect
Steuben Glass Exhibition Factory, Corning, N.Y., Arthur Houghton, president
Corning Museum of Ancient Glass, Corning, N.Y., Thomas Buechner, director

1953
Burton Tremaine House, new wing, Madison, Conn., Philip Johnson, architect
Schlumberger and Company (office building), Ridgefield, Conn., with Philip Johnson, architect
Eliot Noyes House, New Canaan, Conn., Eliot Noyes, architect
Candlelight Restaurant of Westchester, N.Y., Nathalie Rahv, architect

1954
Lincoln Kirstein House (rebuilt), New York, Richard Kelly, architectural designer
Robert Wiley House, New Canaan, Conn., Philip Johnson, architect
William Burden Apartment, New York, Philip Johnson, architect
Independence Mall, Philadelphia, Pa., Harbison, Hough, Livingston, and Larson, architects
U.S. Embassy, Oslo, Norway, Eero Saarinen, architect

1955
Yale University Art Gallery, New Haven, Conn., Louis I. Kahn, architect
Illinois Institute of Technology, Chapel, Ludwig Mies van der Rohe, architect
IBM World Headquarters, Madison Avenue and Fifty-seventh Street, New York, Eliot Noyes, architect

1956
General Motors Technical Center (entire complex), Warren, Mich., Eero Saarinen, architect
American Academy of Music, Philadelphia, Pa.
Kneses Tifereth Israel Temple, Port Chester, N.Y., Philip Johnson, architect
Museum of Contemporary Crafts, New York, David Campbell, architect

1957
Boissonas House, Darien, Conn., Philip Johnson, architect
Richard Davis House, Minneapolis, Minn., Philip Johnson, architect
American Room, UNESCO, Paris, France, Philip Johnson, architect
Seagram Building, New York, Philip Johnson and Ludwig Mies van der Rohe, architect
Transportation Building (lobbies), Philadelphia, Pa., Vincent Kling, architect
Greyhound Post House (restaurant), Philadelphia, Pa., Vincent Kling, architect

1958
Temple Emanu-El, Dallas, Tex., William Wilson Wurster, consultant architect
Concordia Senior College (entire new campus and buildings), Eero Saarinen, architect
Harvard University, Quincy House, Cambridge, Mass., Shepley, Bulfinch, Richardson, Abbott, architects
The Lido Hotel, Las Vegas, Nev., Jac Lessman, architectural designer (Kelly misremembered the name: it was the Lido de Paris nightclub at the Sands Hotel in Las Vegas)

1959
The Four Seasons restaurant at House of Seagram, New York, Philip Johnson, architect (with Edison Price)
Chase Manhattan Bank, New York, Skidmore, Owings, and Merrill, architects
Asia House (museum and office building), New York, Philip Johnson, architect
Nelson Rockefeller House, Pocantico Hills, N.Y., with Harrison and Abramovitz, architects

1960s

Boissonas House, Cap Ferrat, France, with Philip Johnson, architect

1960

Leverett House, Harvard University, Cambridge, Mass., Shepley, Bulfinch, Richardson, Abbott, architects

Munson-Williams-Proctor Institute (museum), Utica, N.Y., Philip Johnson, architect

John Deere and Company, New Jersey, with Eero Saarinen, architect

Sun Life Assurance (building), John B. Parkin Associates, architects

1961

Museum of Western Art (Amon Carter Museum), Fort Worth, Tex., Philip Johnson, architect

La Fonda del Sol (restaurant), New York, Alexander Girard, architect

1962

Bell Telephone Laboratories, Holmdel, N.J., with Eero Saarinen, architect

1789 Restaurant, Georgetown, Washington, D.C., Richard McCooey, owner

1963

Clowes Memorial Auditorium, Indianapolis, Ind., John Johansen, architect

Lincoln Center, Philharmonic Hall, New York, Max Abramovitz, architect

Petroleum Club of Houston, Houston, Tex., George Pierce, architect

Cornell University, Willard Straight Hall, Ithaca, N.Y., Richard Kelly, architectural designer

Dulles International Airport, Washington, D.C., Eero Saarinen, architect

Bankers Trust Building (headquarters), New York, Henry Dreyfuss, architectural designer, Shreve, Lamb, and Harmon; Emery Roth and Sons, associate architects

Sheldon Art Gallery, Lincoln, Neb., Philip Johnson, architect

Henry L. Beck House, Dallas, Tex., Philip Johnson, architect

Place Ville Marie, Montreal, Canada, I. M. Pei, architect

Royal Bank of Canada (headquarters), Montreal, Canada, I. M. Pei, architect

Eliot Noyes House (later), New Canaan, Conn., Eliot Noyes, architect

1964

Pier 66 Hotel and Marina, Fort Lauderdale, Fla., Philips Petroleum Architectural Department, George Downs and Milton Dornblaser, architects

New York State Theater, Lincoln Center, New York, Philip Johnson, architect

New York World's Fair, New York State Pavilion, Philip Johnson, architect

Northern Trust Company (bank building), Chicago, Ill., C. F. Murphy, architect

Travelers Tower and Square, Hartford, Conn., Voorhees, Walker, Smith, Smith, Haines, architects

Constitution Plaza, Hartford, Conn., Charles DuBose, coordinating architect

Travelers Cliff House, Avon, Conn., Moore and Salsbury, architects

Phoenix Building and Plaza, Hartford, Conn., Harrison and Abramovitz, architects

Princeton University, School of Architecture building, Princeton, N.J., Fisher, Nes, Campbell, architects

Dumbarton Oaks (Museum Pavilion), Washington, D.C., Philip Johnson, architect

Museum of Modern Art, new first floor remodeled galleries, new Fifty-fourth Street building, new East Wing, and new garden, N.Y., Philip Johnson, architect

Yale University, Kline Geological Building, Philip Johnson, architect

1965

University of Texas Art Gallery, Austin, Tex., Brooks and Barr, architects

Timken Art Gallery, San Diego, Frank Hope and Associates, architects

230 Peachtree Building, Atlanta, Ga., Edwards and Portman, architects

Greenbriar Shopping Center, Atlanta, Ga., Edwards and Portman, architects

Lincoln Center Repertory Theater, New York, Eero Saarinen, architect

St. Michael's College Chapel, Winooski, Vt., Freeman, French, Freeman, architects

Toronto City Hall, Toronto, Canada, Viljo Revell, architect, John B. Parkin Associates

National Museum of Israel, Jerusalem, Israel, Dora Gad, architect

Squaw Valley Inn, Squaw Valley, Calif., Shepley, Bulfinch, Richardson, and Abbott, architects

Atomic Reactor Center, Tel Aviv, Israel, Philip Johnson, architect

Flamengo Park (O Parque do Flamengo), Rio de Janeiro, Brazil

Sugarloaf Mountain, Rio de Janeiro, Brazil

Michelson Hall, United States Naval Academy, Annapolis, Md., John Carl Warneke and Associates, architects

United Illuminating Company, Bridgeport, Conn., Fletcher-Thompson, Inc., architects

Squaw Valley, Opening of Summer Festival "High Camp," Alexander Cushing, owner

Budd Company, Philadelphia, Pa., the Metroliner's railroad car design and full-size models

1967

The Brooklyn Museum, Kevorkian Gallery, Brooklyn, N.Y., Thomas Buechner, director

1969

First National Bank, Chicago, C. F. Murphy, architect

1971

First Church of Christ, Scientist, New York; first completed 1901, restored 1971; Richard Kelly also architect of new work

1972

Exeter College Library, Exeter, New Hampshire, with Louis I. Kahn, architect

Kimbell Museum of Fine Art, Fort Worth, Tex., with Louis I. Kahn, architect

1974

Yale Center for British Art and British Studies, New Haven, Conn., with Louis I. Kahn, architect

Acknowledgments

This volume and the exhibition in the fall of 2010 at Yale's architecture school would not have been possible without the generosity, patience, and time commitment of many collaborators, correspondents, and helpers along the way. Dean Robert A. M. Stern initiated the project and was, as always, very generous and helpful with funds and advice. But the entire project could not have happened without Addison Kelly, who, together with her brother Scott, decided to give her father's papers in their entirety to Yale University, and was also enormously helpful in loaning additional material for the exhibition and very generous with her time. Thanks to Addison Kelly, material from an earlier exhibition about Kelly (organized by IESNY in 1996 by Matthew Tanteri, Renee Cooley, and others) was made available for our project, simplifying some of its aspects greatly.

Countless hours were spent by Seher Erdogan over the summer of 2009 in the Yale Manuscripts and Archives Division, working on a detailed account of the Richard Kelly Papers. This extensive document will be made available to the Manuscripts and Special Collections Department and will be of enormous help to scholars of midcentury architecture in the future. Seher had been a student in my "Light, Screens, and Architecture" seminar at the Yale School of Architecture in the spring of 2009. Several other students also got involved, in particular Eliza Higgins, who supported Seher as we were approaching the deadline, along with Trisha Snyder, Travis Eby, Elijah Porter, Reuben Herzl, and Mark Gausepohl. Amina Blacksher, another Yale student working at the archive as an intern, discovered and processed additional material. Laura Tatum, the architectural records archivist, arranged for uncomplicated access to the huge amounts of material. She is part of a remarkable team (Cynthia Ostroff, Diane E. Kaplan, Michael Frost, Kristen McDonald, Stephen Ross, Sarah Kraus, and Dika Goloweiko-Nussberg), who all were a pleasure to work with. Many lighting designers were immensely helpful with advice and explanations, such as Howard Brandston, OVI's Enrique Peiniger and Jean Sundin, Yann Kersalé in Paris, Yale's Jennifer Tipton, Mark Major in London, and Tim and Jan Edler in Berlin.

In some aspects the preparation of the exhibition and catalog was also a collaboration between two institutions. The lion's share was carried by Yale, but Brown University's Royce Family Research and travel funds were immensely helpful. The team at Brown was led by the incomparable Karen Bouchard, associate curator at the Art Slide Library, who spent many weekends and evenings and much vacation time handling all the illustrations, rights, and research for our extensive working bibliography and generally kept track of everything. In addition she wrote, cowrote, and edited many of the catalog entries. She was ably supported by senior library associate Jodie Goodnough, as well as Kristen Oehlrich, a graduate student in the Department of the History of Art and Architecture. My colleagues and friends Margaret Maile Petty and Sandy Isenstadt were both immensely helpful and generous with their time, advising, proofreading, and editing several phases of this project.

Several archivists and librarians went out of their way to accommodate our requests and helped quickly and unbureaucratically with images and rights clearance, such as P. Toby Graham of the Georgia Digital Archive, Lynn Eaton of the Rare Book, Manuscript, and Special Collections Library at Duke University, Robert Provost, assistant to Phyllis Lambert, Suzanne Oatey of the Huntington Library, Eva Walters of the Ellsworth Kelly estate, and Andy Walles in the office of John Portman and Russell Flinchum at the Century Association Archive. Friends and colleagues helped with knowledge, advice, and access to information, such as Janet Parks, Christy McLear, Mardges Bacon, Kevin Harrington, John Marsteller, Jürgen Commerend, Tom Beeby, Barbara Lamprecht, and Alec Purves.

The exhibition profited greatly from the spirited and friendly responses to our often unusual loan requests, and I would like to thank Addison Kelly, Alex von Bidder of the Four Seasons Restaurant, Belmont Freeman, its restoration architect, Wolf Tegethoff and Uli Fischer of the Zentralinstitut für Kunstgeschichte, Jan and Tim Edler of Realities:United in Berlin, Enrique Peiniger and Jean Sundin of OVI, Emma Price of Edison Price Lighting, Yann Kersalé in Paris, Rogier van der Heide, and James Carpenter in New York City.

I would also like to thank Michelle Komie of Yale University Press for taking on this unusual project and seeing it through with cheerfulness and patience, manuscript editor Philip King for his attentive and careful reading of the text, and Sarah Henry for producing the book; all have been incredibly helpful throughout. The beautiful design by Jena Sher brilliantly captures the "nocturnal modernity" that Richard Kelly's work helped to formulate.

Index

Illustration Credits

Nasser Abulhassan: Addington fig. 8
Michelle Addington: Addington figs. 7, 9
Ellen Bean: Philip Johnson Brick House fig. 2
Century Archives Foundation: Neumann fig. 7
Louis Faurer: Lambert figs. 8, 9
Lionel Freedman: Yale University Art Gallery fig. 3
Alexandre Georges: Lambert figs. 4, 7a; Petty fig. 26
Emilio Guerra: Rockefeller Guest House fig. 2
Scott Hyde: Singer Showroom fig. 1
Philip Johnson Glass House: Lambert fig. 6.
Addison Kelly Collection: Introduction figs. 1, 2; Neumann figs. 19, 25; Thompson Office fig. 1; Pace-Setter House figs. 3, 4; Candlelight Restaurant fig. 1; Franklin Bank fig. 1; Burden Apartment fig. 1; Barbizon Hotel fig. 2; General Motors figs. 1, 2; Frick Collection fig. 1; Idlewild fig. 1; Penn Transportation Center fig. 2; IBM Headquarters fig. 1; Harvard Quincy House figs. 1, 2; Lincoln Center Philharmonic figs. 1, 2; Bankers Trust fig. 1; Lincoln Center New York State Theater fig. 1; Kimbell fig. 2; Yale Center for British Art fig. 2; Lamp Designs figs. 1, 3, 4, 6, 8
Dietrich Neumann: Petty figs. 1, 4; Isenstadt fig. 3; Lake Shore Drive fig. 1
Eliot Noyes Archive: Petty figs. 16, 22, 23, 24
Louis Reens: Lambert figs. 12, 15; La Fonda del Sol fig. 1
Robert Yarnell Ritchie: Bankers Trust fig. 2
John Ross: Idlewild fig. 2
David E. Sherman: MoMA Sculpture Garden fig. 1
Matthew Tanteri: Tanteri figs. 1, 2, 3, 4, 6
Lawrence S. Williams: Penn Center Transportation Building figs. 1, 3
Yale University Library, Manuscripts and Archives, Richard Kelly Papers: frontispiece (photographer, Antony Di Gesú); Addington figs. 3, 4, 5, 6; Isenstadt figs. 6, 8, 9, 10, 11, 12, 13, 14, 18; Neumann figs. 18, 20; Petty figs. 17, 20, 25; Tanteri fig. 7; Bonwit Teller fig. 1; Ain House fig. 1; Graef House fig. 1; Ault House figs. 1, 2; Morosani House fig. 1; Knoedler Gallery fig. 3; NYU Duke House fig. 1; Humble Oil fig. 1, 2; Lincoln Center, New York State Theater fig. 3; Lamp Designs fig. 5